WHEN MBAs
RULE THE
NEWSROOM

WHEN MBAS RULE THE NEWSROOM

How the

Marketers and

Managers

Are Reshaping

Today's Media

Doug Underwood

COLUMBIA UNIVERSITY PRESS   **NEW YORK**

Columbia University Press
New York   Chichester, West Sussex

Library of Congress Cataloging-in-Publication Data

Underwood, Doug.
    When MBAs rule the newsroom : how the marketers
and managers are reshaping today's media / Doug Underwood.
        p.   cm.
    Includes bibliographical references and index.
    ISBN 0–231–08048–4 ISBN 0–231–08049–2 (pbk.)
    1. Newspapers—Marketing.   2. Newspapers—Man-
agement.   3. Newspaper publishing.   I. Title.
  PN4737.U63   1993
  070.4'068'8—dc20   92-40020
                                                    CIP

Casebound editions of Columbia University Press Books are
printed on permanent and durable acid-free paper

Printed in the United States of America
c 10 9 8 7 6 5 4 3 2 1
p 10 9 8 7 6 5 4 3

To my parents

CONTENTS

PREFACE TO THE
PAPERBACK EDITION

AN advertisement ran recently in the *Columbia Journalism Review* recruiting journalists for the Frank Batten fellowships—a two-year MBA degree program at the University of Virginia designed to train future leaders of the media industry. When I first wrote about MBAs running newsrooms back in 1988, I used the term as a metaphor for the "customer-driven" or "reader-friendly" approach to journalism that was sweeping through the newspaper business. Today the marketing-oriented style of newspapering is so entrenched that a media executive like Batten, chairman of Landmark Communications, which controls more than forty newspapers and broadcast properties mostly in the southeast U.S., has gone so far as to underwrite MBA training as a way to prepare would-be media managers.

Whether they are led by editors who actually have earned MBAs, virtually every daily newspaper has been touched, if not thoroughly revolutionized, by the phenomenon I have dubbed MBA journalism.

Legendary editors like Ben Bradlee, Jim Bellows, Bill Kovach, and Gene Roberts are gone from the newspapers where they made their reputation, and a new breed of editor now dominates the industry—the manager-technocrats who have come up in the corporate culture of big media companies and whose loyalty to corporate profit and marketing goals now infuses every level of newsroom decision making.

The transformation of the business was captured recently by a veteran Philadelphia journalist explaining why the Knight-Ridder–owned *Philadelphia Inquirer*—winner of seventeen Pulitzer prizes in eighteen years under Roberts's editorship—hasn't won the prize since Roberts resigned in 1990 to go into teaching (and more recently to take a temporary top editing position with the *New York Times*). "Gene left because it wasn't the paper he wanted it to be anymore," this reporter told the *American Journalism Review*. "The business has changed. Decisions in the newsroom are made for business rather than editorial considerations. It's the company and the industry, not Gene or Max [Maxwell E. P. King, Roberts's successor]."

It is true that other pressures also have come along to distract MBA editors from their single-minded focus on the newspaper's marketing plan: campaigns to add minorities to newsroom staffs; growing experimentation with multimedia and other forms of electronic news delivery; and the rapid expansion of computer layout and design systems that have moved backshop production functions into the newsroom and put a strain on copy desks.

But the turbulence of newspapering in the 1990s is happening in an environment where newsrooms are micromanaged to meet the business agenda of top management and where the consequences of market research are everywhere in evidence. In today's newsrooms you will encounter team journalism, where editors, reporters, and graphic designers work together to produce a slick and stylized editorial product; a meeting culture where newsroom managers spend hours planning the news and issuing instructions to reporters; newsroom hierarchies restructured around trendy new concepts such as "circular management" and "newsrooms without walls" and editors with new titles such as "change facilitators"; and a system of tight newsroom oversight where employees can't forget they are working in service to the newspaper's circulation and marketing goals. From city to city, daily newspapers read with sameness and homogeneity. There are high concept art and graphics produced by design desks and presentation teams; news-you-can-use and eye-catching gimmicks aimed at readers with short attention spans; new beats with snappy new names such as the "Real Life Team" and the "911 Jump Team"; fad-driven coverage of workplace, family, and other issues perceived to be of interest to a changing readership; and celebrity news and crime and violence stories to compete with local television.

Since *When MBAs Rule the Newsroom* was published in 1993, I have been involved in two projects that show just how completely the daily newspaper business has changed even from when I left it in 1987. Not long ago, I performed an in-depth analysis of the impact of Gannett's News 2000 program—a company-wide campaign to reconnect Gannett's eighty-three daily newspapers with their communities by involving readers in the news production process—at the *Olympian* in Washington state's capital city. At the *Olympian:*

- Editors used coupon forms from readers, community forum meetings, reader panels, and the results of reporter surveys at shopping malls and other public places as a blueprint for redesigning the newspaper's beat system. Break-out boxes fill up the newspaper, stories seldom jump off the front page, and editors believe in the use of multiple "points of entry," which means breaking up longer stories into a series of brief articles accompanied by lots of reader service information—all under the theory that busy readers have less time for the newspaper.
- Reporters are expected to write memos updating story ideas as often as five times a day, with additional files geared toward what they are writing for the weekend, the following week, and long-term projects, to keep editors briefed for their myriad rounds of editorial planning meetings.
- Top editors are held to a strict accountability system by Gannett headquarters, where every six months a panel of corporate officials uses a 100-point scale to rate editors on how well they are following the News 2000 formula. These editors in turn make it clear that their employees' job evaluations depend on how well they adapt to the system.
- A circulation person routinely sits in on news meetings, and newsroom employees are required to participate in the company's marketing campaigns. Gannett's ADvance program, for example, established a series of marketing workshops to devise schemes to sell more ads, and reporters and editors are assigned to the paper's ADvance committees.
- Gannett's "mainstreaming" program, aimed at getting more minority views into the news pages and marketing the newspaper in the minority community, requires reporters to include as many minority sources as possible in stories and identify quotes from minorities so they won't be cut out. Tearsheets are sent to Gannett headquarters, where a report is prepared that compares the performance of each Gannett newspaper. Reporters applaud the idea of

getting more minority sources into the paper, but they say the
rigid requirements make a mockery of a worthy goal. They complain that minority sources often end up in stories no matter how
qualified to comment they are.

While *Olympian* executives point to circulation gains and improved
reader satisfaction surveys as signs of success, many of the paper's
reporters complain that it is difficult to do good journalism under the
constraints of News 2000. The system, complains one reporter, is run
by careerist editors who have "bought the company line" and just
want to advance. "We've become functionaries," he says. Another reporter who has left the newspaper adds: "Journalism there just became more and more like clerical work."

Two years ago, my University of Washington colleagues Keith
Stamm and Tony Giffard and I surveyed 187 editors at 13 daily newspapers in Washington state to see how they were adjusting to the new
pagination systems where newspaper pages are designed, laid out,
and edited directly on the computer screen—systems that have helped
cut costs and made it easier to put out the planned and packaged
newspaper of today.

Not surprisingly, we discovered that editors viewed the advent of
pagination, which has added new and complex burdens to their tasks,
with ambivalence and concern. While a majority of editors praised the
new systems for improving quality control and making newspapers
more attractive, an equally sizeable number complained that the time
they spend on computerized production tasks takes away from traditional journalistic activities such as fact-checking, editing for accuracy, and improving text. A common concern was that pagination has
accelerated the trend, so prevalent elsewhere in the business, of emphasizing form over content. "It looks pretty," said one editor. "But
does it say anything?"

In fact, it seems that everything—the forces of fast-changing technology, economic pressures, and social and demographic changes—is
converging to complicate the life of even the most dedicated MBA
editor. The newspaper business has bounced back from the recession
of the late 1980s and early 1990s, and, while not at the lofty levels of
the past, profits are back up. But the improved profitability has been
due in good part to cost-cutting and downsizing, including employee
layoffs in some places. Rising newsprint costs, combined with flat-to-
declining readership rates, still leave newspaper executives looking to
the future with anxiety.

At the same time, the newspaper companies are taking seriously
the implications for the industry posed by the emerging electronic In-

formation Superhighway. Industry publications are filled with stories about the "convergence" of traditional media and new "interactive" services and "multimedia" experimentation. High-technology beats are all the rage and reporters now cover—some would say overcover—the jockeying by television, telephone, satellite, and computer software companies to see which will bring the much-touted 500 channels of electronic information into the homes of America.

On one level, the newspaper industry, which can't afford the billions in investment required to build the Information Superhighway, looks like a piker in this high-stakes game. Many newspaper companies are waiting warily on the sidelines, hoping that as the producers of news and information they will play a role in tomorrow's wired world. But more enterprising media organizations—led by big companies such as Knight-Ridder and the Chicago Tribune Co. and individual newspapers such as the *San Jose Mercury News* and the Raleigh *News and Observer*—have pioneered the development of portable electronic newspapers, new on-line services, digitized and interactive information channels, and news-gathering and dissemination systems that merge print, video, and audio journalism (even though these new services aren't expected to generate any significant revenue in the near future).

From the standpoint of news content, newspapers, like the rest of the country, are suffering in a chaotic atmosphere of radio talk show chatter, saturation coverage of the O.J. Simpson case, and the proliferation of new forms of video info-tainment. It is no easy task for newspapers to find their niche in a world where people can tune into live coverage of the Bobbitt trial and where local television news has descended ever deeper into the tabloid depths of crime, violence, and gossip from the entertainment world.

Still, there are hopeful signs. Computerized investigative reporting is catching on in a big way at newspapers everywhere. Editors have begun to notice that the public expects leadership from newspapers, and community agenda-setting and public journalism have become new bywords in the business. The most respected newspapers, like the *New York Times,* the *Washington Post,* the *Chicago Tribune,* and the *Boston Globe,* appear to have decided that their future lies in providing intelligent journalism to a sophisticated audience rather than *USA Today*-style once-over-lightly coverage. Even at my old newspaper, the *Seattle Times,* top editors seem to have lost some of their infatuation with MBA tactics and are putting a renewed emphasis on the in-depth journalism "you can't get anywhere else" (as the newspaper's slogan goes).

And yet I caution anyone who believes that a new era of substantial journalism awaits us. It is naive to believe that MBA journalism will prove to be just another passing fad or that, as newspaper analyst John Morton claims, it has made newspapers more fit to face the future. It may be that today's newspaper journalist, whipsawed by economic and technological pressures and weighed down by all the talk that the field is in decline, has grown too weary to protest when one more MBA management scheme makes its way into the newsroom. But the reality is that anyone who wants to understand the threats to the cause of serious journalism must continue to pay close attention to what's going on in the ubiquitous meetings of the media's marketers and managers.

ACKNOWLEDGMENTS

In the writing of this book, as well as in the struggles both within myself and my profession that led up to it, I've been strongly supported by my family, whose own struggles with the way the world is and the way it should be have had much to do with the kind of journalist I was and with the thrust of this book. I've received encouragement, inspiration, and fine counsel from such journalists and friends as Steve Gettinger, Henry Breithaupt, Carolyn McManus, Chris Collins, Bob Partlow, Louis Peck, Walter Hatch, Lee Moriwaki, Mickey Edgerton, Sylvia Nogaki, Dick Clever, David Jay, John Jamison, Bart Wilson, and Ian Joeck (whose own brave struggle with illness taught me much about faith and friendship and the real values of life). I also wish to thank the editors at the *Columbia Journalism Review,* and Spencer Klaw and Jon Swan in particular, for encouraging me to articulate my concerns about what was happening to the profession—and for standing behind me even when I faltered in that articulation. Ann Miller's faith in the book helped make it a reality.

Here at the University of Washington, I appreciate the help I received in the development of the manuscript from Keith Stamm, Judy Hucka, Pat Dinning, Don Pember, Richard Kielbowicz, Jerry Baldasty, Richard Labunski, Kurt and Gladys Lang, Tony Giffard, Roger Simpson, Richard Carter, and Ed Bassett. And, of course, I've taken great satisfaction from my students who have embraced me as a mentor, valued my "war stories," welcomed my advice, and whose continued enthusiasm for the profession makes me believe firmly in the future of newspapers.

INTRODUCTION

> We need to remember that the Founding Fathers did not set up a First Amendment Fund to pay for inquisitive reporters or thoughtful editors or courageous publishers. That honor is left for newspapers' customers—our readers and advertisers.
>
> —James Batten, chairman/CEO
> Knight-Ridder, Inc.

> It's past time that newspapers woke up. We are dealing in a world of marketing, and it isn't something that is going to go away.... The reality is that if you don't give the readers what they want, they'll find it someplace else.
>
> —Kathy Kozdemba, an MBA from Syracuse University and a top news official with the Gannett Corporation

> We aren't a candy bar and we aren't a bar of soap. But, damn, we are a product.
>
> —Chris Anderson, editor of
> the *Orange County Register*

> In today's world, it's bottom-line journalism. Marketing? I never knew what the fucking word meant. We were just out after the fucking readers and to have fun.
>
> —Jim Bellows, former editor of the now deceased *Washington Star* and the deceased *Los Angeles Herald Examiner*

IN 1986, when executive editor Mike Fancher outlined his annual goals for *Seattle Times* publisher Frank Blethen, he sounded like any other striving, young organization man on the fast track, fresh from the University of Washington with an MBA in hand. In his memo, Fancher talked about overseeing a reorganization of newsroom management, coordinating the news department's role in marketing the newspaper, keeping the newsroom budget in line, and serving as liaison with the circulation department to help the *Times* accomplish its circulation goals.[1]

Nowhere in the memo did Fancher talk about the news—overseeing the direction of the newspaper's coverage, participating in news decisions, or helping to develop story ideas.

Welcome to the world of the editor of a modern daily newspaper, a person who, as likely as not, is going to be immersed in readership surveys, marketing plans, memos on management training, and budget planning goals—the new trappings of a business where marketing the newspaper has become the top goal of newspaper managers and where attention to the bottom line has replaced many of the tasks that once occupied editors' time.

The daily newspaper business has undergone a remarkable transformation from the days when editors in green eyeshades made seat-of-the-pants news judgments and readers were noticed only when they wrote a letter to the newspaper. Today's market-savvy newspapers are planned and packaged to "give readers what they want"; newspaper content is geared to the results of readership surveys, and newsroom organization has been reshaped by newspaper managers whose commitment to the marketing ethic is hardly distinguishable from their vision of what journalism is.

The proselytizers of market-oriented journalism view their mission as nothing less than the salvation of daily newspapers. The newspaper business is in trouble—as anyone who has watched the collapse of newspapers' retail advertising base and the rash of closings of big city dailies knows. Although emerging from the 1980s as one of the most profitable industries in America, daily newspapers were already suffering from the ills that began to catch up with them in the 1990s.[2] Four decades of stagnant circulation have translated into a desperate worry about readership as it has become clear that many Americans—busy, distracted, and wedded to television and other forms of electronic entertainment—simply aren't reading daily newspapers anymore. Growing consolidation and chain control of newspapers, intense profit expectations, economic stagnation, the financial woes of big retail advertisers, the competition from weeklies and specialized magazines, and the proliferation of electronic competitors all have combined to darken the outlook of an industry that some predict does not have much of a future in the new Information Age of computers, VCRs, digital television, and multimedia purveyors of electronic data.[3]

The urgency felt by newspaper executives to adopt marketing solutions to their market problems is neatly expressed by Fancher in an article he wrote called "Metamorphosis of the Newspaper Editor." "Change or be changed," Fancher warns his fellow newspaper executives in the piece, explaining that the modern newspaper editor is expected to be a marketing expert as well as an editor. "Some editors resist getting involved in the business of newspapering, fearful they will be tainted by filthy lucre," he says. "I believe those editors are doomed. Sooner or later, their journalistic options will be proscribed by someone else's bottom line. It's a fact of modern business life."[4]

In fact, this kind of advice has become gospel at newspaper conferences and workshops, editors' gatherings, and in the columns of industry publications. The intense focus on the marketing of the newspaper has led to the adoption of techniques—such as briefs and packaged information, entertainment news, and visually appealing formats—that newspaper executives hope will lure back readers. Reader-driven or customer-driven newspapering, as it has become known, has spawned a host of new features that sprang from readership surveys and public focus groups: more escape and upbeat stories, more news-you-can-use features, and more quick reads, capsules, and indexes.[5]

This fixation on the reader has become the centerpiece of campaigns by newspaper companies desperate to find the formula to turn around the fortunes of the daily newspaper. Gannett has led the way with its test-marketed, television-in-newspaper-form *USA Today* and its "News 2000" program, leading many of its newspapers to quite literally remold their beat structures, their news pages, and their newsroom organization in response to perceived reader interests.[6] Knight-Ridder has launched a companywide "customer-obsession" campaign and unveiled its own experimental newspaper in Boca Raton, Florida, with its reader-tested formula of news nuggets, pastel decor, multiple graphics, and easily scannable indexes and service boxes.[7] The trend-setting *Orange County Register* introduced an array of reader-written features, such as columns about dreams and favorite vacations, and scrapped its old coverage for such reader-friendly beats as "malls" and "shopping" and "car culture."[8] Even staid, traditional newspapers, like the *Los Angeles Times* and the *New York Times,* have launched major redesigns, tightened writing, and made readers a top priority.[9]

Today's editors, says Susan Miller, Scripps Howard's vice president/editorial, have come to believe that reader-driven newspapering can be "a higher calling." The vast majority of staffers are becoming accustomed to the idea that "newspapers are to be of service to readers and are not staffed by a Brahmin class that was chosen to lecture the population," she says, adding, "people who refuse to be service-oriented will leave in disgust and say we're pandering and will call us bad names—but they will leave."[10]

And yet there is little evidence that for all the fervency with which it has been promoted reader-driven newspapering has done much to improve newspapers' prospects. The weekday circulation of daily newspapers in the U.S., amounting to just over sixty million in 1990, has barely budged since 1970 even though during the same period the population has increased by more than 20 percent and the number of households by almost 50 percent.[11] Without including *USA Today* in the calculation, the number of Americans reading a newspaper on a daily basis has actually declined since the early 1980s.

Sadly, what the marketing movement has accomplished—as Miller predicted—is to drive many committed and creative journalists out of the newspaper business and to leave many of those who remain lamenting what has happened to their craft. At many of today's market-minded newspapers, good writing and reporting have been forgotten amid the marketing gimmicks, readership studies, and predictable journalism. Newspaper professionals who are not caught up in the readership revolution complain that today's customer-obsessed editors devote too much energy to marketing and bottom-line concerns; they are too willing to squeeze news resources and the space for news in service to corporate demands and the pressures of Wall Street; they suppress aggressive and in-depth reporting for the sake of formula journalism; and they have created a newsroom environment increasingly inhospitable to the independent, irreverent, and change-the-world personalities that have traditionally been attracted to the profession of daily newspapering.[12] In the minds of these critics, daily newspapers caught up in reader-friendly journalism are in danger of losing the true spirit of the journalistic mission—the commitment to community service, the passion for probing injustice, the love of good writing, and the devotion to enterprising reporting.

Bill Walker, a former reporter with the *Sacramento Bee,* the *Denver Post,* and the *Fort Worth Star Telegram,* expresses the feelings of many of today's frustrated newspaper journalists in his swan-song piece, *Why I Quit,* in the *San Francisco Bay Guardian:*

> Nowadays, editors spend their days taking meetings in glass offices, emerging only to issue reporters instructions like this: "Get me a 12–inch A1 box on the city's reaction to the tragedy. Talk to teachers, kids, the mayor, the bishop. Focus on the shock, the sadness, the brave determination to move on. And don't forget the homeless. We've got color art from the shelter." Meanwhile, the promotions director is already producing a cheery drive-time radio spot to plug the story. . . . We used to have a saying: No matter how bad journalism was, it beat selling insurance for a living. But no more.[13]

I have written this book first and foremost from my own experience in the daily newspaper business that I loved but also left. As a Washington, D.C., correspondent with Gannett during its heyday of corporate growth and acquisitions (I left just months before the unveiling of *USA Today*) as well as a reporter who worked at the *Seattle Times* while Mike Fancher turned the newspaper into a model of reader-friendliness during the 1980s, I learned firsthand how impossible it had become to escape the brave new world of marketplace newspapering.[14] At Gannett, I watched in trepidation as the new breed of Gannett executives evolved a journalistic vision that contains a unique mix of Babbitt-like boosterism, nouveau-riche corporate values, sophisticated marketing opinion research, and a philosophy of public pandering once associated with television rather than with newspapers.[15] I labored under the Fancher regime at the *Seattle Times,* where (at about the time he embarked upon his MBA program at the University of Washington) he installed a large and pervasive bureaucracy of midlevel editors, tightened the reins on reporters, redesigned sections of the newspaper based on readership surveys, target-marketed to upscale readers with light features and how-to sections, and produced a slickly packaged newspaper that has won three Pulitzer prizes under his leadership. But the *Times* also evolved into a place where one of those Pulitzer-winning reporters left the newspaper, complaining that Fancher's goal was to drive away committed, enterprising reporters like himself and to "clone" the *Times*'s newsroom into an organization where everybody thinks and acts alike.[16] Needless to say, I exited the profession with my own deep concerns about what was happening to a business that had been transformed into a carefully planned, marketplace-driven, profit-fueled model of modern, corporate engineering— and that was in danger of losing its professional bearings and its journalistic soul.

A plethora of books tells editors and editors-to-be how to become better managers in this day of target-marketing, scientific surveys, and reader-driven newspapers.[17] But the purpose of this book is a different one. What I have attempted to do is to measure—using the methods of journalistic investigation and those of social science research—the impact of the new market-oriented journalism on the newsroom, on the daily newspaper, and on the morale and attitudes of newspaper journalists. When I first wrote about the subject of marketplace journalism for the *Columbia Journalism Review* in 1988, I discovered that many journalists shared my concerns about the excessive emphasis on marketing and managerialism in their newsrooms.[18] And yet I know that editors have a habit of simply dismissing newsroom protesters who resist joining the marketing team as dissidents obstructing progress. So I felt it was important to ground my analysis in the forms of quantitative research that have a certain claim to the objectivity of science (even among editors who scoff at social science methods while duly reporting their results at every opportunity). This also had the salutary effect of showing my academic colleagues (many of whom are equally suspicious of what they call "journalistic inquiry") that there is a real basis for paying attention to the phenomenon of market-driven journalism. Despite my misgivings about the changes taking place in the newspaper industry, I embarked on my research with an open mind. After all, the daily newspaper industry faces unprecedented challenges in the years ahead, and I wasn't about to dismiss out-of-hand the techniques that so many newspaper executives (including some I respect a good deal) feel are necessary to preserve the daily newspaper.

In the first examination, underwritten by the Fund for Investigative Journalism and published in the *Columbia Journalism Review,* I interviewed more than one hundred newspaper editors, reporters, and newspaper consultants to see if they identified—and, if so, how they were adjusting to—the marketing and management pressures.[19] This was followed by a three-year study using the quantitative methods of social science research, which is published in the communications journal, *Journalism Quarterly.*[20] From 1989 to 1991, my University of Washington colleague Keith Stamm and I developed a management policy survey and administered it to 429 newsroom employees at 12 daily newspapers in three Western states. We were particularly interested to see how many journalists shared my concerns—and, if so, whether they felt the changes were merely matters of management style and needed adjustments to an evolving media environment, as many newspaper executives assured us, or whether they had the potential to alter the nature of the news and the fundamental traditions of the newspaper profession.

While our findings did confirm many of my suspicions about the impact of market-driven journalism, they also suggest that a complex phenomenon is taking place in the daily newspaper industry. Newspapers clearly are catering to the marketplace with their greater emphasis on customer-oriented journalism. But they appear to be doing this while trying to preserve some form of the traditional journalistic values of editorial autonomy and community service so prized by news workers. This is an encouraging finding—at least for someone like myself, who worries that journalism as a higher calling may be abandoned in the rush to embrace marketing principles. But the push toward market-thinking in the newsroom also appears to be creating serious stress within newspaper staffs, especially in the newsrooms of chain newspapers where staffers are under particularly strong pressure to adapt to the new market-oriented environment.

As one who was making my first foray into the complex world of social science research, I deeply appreciate the invaluable support in this venture from Keith Stamm without whose partnership I could never have found my bearings. Well-meaning people in both newsrooms and academic communications departments have often lamented that the "communication" between the practitioners in the two fields is so poor and that their appreciation for each others' work is so minimal. Thanks to Keith's firm guiding hand and his determination to avoid any signs of bias, I hope we have succeeded in showing that a journalist and a research scholar can bridge the gap between journalism and academia to produce something of value to both fields.

The first part of the book examines the background of the readership revolution and the roots of market-driven journalism. Chapter 1 focuses on the fears that gripped newspaper executives in the late 1970s as they confronted stagnant circulations, and it examines the spate of market research studies and industry campaigns designed to regain readership.

Chapter 2 takes a close look at the new breed of business-minded newspaper executive that has emerged to transform the daily newspaper in the name of better marketing, more attention to the bottom line, and more focus on audience interests.

Chapter 3 looks at how the newsroom has changed as the walls between the news and marketing departments have been knocked down, and it explores what newsroom employees think about the new systems that have been installed to improve the planning, packaging, and profitability of the newspaper.

Chapter 4 takes a look at the historical role of commercialism in the operation of daily newspapers and traces the use of bottom-line management techniques from the advent of the penny press through today's global restructuring of the media.

Chapter 5 looks at the television industry and how television's techniques to lure the audience both preceded and inspired the daily newspaper industry's push to embrace marketing as its salvation.

Chapter 6 examines the role of new technology in the newsroom and looks at the way computers have helped managers tighten up administrative oversight, spurred the design and graphics revolution, and spawned the transformation of news into the commodity of information.

Chapter 7 takes a look at the way the newspaper industry think tanks, foundations, professional organizations, and industry publications have helped spread the gospel of managerialism and market-oriented journalism.

Chapter 8 focuses on *USA Today* and the leading role the Gannett

Company has played in revamping the newspaper industry's attitudes toward the use of color and design in the news pages, the role of market research, and the importance of the reader.

The second part of the book presents the conclusions we reached after surveying journalists' attitudes about the marketing and management changes that are reshaping their industry. Chapter 9 examines the academic scholarship of newsroom management and asks why communications researchers—like newspapers themselves—have paid so little attention to the marketing and readership phenomena.

Chapter 10 summarizes our newsroom policy survey. It examines the management changes our respondents identified as taking place in their newsrooms, the impact of those changes on the perceived quality of their newspapers, and the implications of the findings on job satisfaction.

The third part of the book examines the consequences for the journalism professional—and for the newspaper reader—of a business that is being transformed in the name of better marketing and the bottom line. Chapter 11 looks at the changing nature of the news and the way market-oriented newspapering is making it easier for powerful business organizations and the media organizations that are intertwined with them to shape the news and evade serious scrutiny.

Chapter 12 takes a glimpse into the future and looks at the advances in technology, the proliferation of electronic competitors, and the predictions of doom for the daily newspaper—and how the anxieties about the future are pressuring newspapers to "reinvent" themselves in ways that are having profound consequences for the profession.

Chapter 13 examines the pressures that market-oriented journalism has brought to the lives of news workers and offers some thoughts on how committed newspaper professionals might survive in the world of marketplace journalism.

Chapter 14 ponders the future of the printed word in this Information Age of wired cities, instant global communications, video wizardry, and rapid advances in computers, fiber optics, and fax machines, and concludes with some hopeful words.

Marketing, of course, surrounds us everywhere these days. With the philosophies of deregulation and free-market thinking in ascendancy, we are seeing marketing pressures invade virtually all our institutions. Hospitals, medical clinics, day-care centers, charities, educational institutions—there are virtually no services so basic and no social activities so sacred that they can't be put into the hands of the marketers and the profit maximizers. And, as corporations have extended their hold on U.S. newspapers, it is probably unrealistic to expect newspapers to be immune to this trend.

There is no question that the economic and technological challenges facing daily newspapers are very real—and very serious. Advocates of change always say that history, economics, and technology are on their side and that those who don't adapt will be brushed aside. But those of us who are troubled by the trends of market-driven newspapering protest that we aren't just a bunch of romantic nostalgics, longing for an era of paste pots, sloppy management, and hack journalism. What worries us is whether the true values of the business—the craft of writing, the vigor of investigating, the sense of fairness and equity, the gut-level impulse to want to right wrongs—will survive in the new, scientifically managed, MBA-run newsrooms.

This book was conceived in that spirit and written for my former colleagues who are suffering through the changes and, I know, worry with me.

WHEN MBAS
RULE THE
NEWSROOM

PART ONE

CHAPTER ONE

The Party Is Over— Where Are the Readers?

I'm certainly not suggesting turning over the editorial direction ... to the business department. ... But the goal must be to provide what readers want, not what the editors or the reporters or even the publisher thinks would be in the ideal newspaper.

—Bob Comstock, former executive editor, the *Record,* Hackensack, N.J.

We're not in this business to lick the public's hand. We're here to tell people what they need to know.

—Eugene Patterson, retired chairman/publisher of the *St. Petersburg Times*

We did this together. That's the type of thing—I almost said "product," which is a word an editor could get shot for using some years ago—that comes out of talking with the chief financial officer and the marketing committee.

—Ben J. Bowers, executive editor of the *Greensboro (N.C.) News and Record*

The press has never been and never should be in business to give the people just what they want. The editor who does his editing predominantly from market research returns isn't worth a damn.

—William Hornby, former executive editor of the *Denver Post*

THE usual crisis atmosphere pervaded the gathering of top daily newspaper executives in Miami in February 1989. The late Steve Star, a member of MIT's Sloan program at the time and a long-time guru on the subject of the business troubles of newspapers, was telling the executives that if something didn't happen to turn around the long-term decline in daily newspaper readership, the future of their industry looked bleak. "It seems to me that any position other than one of extreme alarm is being a Pollyanna," Star said. "I think it is terribly important that we recognize that we are not talking about modest problems but we are talking about an impending crisis."[1]

Star was looking at figures that showed a precipitous drop in the trend line—already on a four decade long decline—measuring the percentage of adults in this country who say they read a daily newspaper during the week.[2] Yet, alarming as Star's message was, it was hardly a new one.

Since he was first hired by the American Newspaper Publishers Association (ANPA) in the late 1970s to conduct a series of newspaper marketing and strategic planning seminars around the country, Star had been warning newspaper editors that an industry that is experiencing a decline in readership is in deep trouble.[3] So it was probably no surprise to hear the newspaper executives kicking around many of the same themes—more target marketing, more research of the marketplace, more attention to the readers—that have become mainstays of the industry's response to its readership problems.

Still, if there was anything new at the Miami gathering, it was a new aggressiveness in the approach of the editors in attendance—and their total lack of reticence in unabashedly touting marketing and the principles of the marketplace as the keys to newspapers' financial future. In fact, *Presstime,* the magazine of the ANPA, which sponsored the Miami gathering, called the meeting a "turning point" in convincing editors that they must remake their newspapers in the name of better reader relations and improved customer service.[4]

Burl Osborne, the publisher and editor of the *Dallas Morning News,* set the tone when he told his convention colleagues that the term "customer"—the "C" word, as he put it—shouldn't be treated as a dirty word in the newsroom. " 'Good journalists' say marketing like they just bit into an apple and found half a worm," Osborne said. And that, he said, must change.[5]

Unfortunately, despite all the brave and hopeful talk about better marketing and more active courtship of readers, the economic situation of the daily newspaper has only deteriorated since that gathering of ANPA members in 1989. A long recession, financial turmoil among their big retail advertisers, and a continuing drop-off in advertising revenues wracked the newspaper business in the early 1990s and left many newsroom employees reeling from slashed newsroom budgets, staff layoffs, and cutbacks in the newshole.[6]

Two years later, at the April 1991 gathering of ANPA's sister group, the American Society of Newspaper Editors (ASNE), a committee of editors issued yet another study about the plight of the industry, this one entitled "Keys to Our Survival," that outlined ways to hold on to readers and to lure back the 45 percent of the population that no longer reads newspapers or is considering stopping.[7]

The heart of the report, produced for ASNE by MORI research, urged newspaper editors to keep stories short enough so they don't jump from page to page, run more briefs and summaries, focus on people rather than events, and run more entertaining material—recommendations MORI and other newspaper consulting firms had been advocating for years. But then MORI went on to urge newspapers to do more in-depth stories, more explanations of complex issues, and more follow-up reports—all in apparent contradiction of the view, long held as gospel in many newspaper quarters, that busy readers don't have time for anything but briefs, summaries, graphics, and stories that entertain or directly relate to their lives.

Virtually at the same time, *Presstime* reported that the cosmetic surgery of the 1980s had not proven effective in stemming the readership slide, and now newspapers were "preparing for heart transplants—radical changes in editorial presentation." The magazine detailed the efforts to "reinvent" newspapers around the country as editors tried to interpret the often confusing results of what they discerned readers wanted from their newspapers.[8] Some editors were putting even greater emphasis on the reader-friendly tactics—easy access, quick-read display, shorter stories, more local information out front, more uses of scanning devices and summary boxes—that have been in vogue the last decade.[9] But others complained that the "cookie-cutter" approach and design gimmicks hadn't worked and readers wanted more in-depth explanations of complex issues. And still others, like the *St. Paul Pioneer Press* with its "Read-It-Fast, Read-It-Slow" format, were trying to appeal to readers who wanted their news in capsule form as well as to those who wanted it in-depth.

What all this means, says Gary Watson, president of Gannett's newspaper division, is that after years of thinking they were giving readers what they wanted, editors "are now finding out they're not— and it's a very difficult pill for some editors to swallow."[10]

Newspaper executives can hardly be blamed if they are perplexed by what the readers—as well as the consultants—are telling them. Readers seem to be telling newspapers that they want more of everything—more foreign and national news, more local news, more investigative pieces and analytical journalism, more briefs and capsules, more relevant stories, more entertainment and help-me-cope information. And then when you give it to them, as frustrated editors complain, they still don't read newspapers.

Yet if there has been one constant within the troubled newspaper industry, it is the willingness, to the point of desperation, of newspaper executives to keep trying to find the magic formula to lure back the elusive reader—and to adopt the marketplace mentality necessary to succeed at it.

While the solutions may be elusive, the readership problems themselves are well understood.[11] By now, daily newspaper executives can tick off the demographic and social changes behind the readership slide as surely as they can the names of their children: television and video-oriented younger people are reading newspapers in alarmingly low percentages, a busy population has less time to read, women are working outside the home, people are moving around more and identifying less with their community, there is more competition for less leisure time, income and education are leveling off, the prime newspaper-reading population is aging, minority groups and a growing wave of foreign-born people don't identify with newspapers.

When they look to the future, executives at daily newspapers feel positively assailed. The proliferation of competitors for people's attention—television, cable TVs, specialty magazines, free shoppers, direct mail, weekly newspapers, home satellite systems—promises to take bigger and bigger bites out of their market every year. And technology continues to keep delivering new problems—desktop publications, digital television, interactive data base delivery systems, home computer shopping, Baby Bell-run electronic information services, fiber optic transmission, and ever smaller and more portable computers.[12]

To make matters worse, the recession has left newspaper executives no longer able to earn profits at the astronomical rates of the past. As late as 1989 the top eight newspaper publishers listed in *Forbes* annual report on American industry ranked second only to soft drink makers in long-term return on equity.[13] But now even in once "safe," monopoly, one-newspaper town markets—which have served as cashboxes for their owners—the advertising revenues are growing less secure. Particularly frightening for newspaper people are the ills that have befallen big retail department stores, which grew up with the daily commercial press and historically have been newspapers' biggest advertisers.[14]

This combination—anxiety about an eroding marketplace, an unrelenting demand for big profits, and a deep fear of what the future holds—has proved to be a potent force in changing the way newspapers are run. The editors of today's newspapers have not only adjusted to the realities of the modern corporate world of financial planning, product packaging, and aggressive marketing—they are doing it with an almost frantic enthusiasm. "Real editors are a dying breed," says Scripps Howard's Susan Miller. "Motivated in part by economic necessity, editors are learning that they are members of a team—the team of departments that produces the daily newspaper. Once upon a time, editors may have had the ability or the luxury to take no interest in the workings of other departments. Now, editors are learning that they must."[15]

The roots of this revolution in modern newspaper management and marketing go back to the late 1970s when newspaper executives began to grow alarmed as readership rates—which had been in decline since the 1950s—began to drop even more steeply. The plunge was particularly noticeable among young readers, who are of vital interest to advertisers—and who, newspaper executives know, are instrumental to the industry's long-term prospects.

In 1977, with the birth of the Newspaper Readership Project, the industry launched a campaign to address the problem in a big way. Spearheaded by ANPA, ASNE, and the Newspaper Advertising Bureau, the project sponsored more than seventy research studies, ten regional gatherings, research training for more than two hundred editors, and dozens of other marketing and education programs.[16]

The part of the $4 million Readership project that spawned many of the changes at newspapers in the last fifteen years was a study commissioned by the American Society of Newspaper Editors, called "Changing Needs of Changing Readers."[17] The study, performed by researcher Ruth Clark and distributed to 3,500 members of seven professional newspaper organizations, urged editors to revamp news content to satisfy the self-fulfillment interests of the 1970s "Me Generation" and respond to readers' desire for help in coping with their personal lives. If society was growing more solipsistic and inward looking, then newspapers must follow, Clark's reasoning went.

Clark's recommendations were the hallmarks of the typical redesigned newspaper of the 1980s. Readers, she said, are hungry for good news, not just bad news. Readers are busy and want their news in brief, easy-to-digest ways. Readers like a newspaper that is well-organized, well-designed, and gives them indices, anchored features, and standardized placement of articles. Clark's message, as many newspaper executives interpreted it, was that newspapers were to find out what readers wanted to read—and then present it to them in their news columns.

Clark's study was just one element of an already ongoing revolution—spurred in large part by advances in printing and computer technology—in newspaper design, graphics, and packaging. While

Clark's recommendations were aimed at the content of the news pages, they also made explicit what had been on the mind of many of the newspaper's financial executives. Relating better to readers and worrying about the needs of the marketplace were familiar concepts to newspaper advertising and marketing directors. But now the readership project made it "respectable—and ultimately de rigueur—for newspaper editors to concern themselves with business questions," as Miller put it.[18]

Madelyn Jennings, Gannett's senior vice president for personnel, captured what rapidly became consensus thinking within the daily newspaper business. "Within the newspaper office we need to remove walls," she wrote in one industry publication.

> Though we preach total newspapering, many of our newsrooms are posting journalism awards but wouldn't dream of posting circulation figures on the bulletin board. Too many of our promotion people wouldn't dream of asking the newsroom to join them in a brainstorming creativity session; and too many of our advertising people don't take the time to tell the press room supervisor how important that clean, on-time press run was to local advertisers.[19]

As part of the new marketing effort, ANPA hired Star to conduct his seminars on how to better market and manage the modern newspaper. In fact, Clark and Star were simply early entrants in the booming field of newspaper consultants, where demand rose steadily in the 1970s and has remained strong in the 1980s and 1990s. No one knows just how many newspaper consultants serve the newspaper business, *Presstime* magazine reports, but the estimates run into the hundreds.[20]

The marketing spirit that swept through newspapers is illustrated in a 1980 essay by Larry D. Franklin, now president and CEO of Harte-Hanks Communications. Newspapers, he says, must become more effective in targeting products to a diverse market. That can be achieved through more effective research that will tell newspapers more about readers and help advertisers reach them. "Newspapers can no longer get by with printing just the news," Franklin said. "They must provide information for coping and for helping the new-value consumer seek self-fulfillment. They must also provide information for escaping and for helping the new-value consumer seek the full, rich life."[21]

The key to this comprehensive marketing strategy is "target marketing," Franklin says, in which advertisers will count on newspapers to help them reach their target market segments. Although neither marketing nor target marketing were new concepts in the newspaper business, the late 1970s and early 1980s saw a virtual stampede by the industry to become more marketing smart.

This fixation on research and marketing burgeoned in the late 1970s. By 1981 about 200 of ANPA's more than 1,400 newspapers had at least one executive with a marketing title, with another 200 served by marketing executives at the group level.[22] And research, once confined to advertising, spread to all phases of the newspaper operation. In the ten years following the forming of the Newspaper Research Council in 1977, its membership jumped from 90 to 240 members.[23] "Enter the computer, the in-depth poll, the MBA," wrote Elise Burroughs in *Presstime* in 1981. "Today, more and more newspaper executives are talking about editorial 'products,' target audiences, market segmentation, shares of advertising, and other formal marketing concepts. And after talking about them, they are making decisions based on them."[24]

Newspaper executives have been encouraged to view the newspaper as a product in the marketplace by marketing people in other segments of the economy—some of whom made a strong impression on their colleagues in publishing. Marketing consultant Gordon Wade told a marketing session for senior newspaper executives in 1986 to follow the "trend analysis" used by other manufacturers to generate new products. "Look for trends and look where they intersect," Wade said. "That's where the opportunity and profits exist. In other industries, this process has led to successes such as Lean Cuisine, Precision Lens Crafters, The Sharper Image, Benetton, Fiber One, and the tripling of cruise business in the past 15 years."[25]

It is no longer surprising to find newspaper executives admitting openly that today's newspapers are edited for the marketplace—and with a keen eye on readership surveys. For example, Frederick Hebert, former marketing director of the *Central New Jersey Home News* in New Brunswick, New Jersey, told *Presstime* about two research projects that he said were designed to help his newspaper's news editors determine the best way to attract and retain readers. "Maybe we will try to attract them with human-interest stories," Hebert said. "Maybe we'll try to get them interested in local news. We just don't know. We have to find out."[26]

As far back as 1978, Arnold Ismach, now dean of the journalism school at the University of Oregon, noted that newspaper owners were launching studies to find out what is needed to attract the elusive reader and tailoring the newspaper to reader interest.

> Research has come into its own in the newsrooms of America, often to the dismay of practicing journalists. Service-oriented stories are blossoming in papers large and small: how to manage your budget, the eleven best pizza parlors in town, techniques for getting along with your spouse [or your friends or yourself], how to keep fit and

happy at forty. Reporters and editors, faced with the imperative of attracting an audience no longer loyal to their traditional efforts, grumble about the change in focus. . . . As a solution to declining readership, they say, the new orientation is like throwing the baby out with the bath water.[27]

Leo Bogart, the recently retired executive vice-president of the Newspaper Advertising Bureau and the newspaper industry's research guru, has shown how dramatically this push for better marketing translated into changes in newspaper content and design. Bogart surveyed 1,310 newspapers in the spring of 1983 and found that two out of three had made substantial changes in editorial content and 71 percent in graphics and layout since 1979.[28] Even before the launching of *USA Today*, color was on the increase, with only 17 percent of the newspapers surveyed not using color and 28 percent using full color, Bogart reported. One-third of newspapers made big changes in the ratio of hard news to features, with the ratio running two-to-one for more features. And Bogart said newspapers were doing much more sectionalizing, regional zoning, and target marketing aimed at upscale consumers.[29] However, Bogart also noted that this trend toward "reader-driven" newspapers hadn't stemmed the decline in readership rates.[30]

The move toward more aggressive marketing can be measured not only by the changes in newspapers, but by what's on the minds of top newspaper executives, too. One of the most interesting pieces of research during this period was done by Ray Laakaniemi, who analyzed the speeches given by editors, researchers, and newspaper executives at trade conferences between 1982 and 1986. Laakaniemi reported that some of the executives' most strongly advocated ways to "improve" newspapers were: (1) to use more marketing research to better understand the different needs of the reading audience; (2) to use news items that would be of greater help to readers; (3) to close the editor-reader gap; (4) to create a "friendlier" newspaper by adding a personal touch; (5) to pay attention to the busy lives of readers by creating newspapers they can read quickly; (6) to recognize that reader interests have shifted to the suburbs; (7) to add more charts and indexes; (8) to balance the bad news with more good news.[31]

However, as was to become commonplace in the years ahead, editors barely had time to digest the advice of one market study before they were faced with new conclusions about what readers wanted. The recommendations of Clark's first study were still being implemented throughout the industry when she delivered what's become known as "Ruth Clark II," which she presented to the ASNE's annual convention in 1984.[32] This time, Clark discarded her advice that readers wanted self-help and help-me-cope information and told the editors readers now sought hard news, real news, facts about health, science, technology. This about-face in reader attitudes, she explained in the *Bulletin* of ASNE, was caused by the economic and foreign policy problems that embroiled the country in the late 1970s and early 1980s. The recession of the early 1980s and the country's overseas troubles had led to a "new realism" about society and the economy's limits, she said. People were worried about nuclear war, AIDS, crime, toxic waste, U.S. global trade problems, and they wanted to be kept well-informed about the fast pace of change.[33]

By the mid-1980s, Clark wasn't the only one cautioning newspaper executives that they should get back to the basics of news delivery and worry less about marketing solutions. Bogart also concluded that newspaper's new emphasis on brief text, softer news, personality journalism, entertainment features, and help-me-cope articles was running counter to readership data showing readers were more interested in what is going on in the world.[34] Bogart said research even shows that readership is high for longer articles—demonstrating, he said, that people will read what's relevant to them regardless of length.[35]

In fact, Bogart has been a consistent voice of caution in the face of the changes sweeping through newspapers. As early as 1981 Bogart was warning in his book *Press and Public* against "market thinkers" who try to give readers what they want as measured in readership surveys. Bogart says, among other things, that editors should be shaping not following public taste; that professional newspeople substantially underestimate the levels of reader interest in serious news; and that the impact of changes in editorial content are hard to sort out from the other social and economic forces affecting newspapers. Bogart says editors should be happy to know that they have a "wide range of options" in handling content because the real critical issues for newspaper survival involve pricing, delivery, service, and other conditions "over which they have no control."[36]

Bogart concluded that newspapers have the best chance of attracting readers if they perform their traditional functions of explaining the world very well and do not try to find salvation in marketing gimmicks. "It is fantasy to believe that a newspaper can be designed and packaged like a bar of soap or a can of dogfood or even like a television news program," Bogart says. "Its symbolic texture is too complex for that; its elements are too rich."[37]

Interestingly, Bogart is joined in his advice by Christine Urban, one of the leaders among newspaper consultants who have helped bring the principles of marketing to newspapers. Urban outlined "10 Myths about readers" in a 1986 *Bulletin* of ASNE, including the "myths" that readers want short stories (readers think important stories should be long, less important ones short, she says); more color and graphics will attract circulation (readers think color improves newspapers, but it's unlikely to attract new readers); upscale individuals are better newspaper readers (blue collar and middle income readers are the mainstay of newspapers as a mass medium); TV is taking away readers (studies show that newspapers aren't direct competitors of TV, and, in fact, TV may stimulate people to buy newspapers); readers want gossip and sensationalism (readers want the same kind of good journalism as do most journalists); content changes and gimmicks can attract readers (research shows that the back-to-basics strategy of doing a better job of a newspaper's primary mission of reporting the news is a good one); redesigns, special sections, and content changes that are a success at one newspaper can be transferred to another (they can't).[38]

There is some irony, of course, in finding the industry's own researchers questioning the trends they have helped launch. But for the most part newspaper executives aren't about to be broken of their addiction to marketing studies or dissuaded from their quest for the reader-friendly newspaper. If nothing else, the marketing philosophy has become ingrained into the newspaper structure during the past decade, with marketing managers, design and graphics editors, survey researchers, and financial consultants now an integral part of the management team in many newsrooms.

People like Frank McCulloch, a former McClatchy and *Time* magazine top editor, and the recently retired managing editor of the *San Francisco Examiner*, laments what he calls the "invidious pressure" of the "MBA mentality" that has come to dominate the newspaper business.[39] "I don't think editors are as good or as powerful as they were 10–15 years ago," adds David Burgin, who recently left his post as editor of the *Houston Post*. "The new power in the industry is the marketing director. I want to see more swashbuckling editors, like Ben Bradlee or Jim Bellows. But those days are dead. Now it's target marketing and target marketing and more marketing."[40]

Like McCulloch and Burgin, few observers believe that the setbacks experienced by the new breed of corporate editors—the underlying financial troubles shaking the newspaper industry, growing frustration at the inconclusiveness of much market research, or more vain campaigns to lure elusive readers—are going to stem the trend toward more marketing and managerialism. This is particularly true, they note, as the newspaper industry, like other American industries, becomes increasingly dominated by ever more concentrated, corporate ownership.

As Ellis Cose, the author of *The Press*, puts it, the next generation of executives—the MBA babies—will be more comfortable with financial management and marketing strategies. In the 1990s, he predicts, newsrooms will be more objective about what it means when the barriers between the business side and the news side of the newspaper have crumbled.[41] Newspapers in the future "will be less tolerant of oddballs and erratic visionaries—brilliant though they may be," Cose writes. "The emphasis will be on collaboration, on building compatible teams, on taking fewer risks. An increasing number of newsroom executives will come from finance or general management and have responsibility for controlling costs and managing process. Though they will not be editors, they will inevitably force editors to question some of the practices followed in the past."[42]

CHAPTER TWO

The Marketers
and Managers
Move In

There has developed a new breed of editors . . . who are less defensive about their prerogatives. . . . There is more commitment . . . that the newspaper is being put out for the benefit of readers instead of for the benefit of the Pulitzer Prize Committee.
—Al Gollin, vice-president of research for the Newspaper Advertising Bureau

There is a fallacy in that calculation. . . . The fallacy is if you edit that way, to give back to readers only what they think they want, you'll never give them something new they don't know about. You stagnate. . . . The whole thing begins to be circular. Creativity and originality and spontaneity goes out of it.
—William Shawn, former editor of the *New Yorker*

A manager is a manager. Modern professional managerial techniques apply to whatever the product is.
—Francis Dale, former publisher of the now defunct *Los Angeles Herald Examiner*

The challenge of American newspapers "is not to stay in business—it is to stay in journalism."
—Harold Evans, former editor of the *Times* of London, England

STUART SCHWARTZ is a marketing executive who has always done unabashedly what most newspaper marketers do quietly, behind-the-scenes, without advertising their impact on the news product. Schwartz, the corporate director of marketing and sales for Lee Enterprises, once circulated charts showing which of the chain's papers had the highest story counts, the shortest stories, the most page-one refers (reference lines to similar stories), and the fewest page-one jumps.

Schwartz's charts—part of a program called "Meeting Our Readers'

Expectations"—could be found hanging on the bulletin board at the *Quad City Times* of Davenport, Iowa, Lee's flagship newspaper, and were circulated to the editors at Lee's dailies in seventeen other cities.[1] And Schwartz points proudly to the work of the executives at Quad City, who have "quantitative goals" to meet, as Schwartz put it: shorter stories, a greater variety of headlines, higher story counts, more refers, and more design devices to draw readers into the page. The point of the program, says John Gardner, the former Quad City publisher, is "to listen and tailor our product to the marketplace. Our readers tell us, 'We don't want to work very hard, we don't want to struggle through what you're trying to tell us.' They like stories they can use for their coffee-break talk."[2]

In some circles, Lee and its executives are viewed as zealots on the topic of marketing and an embarrassment to the industry. But while Schwartz's efforts at standardizing the company's marketing program may seem excessive, he is only an outspoken—and, some would say, openly honest—advocate of a trend that has pushed newspapers into the business of marketing and reshaped newsrooms to dovetail with those marketing goals. "Newspapers will be with us at the turn of the century but many of the traditional jobs will not," warns Richard Handt, systems editor of the *Daily News* of Los Angeles. "The management teams that can read the public's mood and adapt quickly enough to give the reader what he or she wants—at the right price—will have their products on the market when the 21st century arrives."[3]

It's probably no surprise that in an era of mass media conglomerates, big chain expansion, and multimillion dollar newspaper buy-outs, the editors of daily newspapers have begun to behave more and more like the managers of any other corporate entity. And it's understandable, too, that after more than a decade of Ronald Reagan and George Bush's laissez-faire leadership and an anything-goes ethic in the boardroom, the executives of today's daily newspapers have decided to treat their readership as a market and the news as a product to appeal to that market.

These marketplace pressures have led to the appearance of a new kind of editor, a cross between an editor and a marketing official. The model of this hybrid editor as part of a marketing team—and, in some cases, the leader of the team—has gained great popularity in newspaper circles over the last decade.[4] The new, marketing-oriented editor is an outgrowth of a concept known as "The Total Newspaper," where newspaper executives are urged to coordinate the news and business departments and work together to market the newspaper as a total product. In the book *Promoting The Total Newspaper*, Paul Hirt, formerly senior vice president of the *Chicago Sun-Times*, writes that newspaper departments used to be run as "fiefdoms" where "hostility" and "adversarial relations" between department heads were common.[5] In contrast, the "Total Newspaper" is a place, Hirt explains, where editorial, advertising, circulation, research, and promotion functions are all coordinated around marketing concerns.

Not surprisingly, the concept of "total newspapering" is embraced by the newspaper's marketing people who not only developed the idea in the early 1970s but have increasingly sold it to their counterparts on the editorial side. Clearly, the concept has been a boon to the business-side people, whose influence within the news organization has expanded greatly. "No more sitting in the basement counting beans," says Robert Kasabian, executive director of the International Newspaper Financial Executives. "Financial officers are in the board rooms. We're in the publishers' offices, helping make decisions."[6]

Philip Meyer, a former Knight-Ridder executive who now teaches at the University of North Carolina, has emerged as a strong advocate for the idea of total newspapering—albeit a cautious one. In his *Newspaper Survival Book*, Meyer writes that editors must consider using some "salesmanship" in their job. "An editor should at least approach the market ethic with an open mind and give some tentative consideration to the possibility that there might be some value in it," Meyer writes.[7]

Some editors are as sheepish-sounding as Meyer in advocating the cause of marketing the newspaper. But a growing number of newspaper executives who came up on the news side now define their job in terms of the marketplace—and some, such as Mike Fancher of the *Seattle Times*, Burl Osborne of the *Dallas Morning News*, David Lawrence of the *Miami Herald*, Larry Jinks of the *San Jose Mercury News*, and Knight-Ridder's James Batten have earned MBAs or spent time in business school programs as a way to improve their financial acumen.[8]

Ben J. Bowers, executive editor of the *Greensboro (N.C.) News and Record* who attended a special executive management program at Harvard business school, acknowledges that in his job he talks with financial, advertising, and marketing people as a matter of course. "I'm still not a number cruncher, but finance very definitely is part of the overall strategic planning," Bowers says.[9]

Fancher has become quite influential in industry circles by proselytizing that an editor's job is now one of managing—"managing people, managing systems, and managing resources," as he puts it—as much as it is editing. At industry seminars and in industry publications, he urges his fellow editors to abandon the idea that journalistic quality and a marketplace orientation are mutually exclusive. "In the best of worlds, excellence in journalism and success in the marketplace are two sides of one coin," he says.[10]

The implications of this "managing for the market" philosophy have spread into many of the nation's newsrooms, including those of some of the finest newspapers. For example, Gene Roberts, the highly respected former executive editor of Knight-Ridder's award-winning *Philadelphia Inquirer,* was one of a handful of editors who also took on the duties of circulation manager (an experimental move, he says, which he abandoned shortly afterward).[11]

In fact, Roberts has openly lamented the negative consequences of profiteering and superficial journalism and design gimmickery among the media conglomerates since he left the business.[12] But many of his former colleagues in Knight-Ridder—among them some of the most highly regarded executives in the business—have wholeheartedly endorsed the trend toward market-driven journalism. And they have little use for critics—even those inside their own company—who have been appalled at watching a chain that has always prided itself on quality jumping on the marketing bandwagon.

"This industry needs to be changed," replies Lawrence, publisher of Knight-Ridder's flagship newspaper, to the charge that newspapers have become too market-conscious. "My job is to reach people. That means we've got to sell newspapers. I've got enough real things to worry about. That's a straw man." Lawrence adds, "Our business has been through and will continue to go through a lot of change. Some people aren't going to like the pace. But I'm not setting the pace. The marketplace is setting the pace."[13]

In fact, Knight-Ridder chairman Batten has become one of the most prominent proponents of market-based journalism with his companywide "customer-obsession" campaign and with the company's unveiling of the "experimental" Boca Raton *News,* which was designed and test-marketed to appeal to young, busy, upscale readers. *Business Month* magazine profiled Batten under the headline, "Customers First: After a Year as CEO, Jim Batten Is Campaigning to Get Every Knight-Ridder Newspaper Employee Thinking Like a Marketer."[14] The article discussed Batten's crusade to make Knight-Ridder a "customer-obsessed" company "practically the way Allstate was the good hands people." To do this, Batten's top managers have enlisted the help of top management consultants, made the campaign a focus of company training, put "customer-obsessed" logos on company paraphernalia, and held meetings with skeptical journalists who are told that the customer-oriented changes are needed to turn around dipping circulation and household penetration rates.

Knight-Ridder isn't the only high quality, high prestige organization that has been transformed by the push toward market-minded journalism. The *Wall Street Journal* went through a major redesign—with some of the ideas for changing its design growing out of market surveys.[15] The *Los Angeles Times,* once known for its imposing layout and its brilliant but lengthy writing, has also been redesigned under the helm of editor Shelby Coffey III, a move which some saw as a response to upscale competitors like the *Orange County Register,* which had made inroads into the *Times*'s market with its splashy design, its pacesetting graphics, and its formulas for reader-friendly journalism.[16]

Even Max Frankel, the executive editor of the *New York Times,* once thought of as the last bastion of traditional newspaper standards, has metamorphosed into a champion of reader-driven newspapering.[17] Frankel describes how the nation's preeminent newspaper has been trying to make the newspaper's once intimidating news columns a friendlier place to browse by using inside pages that are filled with "blurbs," charts, shadow boxes, balloon captions, shaded graphs, previews, refers.

"People don't read the paper from start to finish; they dip in and out," Frankel says. "It's like a supermarket of great riches; you don't expect readers to be interested in everything any more than you'd expect customers to buy everything in the store." *Times* assistant managing editor Allan M. Siegal adds, "Max thinks we're taking readers' attention too much for granted. We need to be ruthless in admitting how little time readers have for us. If they can't find what they need fast enough or if they get the impression it's just too goddamn much, then they're going to read someone else or not read anything at all."[18]

There are, of course, editors who express discomfort with the move toward marketplace journalism, even as they've been pressured to embrace it. Jim Gannon, who was the editor of the *Des Moines Register* when Gannett purchased the newspaper, maintains that Gannett hasn't done anything to undermine the *Register*'s position as one of the Midwest's most respected publications.[19] Still, Gannon, who is now the Gannett-owned *Detroit News*'s Washington, D.C., bureau chief, acknowledges that there are "pressures on editors to think more like marketers." If readers aren't interested in government and foreign policy, Gannon says, then the job of the modern editor is to "figure out what they are interested in. . . . I think it's a very unhealthy trend,"

Gannon says. "If you couple that with a concern over the level of education of the kids coming out of our schools relative to the Japanese kids, I think there's a definite cause and effect. Everybody talks about this at industry sessions. Sure, they think it's unhealthy. But the bottom line is, the bulldog has to be fed."[20]

Even at newspapers where money has been spent in the newsroom, marketing concerns may be the major motivation. One of the biggest stories in journalism during the last decade was the appointment at the Atlanta *Journal and Constitution* of Bill Kovach, the former *New York Times* Washington, D.C., bureau chief who hoped to bring a more aggressive, in-depth style of coverage to Southern journalism. Kovach eventually quit as editor of the newspapers in a much-celebrated battle with their owner, Cox Newspapers. Kovach insists that resources were never the problem when he was in Atlanta. But he does criticize the marketing motivations of today's newspaper editors who have taken to "pandering, chasing celebrities," as he puts it, at the expense of hard news and covering government institutions.

"Where the pressure comes," Kovach says, "is to make the reporting the staff produces more enticing in order to raise circulation and raise advertising rates. It's pressure to always grow that changes the nature of journalism. It has more territory and wants to offend fewer people."[21]

Not surprisingly, Kovach's successors take a more benign view of the move among newspapers toward market-based strategizing. Atlanta *Journal and Constitution* managing editor John Walter (who works for Kovach's successor, Ron Martin, the first executive editor of *USA Today*), says the new trends are simply a correction for an industry that had become too sober and too out-of-touch with readers. "We're accepting once more, as they did thirty years ago, that there should be interaction between the public and newspapers," he says. "Back then it wasn't faxes and phone numbers. It was that the newspaper people were of the public. But we got overeducated and forgot. Now, with embarrassment, with little apologetic titters, we're gathering up the courage to go back."[22]

In fact, diminished coverage of government has been one fallout of the move toward market-oriented journalism. Carl Sessions Stepp notes that editors have paid close attention to polls that show readers (and particularly young readers) don't "connect" with government news. Stepp quotes journalists who say the public's eyes "glaze over" with boredom at government coverage. "We're covering a great deal less of the turn-of-the-wheel kind of thing," says Davis Merritt, Jr., executive editor of the *Wichita Eagle*. "Nobody gives a damn."[23]

Stepp applauds the move among newspapers away from the mundane, process-oriented coverage of government and toward explanatory journalism that presents issues in a skillful and compelling manner. But he also worries about signs that newspapers are forsaking their social responsibility as monitors of government—particularly, he says, if the motivation comes from marketers tailoring the product to perceived audience taste. In a period of shorter stories and shrunken newshole, he says, it's probably fair to assume that publishers will use public alienation as an excuse to cut government coverage. "Don't rule out a period of retreat during which resource-hungry publishers defang watchdog journalists and snatch reporters and space from the government desk," he says.[24]

The backdrop of the marketing controversy is money, of course, and newspapers haven't been making as much of it in recent years. Former *Wall Street Journal* reporter Jonathan Kwitny has detailed how the financial misfortunes of newspapers have hammered newsroom budgets, cut news coverage at daily newspapers all around the country, and accelerated the trend toward market-based solutions.[25] Kwitny says the pain has been caused by publicly held newspaper companies trying to maintain pretax profits of between 20 and 40 percent despite the economic downturn. Kwitny says these sky-high profit expectations (which he compares to profit margins of between 5.8 and 9.4 percent at Exxon and 10.6 and 15.6 percent at IBM) are the result of the growing phenomenon of one-newspaper markets, the expansion of newspaper chains fixated on the bottom line, and the pressure of Wall Street brokers who have no concern for anything but the performance of newspaper stocks.

While the cutbacks have been particularly traumatic at companies like Knight-Ridder, the budget pressures have wreaked even more havoc at lesser-known chains that have adopted all the latest marketing devices in the service of the bottom line—and little else. For every Knight-Ridder or *Los Angeles Times* or *Wall Street Journal,* where journalists with consciences at least struggle with the implications of market-minded journalism, there are a myriad of high-profit newspaper chains that have adopted design changes and reader-friendly tactics as a cheap way to make their newspapers look improved without spending anything upon (and often slashing) newsroom resources. Some of the worst case scenarios of conglomerate ownership are illustrated in *The Buying and Selling of America's Newspapers,* edited by Loren Ghiglione. In the section on the Worrell company, one of the dozens of little-known chains that have gobbled up independent newspapers around the country in recent years, Ben A. Franklin describes how owner Tom Worrell often elevates the advertising directors of his properties to publisher and puts them on tenuous tenure, tied to profit norms. "A newspaper is a business," Worrell is quoted as saying. "You can't operate a newspaper unless you run it like a business."[26]

In describing how the Ingersoll chain has decimated the *Transcript* of North Adams, Massachusetts, in search of outstanding profits, Ghiglione says newsroom costs were reduced, newshole slashed, and the budget became gospel. Ingersoll's formulas are laid out in a large loose-leaf—"Financial Control Standards"—that set cost and income goals for the news executives at his newspapers. "It's like a military manual," Donald Sprague, Jr., a former *Transcript* publisher, told Ghiglione. "There is absolutely no room for innovative thinking. You're not a publisher or a general manager because you're really not supposed to have any of your own ideas. The bottom line is the deciding factor. If you have to cut newshole, reporters—anything to control the bottom line."[27]

The growth of the newspaper chains in the 1970s and 1980s has made it much easier to spread the cause of marketing and managerialism—and even some of the industry's own top executives have become alarmed. Both the late C. K. McClatchy and Eugene Patterson, former chairman and chief executive officer of the *St. Petersburg Times,* whose well-regarded newspaper company was forced to fend off a takeover bid by a group of leveraged-buy-out artists, spoke out regularly against the growing commercialization of the news business and the bottom-line orientation of many of the U.S.'s more than 150 newspaper chains.

"The news business is exposed to the same virus that's infected the nation's business," said Patterson. "Too often we're taking a financial approach to a creative enterprise: investing for short-term earnings instead of betting on long-term quality, settling for fatness in the bottom line . . . and getting pretty complacent about what's expected of us in the way of public service in return for that constitutional shield we wear."[28]

Ironically, for all the emotion it arouses, journalists simply haven't settled the debate over the impact of chain ownership upon journalism quality. Defenders of chains, such as Larry Fuller, the publisher of Gannett's Sioux Falls, South Dakota, *Argus Leader,* say that only romantics believe that the journalism at independent newspapers is inherently better than that at chain-owned papers. Many of the newspapers that have been purchased by chains were so bad, chain ownership couldn't help but improve them, he says. "We have to change as society changes and everybody has to recognize that," says Fuller. "In my opinion, the problem isn't the newspapers that have changed; it's the problem of newspapers that haven't. You look at many newspapers and they're still frighteningly dull."[29]

In fact, the remaining independent newspapers have been far from immune to the trends of reader-driven journalism and bottom-line management. George Wilson, former president of ANPA and the president of the family-owned *Monitor* in Concord, New Hampshire, maintains that newspapers weren't in such great shape three decades ago—and he believes the change toward improved marketing has been welcome. "What we used to do was throw the thing together," Wilson said. "As much charm as there was twenty-five years ago, there was a hell of a lot of arbitrary decision making going on. If anything, the balance of power has shifted to the reader—and that's a good thing."[30]

Academic studies tend to mirror the ambivalence among journalists about the impact of chain ownership on the quality of newspapers. Some academic studies have found evidence that chains have undermined newspaper quality at their properties; others haven't.[31] "There is no compelling evidence that newspaper readers have been ill served by the trend toward groups," says Benjamin Compaine in summarizing the various studies on the subject. "There are at least as many documented cases in which a paper purchased by a group was substantially improved as there are cases in which a paper was weakened."[32]

Unfortunately, few of the studies have looked very deeply into the way conglomerates manage their properties. In general, the researchers have examined things that are relatively easy to measure—such as the quality of editorial pages or the size of newshole before and after a chain purchase. However, these factors seldom tell the whole story. In fact, chain owners are often quite savvy at implementing the kind of cosmetic improvements that are designed to impress most readers—and apparently many researchers, too.

Critics of the growing conglomeratization of the media, like Ben Bagdikian, argue that many of these academic studies miss the point anyway. The lack of diverse ownership, he says, presents the danger of a narrowing of political and social debate to conform to corporate objectives. Bagdikian argues that it is the homogenization of content—what he calls the "Howard Johnsonizing" of newspapers—that promises to substitute "light entertainment, fantasy, and salesmanship" for "ideas and information."[33]

Bagdikian has virtually made a career out of chronicling the growing domination of the mass media by fewer and fewer companies. In 1982 Bagdikian pointed out that fifty corporations controlled half or more of all U.S. media outlets. In 1984 that number had shrunk to forty-four corporations.[34] In the United States, fifty dailies a year changed hands from 1977 to 1985, most purchased by newspaper groups.[35] While the growth of chains has slowed some in recent years, the inflated prices paid for newspaper properties and the bias in favor of newspaper corporations in the nation's tax laws (which makes it difficult for family-owned companies to pass on properties while letting newspaper corporations perpetually maintain their holdings and reduce their taxes by using profits to buy more newspapers) insure that the trend toward greater concentration in the newspaper industry is unlikely to ease.

Reformers have pushed for changes in the tax laws, urged the government to enforce antitrust laws more aggressively, and called on Congress to put a limit on newspaper holdings. But few special interests have a greater (although quieter) hold on Congress, whose members are deeply aware that newspaper owners have an inordinate say in their political fate. Naturally, the sway of media organizations over government officials is seldom discussed in newspapers, in the same way that other legislative issues that affect the financial prospects of newspapers seldom break into the news columns.

If the galloping growth of newspaper conglomerates was ever a public controversy—and there is doubt that it ever was—it certainly doesn't seem to be a hot topic these days. The last time dust was kicked up over the issue was in 1977 when former Representative Morris Udall, D-Ariz., upset at Gannett's purchase of his hometown *Tucson Citizen,* introduced legislation to break up newspaper chains. It is ironic that John Seigenthaler, then the editor of the *Tennessean* in Nashville, Tennessee, and the strongest voice in favor of independent newspapers, was a key witness against the chains during congressional hearings on concentration in the newspaper industry. However, after Gannett purchased the *Tennessean* in 1979, Seigenthaler went to work for the company and, as editorial director of *USA Today,* became a defender of chain ownership.

Bagdikian is now raising warning flags about the transformation of media into a multinational industry with ownership crossing national boundaries. In his latest report, Bagdikian predicts that by the mid-1990s a handful of mammoth private organizations will control most of the world's newspapers, magazines, books, broadcast stations, movies, recordings, and videocassettes—a trend that he says will exert a dangerously homogenizing power over society's cultures and values. "No small group of organizations is wise enough or unselfish enough to provide most of the news, information, scholarship, literature and entertainment for a whole society, let alone most of the world," he says.[36]

The realities of this corporate world—and the changes wrought by technology, a busy and fickle public, and the demands of Wall Street—

have left even the industry's most thoughtful executives torn between their traditional sense of journalistic responsibility and the pressures to adjust to the times. Anyone who engages today's editors in conversation about the profit and marketing pressures placed on newspapers will often encounter real concerns about the direction of the journalism business. But invariably the conversation will end with the reassuring analysis that it is possible to pursue success in the marketplace without compromising the goals of journalism.

William Winter, a former Knight-Ridder executive and executive director of the American Press Institute, shows how the debate can cut both ways—even in the mind of the same person. In 1988 API unveiled a computer simulation program to teach newspaper executives in a mock setting how to make decisions affecting all departments by manipulating advertising, circulation, and production data.[37] However, despite developing these tools for better management of the "total newspaper," Winter has also expressed his concern about an industry that is looking for "efficient and effective newsroom executives" who are "team builders" and "hawks on the budget" and "button-down managers." In putting such an emphasis on management routine and the intense pursuit of higher profits, Winter laments, "we may be losing our grip on some qualities we won't be able to recoup. . . . It does strike me that twenty years ago, or even ten, there was more personality in our business, less fear of taking chances, less looking back over one's shoulder, waiting for the controller to strike." The compromise, he finally suggests, is to seek newspaper executives who are "efficiency models with a soul."[38]

In fact, this kind of glib analysis sounds convincing coming from the many executives—well schooled in the soothing phrases of consensus management and reader-friendliness—who run the modern newspaper. But there are many journalists who work under editors whose mastery of the buzzwords of modern management theory may sound impressive at journalism panels and before public forums, but whose newsrooms are in a painful transition to the marketplace-oriented newsrooms of the future. Sometimes it takes exposure to the consultants who have proliferated throughout the business to see how the language of "team building" and "resource management" can mask a harsher reality.

At the 1987 Associated Press Managing Editors convention in Seattle, for example, Louis LeHane of Thompson Group, a consulting firm, urged editors "to create a culture" in their newsrooms that will ensure that reporters and midlevel editors will not resist the application of new business management practices. To achieve this end, he suggested that management should set up teams, develop lots of dialogue, and create "win-win situations." LeHane ended his remarks on this note of eerie managementese: "Some of the people may be forced to learn by peer pressure, because in a participatory system, the noncontributors— those who can't go from the rejection to the acceptance stage—really aren't tolerated."[39]

In translation, this means the new newsroom is no place for nonconformists. And, increasingly, it is not.

CHAPTER THREE

Inside the Managed Newsroom

Editors in charge of the newsroom have to build a team and make it clear that, in the best interest of the newsroom, people have to get on the team.

—Bob Giles, editor and publisher of the *Detroit News*

Once the IBM types take over, they'll reward and promote other IBM types.

—Drex Heikes, former metro editor, the *Fresno Bee*

If they say you're meeting-crazy, don't worry. You can't plan too much.

—Walker Lundy, editor of the *St. Paul Pioneer Press*

Papers shouldn't be editor dominated. They [editors] sit in offices and get ideas from what they read. But if you're not reporting out there, you've turned the process around.

—John Kolesar, ex-night-news editor of the *Record* of Hackensack, N.J.

WHEN a new draft of the editorial mission of the *Free Press* in London, Ontario, was announced by top executives, city editor Don Gibb protested. The mission statement said that, among other things, the newsroom was going to be expected to work to enhance the paper's profit picture. The protest by Gibb and others worked—the reference to profit was removed from the mission statement. But shortly thereafter, Gibb resigned. "I don't think profit is a dirty word," Gibb said. "But it does not have a place in the running of the newsroom." [1]

Such purist thinking can get a journalist in trouble—particularly in Canada where press freedoms don't have the same constitutional protections as in the U.S. and where most of the country's daily newspapers are controlled by two highly profitable, business-minded chains, the Southam and Thomson groups.

While MBA journalism may be a relatively new phenomenon in the U.S., Canadian journalists say it is only the latest variation in a long-time tradition of bottom-line management at Canadian newspapers, which are unapologetic in declaring themselves to be profit-centers first and foremost.

Although their methods may be a bit extreme, the moves by the editors of the *Free Press* to adopt the formulas of market-oriented journalism fit a pattern all over the U.S. and Canada as daily newspapers are being reshaped to please readers and advertisers—but often at the expense of upsetting newsroom staffers.

Nowhere were the principles of marketplace newspapering carried out with more enthusiasm—and met with more unhappiness—than at the *Free Press,* where editors, armed with surveys of their readership, virtually overnight revamped the newspaper into a local version of *USA Today* that follows "a McPaper formula, processing bite-sized chunks of easily digestible news that sell well," as Mark Richardson put it in the *Ryerson Review of Journalism.* [2]

In a protest piece, Gibb wrote in *Content* magazine that the newspaper had fallen under the "formula pap" of "MBA journalism" where "profit is the driving force over quality journalism." He said surveys dictate what stories the newspaper will run, graphics and new formats are developed by consultants, and reporters are told by editors what their stories should say before they write them."Today, there is a feeling of despair in the [*Free Press*] newsroom," Gibb wrote. "It has been sapped of enthusiasm, initiative and creativity because reporters feel they have little or no control over what they do." [3]

Editor Philip McLeod said that, despite similarities, the redesigned newspaper isn't an imitation of *USA Today,* but he admitted that its emphasis is on readability rather than on the writing in the newspaper. "Good writing often gets in the way of other things you're trying to do," McLeod said. [4]

Critics of MBA-style journalism say they see a clear pattern when the marketers gain control of a newspaper. Not only does the substance of the newspaper become secondary to the planning, prettifying, and promoting of the newspaper, but newspaper executives often must institute tough newsroom management systems in order to bring along newsworkers reluctant to buy into the philosophy of market-oriented journalism.

Many of those journalists speak with great passion—and much disillusionment—about what is happening to the newspaper business. "If ten, fifteen years ago, you told someone in a newsroom, 'This is our product,' they would have looked at you like you were nuts," says a former *Hartford Courant* reporter quoted in Andrew Kreig's *Spiked.*

"Products were shoes. But now newspapers are thought of as products, marketed as products. It's a different philosophy. And when you change the shape of an industry like that, you're going to have terrible discontent—legitimate discontent—among the people who have been in it."[5]

"Compared to twenty years ago, a lot of the fun has gone out of journalism," adds R. W. "Johnny" Apple, the long-time political writer for the *New York Times* and a headliner in the zany cast of presidential campaign reporters in Timothy Crouse's 1972 classic, *The Boys on the Bus*. "This used to be a business that attracted a lot of nonconformists, oddballs and unusual characters, in terms of interest, background, and appearance. A lot of that seems to have been leached out of the business somehow. I look out around the *New York Times* newsroom [now], it looks like a law firm."[6]

Ironically, even some top news executives admit to the absurdity of becoming overly focused on systems management. "In my corporate career so far, to name a few, I have been through the OR&S Era, the Plan, Organize, Implement, Manage and Control Era, the McGregor X and Y Era, the Blue Collar Blues Era, the T-Group and Sensitivity Training Era, the Managerial Grid Era, and now, the Productivity/Theory Z Era," says Madelyn Jennings, senior vice-president of Gannett Corporation. "Fashions in managerial style come . . . and, much like some politicians who inhabit Washington, they come, and they blow, and they go."[7]

Yet no matter what they call it, the focus on managing people and managing resources means a return to a "strong" editing system in the newsrooms of today's market-oriented newspapers. These days, the newsroom isn't being run by the autocratic publisher or the tough-talking city editor of yore. Modern management philosophy is being ladled out with a heavy dose of sophisticated, business school jargon. But beneath it lies inexorable, technology-driven, and market-driven change. All this has caused considerable stress from the top to the bottom of the news organization. Researcher Ted Pease found in a survey of 1,328 newsroom employees that 46 percent wouldn't want their child to pursue a career in newspaper journalism. "There are a lot of angry people in newsrooms," Pease said. "Regardless of race, color, creed or sex, people say horrible things about their managers. It's not just dissatisfaction; there's real anger about mismanagement."[8]

Interestingly, a survey of 212 editors undertaken for the Associated Press Managing Editors found that corporate expectations, more than the traditional newsroom pressures, were what caused the modern editor stress on the job. The editors in the survey said they found it stimulating to deal with deadlines, problems of accuracy, staff management, and conflict in the newsroom. The most stressful elements of their job, they reported, were when their news values were put into conflict with the company's profit goals.[9]

Bob Giles, then managing editor of Gannett's Rochester newspapers and the person who supervised the study, says,

> Fifteen years ago, editors were editors. Today they are editor-managers. They direct the editing of the newspaper with one hand and, with the other, they are deeply involved in business management. This editor is expected to carry on in the best traditions of journalistic excellence, but also is expected to share the responsibility for the newspaper as a "profit center." Many editors discovered that this dual obligation created unfamiliar stresses.[10]

Giles himself appears to have made the adjustment. Now editor and publisher of the *Detroit News,* he has written a seven-hundred-page tome, *Newsroom Management: A Guide to Theory and Practice,* which, complete with charts on motivation, models of conflict resolution, and graphs on leadership, is designed as a blueprint for how to be a modern newsroom manager.[11] Giles replaced Ben Burns as top editor of the *News* soon after Gannett purchased the newspaper in 1986. Since then, the *News* has become known as one of the country's premier graphics newspapers, with a slick, splashy, color-filled feel to it.[12] And Burns, who teaches in the journalism program at Wayne State University, doesn't mince words in describing what he thinks is happening to the business.

> Modern corporation management and packaging theories are sapping the vitality of creative editors and reporters. It's the General Motors syndrome. In order to survive, newspapers try to look like everybody else. People who stand out from the crowd are at risk. And what you breed out of editors is the willingness to take risks with their careers. Now we think we can create good editors by management training. You end up with a CPA mentality.[13]

If the corporate demands cause stress for top editors, they are causing stress for midlevel editors and reporters, too. As far back as the early 1970s, researcher John W. C. Johnstone and his colleagues discovered how little journalists liked to relinquish control over assignments and editorial freedom—a finding that has been noted by other researchers since.[14] In their nationwide survey of journalists, Johnstone and his colleagues found that the job satisfaction of reporters diminishes in larger organizations, and greater professional autonomy was consistently a predictor of greater career happiness.[15] "The bureaucratization of newswork is an aspect of the contemporary media experience that few journalists regard with warmth, and it is one of the principal sources of job dissatisfaction in journalism today," Johnstone wrote.[16]

In their replications of Johnstone's study in the early 1980s and early 1990s, David H. Weaver and G. Cleveland Wilhoit concluded that the job dissatisfaction has climbed considerably in the years since the Johnstone study.[17] The most likely defectors from newspapers, they concluded, are midcareer journalists with the most education, experience, sense of job autonomy, and altruistic beliefs. The implications, Weaver and Wilhoit say in their 1981–82 study, are that the new technologies and concentration of ownership—along with increased editor authority—have lessened reporter freedom in a way that's a worry for the industry. "That is a disturbing shift," they say. "While the problem should not be exaggerated . . . it is vexing that highly educated, experienced journalists with strong feelings about the role and purpose of the field are overrepresented among those who intend to leave the profession."[18]

Employee morale, in fact, was not a top priority in many newsrooms during the 1980s—and particularly not in those newsrooms where executives felt pressure to implement new management systems despite employee resistance. Many newspaper executives believe—although they seldom say it for public consumption—that change is always painful and, desperate as they believe the economic circumstances of newspapers to be, they can't let their employees' misgivings about marketing journalism slow them down. "Resistance to change exists in every organization, but we may see some of it diminish when our managers and supervisors become part of the change," advised Lee Guittar, a former publisher of the *Dallas Times Herald* and the *Denver Post,* in one publication for industry managers.[19]

Audience-oriented journalism and the corporate management systems that support it have taken their toll on many newsrooms. When John McMillan, a Gannett executive who recently retired as publisher of the Utica, New York, *Observer-Dispatch,* surveyed reporters at eight Western Gannett newspapers, he reported that he found "unanimous dissatisfaction" among reporters with their editorial leadership. In his essay in the *Gannetteer* of January 1982, entitled "It's Time to Reinvent the City Editor," McMillan quoted reporters who complained that no one teaches them anything, no one edits their copy, praise is too loosely given, criticism rare, and they are jerked from assignment to assignment. McMillan reported that these themes and others—low pay, lack of adequate newshole, staff shortages—were becoming prevalent as news organizations rushed to turn editors into administrators.

"We too often have corrupted the city desk with those 'endless imbecilities of high command,' " McMillan concludes. "Instead of talking to a reporter, the city editor audits time cards. Instead of editing copy, the city editor writes a memo about expense accounts. Instead of reading the competition, the city editor goes to a management meeting. . . . I submit that we run the risk of alienating our basic resource—reporters."[20]

Despite this gloomy portrait of newsroom morale, study after study, beginning with Johnstone and confirmed by Weaver and Wilhoit, shows that journalists in large proportions report they love their work.[21] Yet the emphasis needs to be put on work—not on job conditions. For example, 75 percent of the respondents in a 1989 ASNE study of 1,200 newsroom employees from 72 newspapers said their present job meets or exceeds their expectations. However, the respondents were not so positive about their immediate supervisor (42 percent gave very high or outstanding marks, 45 percent adequate or not outstanding, and 13 percent poor or inadequate). When asked about significant newsroom problems, the respondents pinpointed staff morale (29 percent), lack of time to do a good job (25 percent), lack of a clear newsroom mission (22 percent), and lack of resources (20 percent).[22]

"When I mentioned that morale is the biggest problem in our newsroom, I meant it," said one reporter in the ASNE study *The Changing Face of the Newsroom*. "Creative, enthusiastic people are driven away or pushed into mediocrity by bosses who are threatened by their drive and new ideas. Instead of working with people and encouraging them to work harder, middle management stifles subordinates."[23]

In this study, the discontent with their superiors was highest among reporters who intended to leave the newspaper business. And, at least according to one study of Florida journalists, reporters exiting the profession are also likely to find more happiness in their new positions. In a 1988 study by Fred Fedler, Tom Buhr, and Diane Taylor, the journalists (who complained of low salary, bad working conditions, and poor management as the key reasons for leaving the business) said, by roughly 2–1 margins, that their new jobs gave them more freedom and opportunity for creativity and, by 3–1 margins, that they found their new place of employment to be better managed.[24]

A key reason why newspaper executives appear to be bedeviling their reporters is the financial calculations that are increasingly driving newspapers. George Blake, the editor of Gannett's *Cincinnati Enquirer,* says editors who understand their commitment to circulation and to the marketplace "must not be content with a stereotype of the reporter as a liberal hippie freak whose main mission in life is to make people angry enough to cancel their subscriptions." Blake goes on to say: "If you find someone on your staff routinely and frequently badmouthing the product, explain to him or her why decisions are made the way they are. And if you find someone who just never will be happy with the newspaper, urge that person to go elsewhere. He or she is in the wrong business."

Blake says editors and reporters and photographers must maintain the "proper image" and understand that they are the newspapers "link with readers." Blake tells circulation managers: "We must support you in your efforts to provide better service and stronger sales. The modern editor is interested in circulation. And that means we share a mutual interest in promotion."[25]

An equally powerful reason for the tightening of the reins on reporters has been the growing power of editors, backed by a more conservative social climate and the increased strength of management, to demand fealty from their staffs. Guittar puts it bluntly when he cites the technological changes—VDTs, electronic pagination—that have shifted the power away from the Newspaper Guild and toward management. Technological advancements have "turned the tide," Guittar said. "Now more than ever before, the leverage in collective bargaining rests with management."[26]

In fact, newspaper employers have enjoyed a buyer's market since the early 1970s when the Baby Boom generation—imbued with the romantic exploits of Woodward and Bernstein and attracted by the growing allure of a media career—filled the journalism schools with an excess of new talent. Demographics and the lessening of the number of students enrolled in news editorial programs have reduced the publishers' advantage somewhat. But with technology, profit pressures, and economic troubles holding down newsroom hiring, the employment calculus still strongly favors newspaper employers.

There are also signs that even without overt pressure from publishers the younger generation of the Reagan-Bush era reporters is much less likely to cause trouble for its bosses. This is providing an even greater incentive for editors to push out older reporters—particularly those who came of age in the Vietnam War and Watergate eras. Reporters in their thirties and forties, says Karen Schneider of the *Detroit Free Press,* are "part of the post-Watergate generation who went in with reform on our minds. We certainly went in questioning authority. Today what you see are kids coming out of college who are coming from a different generation. There's less questioning of authority. . . . And papers reflect that."[27]

Many analysts say the seeds of this era of strong management systems were sewn as far back as the late 1970s and the early 1980s. Knight-Ridder pioneered the use of management-by-objective goals for management and personality tests for new employees in the 1970s.[28] In *Presstime,* Patricia Renfroe noted that newspapers were tightening up management practices by measuring productivity and efficiency.[29] For example, a 1981 survey of ANPA members showed that performance evaluations, particularly in newsrooms, have become increasingly important to the industry.[30] "Newsrooms have traditionally been difficult to grade on productivity, but lately there has been a greater effort to do so," Renfroe said.[31]

In his study of the *New York Times* in the 1970s, Chris Argyris painted a pessimistic picture of the future for newsroom employees in an era of growing scientific management of newsrooms. Argyris found the executives he studied to be compulsive, insecure, dominating, defensive, emotionally closed, averse to risk-taking, and unwilling to change.[32] Since a management system comes to reflect its managers, Argyris predicted, these problems will only become more deeply interwoven with the more sophisticated systems of planning and control. The adaptation of scientific management techniques means "top managers will react by becoming even 'stronger'; by designing even tighter control systems; and by creating long-range plans which, if examined, are not to manage the future or to learn about it, but to co-opt it," Argyris said. "Long-range planning will become a force to make the system more predictable in the future; that is, to make it ultra-stable. From the viewpoint of the lower-level reporters, editors and other participants, this ultra-stability will be experienced as system rigidity."[33]

Back in 1980 Kenneth Edwards, a journalism professor at the University of Alabama, advised editors in his article "Improving the Profit Plan by Evaluating Newsroom Efficiency."[34] In urging editors to apply a "systems approach" to newsroom management, Edwards suggested they ask themselves these questions: Does your paper have general and specific objectives? Have your editors considered all available information, including opinions of advertising and circulation people as well as readership surveys, as the basis for adopting objectives? Does your news organization have a definite chain of command to establish responsibility and authority? Is there a plan for evaluation of employee performance? Do your editors plan ahead with other department heads, for weeks and months, for special developments or important assignments that may have deep community significance? Do reporters and editors stay within channels of responsibility? Is your newsroom usually a smoothly working, disciplined organization?[35]

Paul McMaster, *USA Today*'s associate editor/editorial page, illustrates how modern managers have adopted Edwards's systems approach and the language of business school management thinking. In ASNE's *Newsroom Management Handbook,* McMaster says that the management-by-objective approach to running a newsroom is a good way for editors to insure that they are meeting clearly defined goals and "maximizing management resources." MBO management "gives an editor more control by allowing him or her to initiate goal ideas and set them in motion," McMaster says. "It involves close, productive communication with the publisher, fellow department heads and newsroom supervisors. . . . The editor using MBO directs more effort toward results, instead of engaging in activities that may keep him or her busy, but often delay or derail progress toward real goals."[36]

Ironically, despite their attempts at more efficient management, many newsrooms are still badly run—and light years behind the industries that have actually begun to implement systems that encourage employee initiative and creativity as a way to improve competitiveness. For example, the more progressive high technology firms emphasize the need for worker flexibility, highlight the employee's role in product innovation, and organize themselves on a nonhierarchical basis. Many newspapers are still run as they were in the 1800s when newspaper managers pioneered the concept of the white collar assembly line. While the daily newspaper was once considered the model of industrial efficiency, the traditional structure—with rigid editorial bureaucracies, the heavy involvement of financial managers in product decisions, and an emphasis on the look and packaging of the product over quality—is reminiscent of the kind of management structures that are now considered outdated in other industries.[37]

Perhaps the most celebrated form of self-conscious newsroom management style was the "creative tension" approach attributed to the recently retired *Washington Post* editor, Ben Bradlee. Joe Nocera describes the "culture" of the *Post* as a businesslike, "IBM" atmosphere where smart, aggressive, ambitious reporters were motivated "not through the inherent excitement and interest in the news . . . but through the internal competitions, those steps up the career ladder, that reward those that do well."[38]

There are some signs that in some quarters newspaper executives are beginning to jettison Bradlee's notion that it's a good idea to keep employees intentionally anxious, off-balance, and insecure. In recent years, there has been a trend toward company morale boosting programs—ranging from "change management" seminars to stress reduction classes to communication improvement sessions between top managers and employees—that are run by human resource managers or company psychologists. In her article, "Managing the Newsroom: Trading Tough Talk for TLC," Susan Miller cites a number of editors who say it's unproductive to foster an atmosphere of backstabbing and free-floating terror.[39] "Creative tension is bullshit," says Angus McEachran, editor of the *Pittsburgh Press.* "There's enough tension. That's the nature of this beast. We don't need anybody to artificially inseminate anything."[40]

However, for many of the new breed newspaper managers the morale of their employees simply isn't a top priority, particularly when their first loyalty is to the corporation and their career within the corporation. The issue of the well-traveled newsroom manager—devoted almost exclusively to his or her success within the framework of the corporation's agenda—has become a troublesome one in this era of chain ownership. One survey of chain editors shows lots of movement and aspirations for promotion to another newspaper.[41] Gannett, for example, makes much of the "local autonomy" of its newspapers. But local autonomy doesn't mean much if the editors of the newspaper know little about—or have little interest in—the community where they are working. Tom Goldstein cites the case of Gary Watson, whose résumé includes three years as editor in Boise, Idaho, three years as editor in Springfield, Missouri, a stint as publisher in Rockford, Illinois, a short stint as president and publisher at the *Cincinnati Enquirer,* before his job at Gannett headquarters.[42]

So how are the folks in the trenches—the reporters and midlevel editors who put the newspapers together—holding up in this era of test marketing, readership surveys, audience targeting, budget planning, and career carousels?

Not always so well, it seems.

Drex Heikes, a former metro editor at the *Fresno Bee* who is now an editor in the *Los Angeles Times*'s Washington, D.C., bureau, describes a budgeting and personnel process at McClatchy Newspapers that has become so burdensome that some editors have little time to do anything else. For example, he points out that McClatchy's financial people required that newsroom budgeting—once an annual exercise—be continually updated. "It seems like the bureaucratic and corporate requirements have reached down to the department heads and editors like me," he says. "Those people are swimming in paperwork. It's a tremendous frustration to deal with that, because we're the people who are the guardians of the quality of the newspaper."[43]

John F. Persinos, a former business reporter for the *Orlando Sentinel,* says the *Sentinel* had evolved into a market-driven, slickly packaged cash machine. In the business department, he says, that meant that the staff spent an inordinate amount of time producing copy for two new weekly supplements devoted to business and to consumer money management. "It's a pernicious trend," he says. "Marketing always came first. You felt like you were a copywriter for the marketing department, cranking out stories so they could sell ads for the sections."[44]

Before the death of the *Times Herald,* the Dallas newspaper scene evolved into a marketing contest in which the city's two dailies tried to appeal to upscale Dallas readers. The *Morning News,* with its puffy special sections and reader-driven formulas for news, was particularly solicitous of affluent readers. "I'm afraid that the *News* and papers like it run the risk of appearing to be slavishly adoring of the power structure," says Brad Bailey, formerly a reporter at the *Dallas Morning News.* "The effect on [newsroom] morale was to realize we weren't part of an art or a sacred responsibility but a business to put out a package that was attractive to a market segment. If most journalists realized they were going into that, they'd go into real estate."[45]

John Kolesar, ex-night-news editor at the *Record* in Bergen County, New Jersey, says that packaging and graphics requirements at a place like the *Record* can also make life at the desk pretty unrewarding. "I think what we do with this packaging can get very damaging," he says. "All the time that's spent in planning and packaging and detail work is time that's taken away from the news and the substance of the news. It's a very corrosive thing. My mother didn't raise me to be an interior decorator. I was interested in the news."[46]

Kolesar's views are echoed by reporters who complain that their jobs have become circumscribed by management's obsession with packaging, marketing, and brief writing. This, they worry, means that as newspapers become more and more visual and scannable, they will become indistinguishable from other media. "I don't write anything readers can't get on television," says one *Record* reporter. "The thing about newspapers is they used to offer an intelligent alternative. Now we're writing for the lowest common denominator. The *Record* and papers like it are running a terrible risk of insulting the readers who've stuck with them for years."[47]

Even at the best of newspapers, such as Knight-Ridder's, some reporters believe that the marketing philosophy of top managers has begun to change the nature of their job. One reporter at the *Miami Herald* says that through their market research his newsroom bosses make it clear to feature writers what kinds of stories they want. Stories that appeal to the yuppie market, suburban readers, and Hispanics are encouraged, while stories that aren't targeted to a special audience get short shrift. This reporter, who entered the business during the social activist days of the 1960s, finds the trend very discouraging. "The change-the-world style of journalism is waning to the point where it's an endangered species," he says. "I don't know but a handful of my friends who are still in the business to make the world a better place."[48]

Ironically, many reporters are feeling that way at a time when newspapers—at least, the better ones—are devoting more resources than ever to investigative teams and big, expensive projects designed to win prestigious prizes. Winning prizes is, of course, an important marketing tool. Kolesar, for example, tells about sitting on a committee at the *Record* that set up a plan for trying to divine what kind of project might win a Pulitzer prize.[49]

Reporters also note that the character of investigations is changing as well as the atmosphere in the newsroom where they are trying to do their work. It is increasingly difficult, they say, to question authority out in the world when they themselves are being pressured to become loyal corporate soldiers inside their organizations. Michael Wagner, formerly an investigative reporter for the *Detroit Free Press*, says that newspapers are a "perfect mirror" of the probusiness government of Ronald Reagan and George Bush and of a population focusing on personal problems. "The appetite these days is for fairly safe, less controversial, sociological investigative stories," says Wagner, who is now at the *Sacramento Bee*. "If you look across the country, you see papers doing a great job of covering prisons and juvenile crime and child abuse. But you don't see people asking how Exxon got to be bigger than five or six countries in the world."[50]

Or as Bailey, formerly of the *Dallas Morning News*, puts it: "Do you see a corporation that's in the business of making money going out and investigating other corporations? I don't."[51]

But perhaps the most poignant predicament is the one facing reporters, many of whom got into newspapering because they love to write, who find themselves forced to fit their work into marketing formulas. Jim Renkes, a veteran reporter-turned-features editor at the *Quad City Times*, says many of his colleagues may not mind seeing the product of their efforts cut and trimmed into "bite-sized nuggets" of information, but he does. Renkes notes that he now works at a newspaper that is fixated upon such design devices as drop-heads, refers, pull-out quotes, perspective lines, breakout boxes, impacts, and points of entry.

"A lot of reporters, I think they got into the business to be writers," Renkes says. "They sure didn't get into it for the money. If you take that away from them—well, they might as well have another job. I'm almost melancholy about the whole thing."[52]

CHAPTER FOUR

The Historical Roots of the Marketing and Management Revolution

Things that shocked Steffens and his readers now are accepted as matter of course. The communications industry today is indeed Big Business . . . and no knowledgeable observer for at least the past fifty years has had the temerity to maintain otherwise.

—Hillier Krieghbaum, *Pressures on the Press*

There is a good deal of benefit to both power and the media in the maintenance of the folklore of the watchdog, the adversary, or the agenda-setter. . . . The joker is the assumption that the press is free and exercises independent power.

—J. Herbert Altschull, *Agents of Power*

Trying to be a first-rate reporter on the average American newspaper is like trying to play Bach's Saint Matthew Passion on a ukulele: the instrument is too crude for the work, for the audience and for the performer.

—Ben Bagdikian, *The Effete Conspiracy*

It seems to us that Dr. Bush hands his students not a sword but a weather vane. Under such conditions, the fourth estate becomes a mere parody of the human intelligence, and had best be turned over to bright birds with split tongues or to monkeys who can make change.

—E. B. White's response to a journalism professor who believes publishers should take a poll before taking an editorial stand

"MARKETING" and "managerialism" have a long tradition in the history of daily newspapers in the United States. Today's practitioners of reader-driven news—and the management systems they have established to support it—have simply put a modern, corporate face on a form of daily newspapering that extends back through the eras of the "yellow press" and the "penny press" to the very foundations of the commercial press in America.

"Run contests, cut prices . . . get the circulation," F. M. Ball, a daily newspaper circulation manager, advised his colleagues back in 1915. "Don't hesitate. . . . Circulation you must have. . . . If you have not got it already, go out and get it by hook or crook."[1]

Early in the twentieth century, the businesslike management of editorial staffs had already left many newsrooms "as regimented as a real estate office," as one writer in *Editor and Publisher* put it.[2] In 1919, for example, the managing editor of one Texas daily had worked out a cost accounting method for analyzing the output of each reporter.[3] And the old *New York Herald Tribune* had devised a statistical system to analyze just how well the work of its staff compared with the competition each day.[4]

In earlier eras, the mass circulation dailies' pursuit of profits, readers, and advertisers was often expressed in cruder and blunter forms than it is by today's smooth-talking corporation managers. Nevertheless, beneath their talk of "MBO" and "human resource management" and reader-friendly journalism, modern newspaper executives are driven by the same anxieties as their counterparts of old: how to capture the attention of readers, how to improve the bottom line, and how to keep newspapers thriving in the midst of a continuously evolving media marketplace.

No one should be surprised to discover that fears about the demise of the daily newspaper are not a recent phenomenon, either. Thirty years ago, Carl Lindstrom entitled his book *The Fading American Newspaper,* and in it he cited a catalog of troubles that certainly sounds familiar to today's daily newspaper executives: readers migrating to other media, lack of money spent on research and development, the use of monopoly and merger tactics.

In fact, Lindstrom prophesied a future for the daily newspaper that sounds remarkably like the predictions of today's doomsayers. Faced with new printing developments and the electronic transmission of news, "it is entirely possible in the not so remote future that it [the daily newspaper] will go the way of the street car," he wrote.[5]

In one respect, the history of the daily newspaper business in this country can be seen as one of pendulum swings, with the ebb and flow of "muckraking" reporting and the up-and-down popularity of entertainment journalism and the fluctuating cycles of "personal" and "objective" reporting. For those who see newspapers caught up in the coming and going of trends, the marketing and management mania that has swept up newspapers in the last decade is simply the return of a way of doing business that has periodically captured the imagination of the newspaper industry, particularly in times of economic turbulence or rapid technological change.

There are others who see the history of newspapers primarily in evolutionary terms, with the relentless arrival of new and cheaper printing techniques, continuously advancing systems of electronic automation, and now computer-generated information technologies altering the structure of the newspaper industry. This scenario sees big city dailies falling in favor of a rising suburban and specialty press; a distracted, indifferent, and video-oriented public increasingly turning away from the printed word; and newspapers of all kinds sinking under the assault of electronic competitors.

This view, held as gospel in many quarters of the newspaper industry, envisions a tomorrow where newspapers are likely to look little the way they do today and where all forms of media will increasingly blend together under the advancing forces of multimedia technology and conglomerate ownership.

But the history of newspapers is also a straight line that, with virtually no fluctuation, points to tenets that are as true today as they were in years past. And two tenets hold particularly true. First, the ownership of newspapers has consistently led to the creation of fortunes for individual entrepreneurs and, increasingly these days, for corporate executives and shareholders. The second tenet is that—despite cycles of good times and bad times—the newspaper industry has emerged each time financially sounder, more entrenched in the economy, and more flexible in facing the future.

For all the fretting about the loss of readers, the worries about its eroding advertising base, and the tales of coming technological and financial woe, the daily newspaper industry is still one of the nation's most prosperous.[6] After weathering the inflationary years of the 1970s and the recession of the early 1980s—which wrung out many of the weak sisters in the business—newspapers roared back to participate fully in the business boom of the Reagan era. With chains like Gannett in the lead, the nation's newspapers showed Wall Street how attractive monopoly markets (as most daily newspapers now are) could be. Some prestige chains, such as Knight-Ridder, Times Mirror, the Washington Post, and Dow Jones, nearly matched the performance of bottom-line oriented groups, such as Donrey, Harte-Hanks and Thomson, which are alleged to have made profit returns at some of their newspapers in the 20 and 30 and even 40 percent range.[7] Thanks to inflation and the nation's tax laws (which benefit chains by making it difficult for individual owners to pass on their properties), the push toward conglomeratization accelerated as dailies fell into chain hands in large numbers from the mid-1970s to the mid-1980s. At the same time, many newspaper groups merged or were bought out by other corporations. Even some of the leaders of the newspaper business were surprised at just how a big force they had become in the economy. David Halberstam, for example, describes the amazement of *Los Angeles Times* publisher Otis Chandler that the banks would actually finance the acquisition spree that has made the *Times* one of the biggest publishing empires of all.[8]

Today, with the spread of the conglomerates and joint operating agreements in force in many big cities, only a handful of cities—among them New York, Chicago, Denver, and Boston—have truly competitive, independently owned and operated, citywide dailies. However, the new capital-conscious, market-driven newspaper companies have found that they aren't in a position to just sit on their riches. With the stock of most of the major companies traded publicly, the pressures of the bottom line have grown even more intense. Wall Street, as publishers have learned, can be insatiable in the demand for earnings growth and unmerciful in hammering a stock if earnings drop.

During the 1970s and 1980s all this led to a disingenuous ritual at industry conferences where, with profits pouring in, newspaper executives continued to badmouth the industry's prospects—a ritual Bagdikian first labelled "hogwash" in his 1973 essay "The Myth of Newspaper Poverty." "American publishers have always felt obligated to pretend that they are an auxiliary of the Little Sisters of the Poor," Bagdikian says. "This was always amusing, but now that so many papers are owned by publicly traded companies which have to disclose their finances it is taking on the air of slapstick."[9]

Nevertheless, the poormouthing of the 1970s and 1980s has grown to a chorus of woe in the 1990s. The Bush era—with its inheritance of the excesses in private and public borrowing and marketplace deregulation of the 1980s—has also been a dues-paying time for the newspaper industry. A shake-out among debt-ridden retailers has fueled a drop-off in newspaper advertising revenue.[10] The recession of the early 1990s with its downturn in auto and real estate and classified advertising has forced some publishers to engage in staff layoffs for the first time in many years. The continued drop-off in readership and household penetration numbers combined with a virtual explosion of electronic entertainment and information system competitors into the marketplace has led some to claim the newspaper industry's long-predicted day of reckoning may be at hand.

"I think newspapers aren't probably ever going to be as profitable as they were back in the '70s and early '80s," says newspaper analyst John Morton. However, he adds that despite the slipping profits of newspaper companies, newspapers are "still going to be a profitable business."[11]

Of course, recessions, laissez-faire economics, and the cold chill of the marketplace were not felt for the first time in the era of Reagan-Bush capitalism. Anyone who wants to understand the dilemma of today's newspapers should look not only to the future but also to the past. In fact, modern marketing and packaging journalism may be seen simply as a more sophisticated way of doing what newspaper executives have traditionally done whenever they were worried about their market share—that is to try to build circulation by giving readers what they want, attract more advertisers by target-marketing customers, and produce a more attractive newspaper by packaging it in more enticing ways.

Some of the most interesting parallels in newspaper history can be drawn between today's marketing mania and the tactics used by newspaper executives throughout the late 1800s and the early 1900s. Gerald Baldasty, a press historian at the University of Washington, points out that by the late nineteenth century a wide variety of businesses—department stores, food processors, bicycle manufacturers, among others—had turned to newspapers as their principal advertising vehicle. The makers of the industrial revolution sought customers for their commodities, and they expected newspapers to reach that market for them. In fact, publishers and advertisers came to see the press in much the same terms—in marketing terms—and were interested in shaping newspapers accordingly. It was an era of crass efforts to manipulate the press, Baldasty says, with department stores receiving free publicity in news columns, advertising agents fighting efforts to segregate news and advertising, and advertisers putting reporters on retainer. At the same time, newspaper owners were often willing participants in the commercialization of their enterprises. "Advertisers deserve much of the blame for this commercialization of the press. . . . But they share the blame with publishers who shared the same vision of the press," Baldasty says.

Since the advent of the penny press in the 1830s—with the transformation of urban newspapers from partisan publications with a limited readership into the low-cost, advertiser-supported, big circulation newspapers of today—there has been a tendency on the part of publishers to focus on the financial side of the newspaper enterprise. Baldasty points out that by the late nineteenth century, the formula of the newspaper-as-business-first-and-foremost was firmly established. Advertisers were willing to pay rates based on circulation, and so publishers paid more attention to readers. Newspaper content was shaped, molded, and packaged to increase its commercial value to readers. It became important for news to be bright and vivid and interesting, and content was tailored to be useful to readers. Baldasty cites the example of an 1898 Sunday edition of the Pittsburgh *Leader* as typical of the era. The newspaper provided articles on how to eat with chopsticks, gold speculation in British Columbia, big game hunting, identical twins in Michigan, spring fashions for men, gossip about former President Cleveland and his family, women polar explorers, amateur baking, egg farming, women fire fighters, prominent species of American trees, and insect life.[12]

Important transformations were also under way inside daily newspaper organizations to support these marketing efforts. By the late nineteenth century, a managerial class had grown up, and business managers took their place beside editors in the newspaper hierarchy. Despite the image of the early captains of the penny press as self-made bootstrappers from lowly origins, by the turn of the century editors had come to resemble other executives in industry; they were largely well educated, from relatively privileged backgrounds, and accomplished at getting ahead in a bureaucratic environment.[13] In fact, the urban newspaper as an organization—with its need for skilled executives, specialized newsgatherers, compartmentalized circulation and finance functions, assembly-line efficiency in the news preparation process, and mass production presses—had become a model of industrial efficiency by the late 1800s. "Facilitated by the industrial and commercial growth of the country and by mechanical and other changes, the managemental structure of dailies came to resemble more and more that of other large manufacturing establishments," writes press historian Alfred McClung Lee.[14]

The situation of reporters was often wretched in an era when they, like much else associated with the emergence of the mass circulation press, were treated as little more than commodities. Low wages drove many reporters—a profession that had emerged as one of the specialized functions of the newspaper by the 1830s—into ill health or leaving the business. Work conditions—the hours, the pressures of production, the treatment by editors—were often barely tolerable. The conflict between editors and reporters was made clear in the memoirs of late nineteenth century reporters, and the horror stories of the miserable life of reporters (and sublevel editors, for that matter) were part of the lore of the profession. Ted Curtis Smythe describes how journalists of the period were exploited by pay-by-the-column-inch systems, urged to gain exclusives, pressured to doctor events with sensational treatment, and tempted by payola and ethically dubious newsgathering practices. "Pay was low, jobs were tenuous, hours were long and arduous," he says. "Reporters—with notable exceptions—knew they were not worth much to their publishers. Reporters, except for the truly talented, were treated as though they 'were machines or privates in an ill-paid army to be thrown in any breach.' . . . Some reporters, but not all, were broken by the management practices and publisher attitudes." [15]

It was also in the nineteenth century that the advertising and public relations industries grew up, a phenomenon that, while it didn't cause mass market newspapers, is inextricably bound up with their development. [16] After the Civil War, advertising in American newspapers increased dramatically and became the predominant source of revenue for most publishers. [17] And the public relations industry grew to a point where press agents became as "familiar in the corridors of newspapers as journalists themselves," as press historian J. Herbert Altschull puts it. [18] In *Captains of Consciousness*, Stuart Ewen notes how businessmen of the industrial revolution, needing to stimulate demand and distribute goods from the new mass market machinery of production, encouraged workers to define their needs and identity in terms of the marketplace. The development of an "ideology of consumption," Ewen says, helped to develop the idea of the consumer marketplace as a modern expression of liberty, and the mass market newspaper certainly played a major role in fostering it. "The vision of freedom which was being offered to Americans was one which continually relegated people to consumption, passivity and spectatorship. . . . More than a vehicle for the good life, self-definition by commodities pointed the way to a safe life," Ewen says. [19]

Press historian Michael Schudson claims that Ewen overstates the self-conscious efforts on the part of the business community to manipulate workers to become consumers. [20] But Schudson notes that in the 1890s the big city newspaper readers did offer advertisers the mass audience that was making mass marketing possible. The mass newspaper readership increasingly looked with curiosity and awe at the urban landscape and wanted a newspaper that entertained and made sense of this curious and somewhat forbidding panoply of life, Schudson says. Joseph Pulitzer's great innovation in St. Louis was the newspaper crusade, which he brought with him to New York when he bought the *New York World*. Pulitzer and his less principled competitors, such as William Randolph Hearst, ushered in the era of the so-called yellow journalism, with its emphasis on cartoons and drawings, liberal use of headline type, and emphasis on relatively simple words and big circulation numbers. "Pulitzer did not talk up the idea of entertainment," Schudson says, "but the *World* came to embody it."[21]

Yet it was Pulitzer—whom Schudson describes as an old-fashioned editor and political thinker rather than a businessman—who helped institutionalize many of our modern professional values when he created the Columbia University Graduate School of Journalism. The highest of those values have since become embodied in the philosophy of the Pulitzer prize awards. There is some irony in this since Pulitzer, despite his interest in "exclusive news," as Theodore Dreiser put it, was not known for treating his overworked and underpaid reporters much better than other publishers of the period. Dreiser called the "internal economy" of the "constantly moralizing" *World* "heartless and savage."[22]

While Hearst and Pulitzer were appealing to the reading masses, Adolph Ochs was demonstrating with the *New York Times* that a newspaper that covered the world in a polite, orderly fashion could be a big market success with wealthier readers.[23] It was Ochs's model that would help in the twentieth century to submerge the brassier mercantile instincts of the newspaper business beneath an emerging rhetoric of objectivity and professionalism and a growing belief that the press should serve as a responsible institution that looked out for the public good. Ochs showed newspapers across the country that they could improve their reputations and advance their economic interests by reducing the partisanship in their news columns and covering the news in a formal, evenhanded manner that wouldn't offend readers of any political stripe. This tendency was buttressed by the empirical outlook of the era, which saw gathering "facts" and following the laws of the natural sciences as the route to truth, and the needs of the Associated Press for simple, fact-oriented writing that would satisfy the needs of its diverse clientele. Still, it was the *New York Times* that—despite its excessive formality, its deference to established institutions, and its dearth of investigative reporting—was and is still held up as the epitome of a professional newspaper.

The newspaper industry—like much of the rest of big business—was the target of the muckraker's wrath around the turn of the century. Upton Sinclair painted a relentlessly bleak picture of the newspapers of his era. In his book *The Brass Check,* Sinclair argued that newspapers weren't interested in principles or crusades or the heritage of the country but in making money—"competing for advertisements of whiskey and cigars and soap," as he put it.[24] Newspapers, he said, "do not represent public interests but private interests; they do not represent humanity, but property; they value a man, not because he is great, or good, or wise, or useful, but because he is wealthy, or of service to vested wealth."[25] Will Irwin wrote a fifteen part series for *Collier's* magazine that blamed the failures of American journalism on greedy publishers and a system of advertising that handicapped the search for truth. He complained that power had shifted from editorial offices to the board rooms and that newspaper editors had become indistinguishable from the captains of industry. By the twentieth century, as Altschull puts it, Irwin felt it was no longer necessary for advertisers to dictate content, for "their allies in the executive offices of newspapers saw things in quite the same way as did the Rockefellers and the Morgans."[26]

Sadly, the muckrakers disappeared almost as quickly as they had appeared. John M. Harrison and Harry H. Stein say muckraking has always had a "ticklish" relationship with the media's need to profit from advertising dollars and maintain a good relationship with the business community.[27] Carey McWilliams says muckraking comes in cycles and appears to be attached to such historical developments as the emergence of a large, well-educated audience interested in public affairs and technological changes designed to make it easier to reach that audience. But most important, he says, muckraking is usually accompanied by a mood of deep social concern and disaffection with the system. In periods of apparent prosperity, muckraking journalism loses its appeal, and "the muckraking journalist is regarded as a spoil-sport or an old-fashioned curmudgeon," McWilliams says.[28]

McWilliams speculates that the muckraking around the turn-of-the-century disappeared with the rise of the Progressive Party, which absorbed many of its goals, and the eruption of World War I. Just as important, he notes that many of the magazines that supported muckraking journalism were run off by other magazines that flocked into the market. McWilliams says that a less visible muckraking tradition has continued, with small magazines like the *Nation,* which he edited, keeping it alive. And there have been occasional flare-ups in the established media—particularly in the 1960s, when the idealism of John Kennedy, the acceleration of the war in Vietnam, and the rebellion of blacks and students created a new market for reform journalism.

In his book *The New Muckrakers,* Leonard Downie, Jr., chronicles the work of Seymour Hersh, who unearthed the My Lai massacre in Vietnam; Bob Woodward and Carl Bernstein, who uncovered many of the Watergate scandals of the Nixon administration; the work of I. F. Stone, Drew Pearson, and Jack Anderson; and modern, computer-oriented investigators like Donald L. Barlett and James B. Steele of the *Philadelphia Inquirer*.[29] However, despite the re-appearance of so-called muckraking in the 1960s and 1970s, Downie notes that few newspapers engage in real investigative reporting, and when they do, private business is almost never examined. He cites an Urban Policy Research Institute study showing that some publishers may allow exposés of "petty payoffs and welfare abuse but draw the line at stories dealing with the institutional foundations of a city or state, the relationships of banks, corporations, elected officials and—perhaps—newspapers."[30]

Denny Walsh, a former *Life* magazine investigative reporter, puts it like this:

> The owner and/or top officers of the newspaper in almost every case have financial, civic, political, and social entanglements with their selected segment of the community in which the paper is located. And this makes it extremely difficult at times for a muckraker to surface the transgressions of this segment of the community, even though there are things about it that should be exposed. You can barely walk through a city room without tripping over some sacred cows.[31]

In fact, prior to the 1960s and the 1970s, the tone of twentieth-century journalism was as placid and noncontroversial as the century was wrenching and traumatic. The earthshaking events of the time—World War I, the Great Depression, World War II, the Korean War, the post-World War II recovery period—seemed to deflect much examination of the practices of U.S. newspapers, certainly within the press itself. Objectivity in covering the news—or at least, the belief in objectivity—had become the operational principle of most daily newspapers. Criticism of the press focused on its "superficiality," as witnessed by the debate set off in the 1920s by Walter Lippmann when he said newspapers were so hopelessly enmeshed in stereotypes, standardization, and routine judgments as to be virtually unable to perceive the truth of things.[32] His disenchantment was so great that he advocated the establishment of a cadre of government experts—which (ignobly as it would turn out in the 1960s and 1970s) he dubbed an "intelligence" corps—to do the job of truth-finding for society.[33] But it wasn't until the 1950s, when the late Senator Joseph McCarthy launched his assault on alleged communists in government, that the press began to reexamine the principles of objectivity, which McCarthy had manipulated to keep his charges in the headlines.

Yet, as Edwin Diamond argues, the press continued to act as "largely pacified members" of the establishment during the war years and the Cold War years that followed.[34] Most critics, Diamond says, would agree that there was no sustained period of muckraking between 1913 and 1970. The people of the press, as Diamond says, were "members of the team" and "with the program." Douglass Cater's book *The Fourth Branch of Government,* portrays the "organization man" era in which most reporters of the 1950s operated. "The Washington correspondent has odd notions about himself," Cater said. "He clings to the image of the reporter as the supreme individual in the age of the organization man. He is the one standing up against the many. He denies stubbornly that the production of news can be likened to the mass production techniques of other large-scale industries."[35]

Still, at least from the perspective of journalists, the story of the twentieth century press was the slow but steady professionalization of the newsroom and of newspaper reporters in particular. While conditions for newsroom employees improved throughout this century, it was in the 1950s, the 1960s, and particularly in the 1970s that newspaper after newspaper began to fully professionalize its operations. The *New York Times* soon found itself challenged for preeminence by such other newly respectable newspapers as Phil Graham's *Washington Post,* Otis Chandler's *Los Angeles Times,* Thomas Winship's *Boston Globe* and the *Chicago Tribune* of the successors of Colonel Robert McCormick, who eased their grip on their newsrooms and turned the reins over to their editors and reporters. Newspapers that aspired to national stature were no longer run as playthings of their publishers. Autocratic decision making, kingmaking in the news pages, and blatant conflicts of interest disappeared from many news organizations. Passive staffs of dutiful scribes were replaced with newsrooms filled with reporters—many graduates of the burgeoning journalism training programs in universities—who saw the business as a place to exercise professional judgment and ethical standards. Increased pay and growing prestige elevated news work to a semiprofessional—and, in the case of the best journalists and the best newspapers—a truly professional activity.

By the early 1960s "most newspapers had lived down their colorful past," as James Boylan put it.[36] Advertisers seldom controlled news content—at least not in the blatant fashion of the past. Most publishers had learned to conceal their hostility to labor. And most offered balanced news and evenhanded political coverage. Younger reporters of the Vietnam War and Watergate eras—many of whom had inherited a long-standing antipathy to authority—were also given more latitude. While balance and fairness were still the watchwords of newsrooms, reporters were given more opportunity to use interpretative techniques and perspective reporting to help readers better analyze events. Professionalism, Boylan says, was the catchword reporters invoked to insulate themselves against their employers. "In part, this was because the battle had been won—newspaper editors had already become more 'permissive,' and objectivity, as a journalistic standard like the straight-edge and compass of classical geometry, was widely accepted as, if not obsolete, then insufficient," Boylan wrote.[37]

While some publishers clearly valued the prestige that went with a more professional operation, their motives weren't always entirely high-minded. The economic worries of stagnant readership—combined with the competition of television—made them also more receptive to reporters' desires for more leeway to do interpretative and investigative reporting.[38] Even more than that, there was a feeling at some newspapers that the public simply was no longer interested in reading newspapers that stuck to rigid formulas or were dominated by the attitudes of the old "lords" of journalism.

For example, Clayton Kirkpatrick, former editor of the *Chicago Tribune,* outlined why a transformation occurred at a newspaper that had been the mouthpiece for the reactionary views of Colonel McCormick for decades. Kirkpatrick notes that in 1968 the *Tribune* commissioned a market study that suggested "prospects of a dwindling audience" because many readers "personified the *Tribune* as a severe old man preaching rigid and arbitrary lessons as if they were the key to eternal truth." In short order, the newspaper's typeface, its format, its news standards, the professionalism of its employees—in short, its entire character, as Kirkpatrick put it—was overhauled and the modern *Tribune* of today emerged.[39]

It is ironic that of all the criticisms that Bagdikian has launched against the press, the one newspaper executives took to heart was his 1972 analysis in *The Effete Conspiracy.* There Bagdikian portrayed newspapers as riding the easy tide, out-of-touch with readers, using archaic accounting methods and Byzantine advertising rates, and resisting basic reforms that readers deserved.[40] The newspaper industry of today has many faults (certainly in Bagdikian's eyes) but, on the whole, obliviousness to its readership problems and the use of old-fashioned accounting techniques aren't among them.

In 1980 Anthony Smith painted an optimistic picture of the journalism of the 1960s that, he says, has left reporting of the 1980s "considerably enriched." He says reporters still retain a deep commitment to straight facts but have been freed to use emotions and experience as a guide to events as well. This, he said, has occurred alongside a gradual internal democratization of the newsroom. "The power of brokerage has thus passed from news editor to correspondent and specialist reporter, and as a result the editor cannot wield the same kind of authority he did in previous generations," Smith said.[41]

But Smith underestimated how deeply newspaper executives were shaken by the polarization of the 1960s and 1970s. The professionalization of the press in the 1960s and 1970s took place against the backdrop of Vietnam War protest and civil rights turmoil, revolutionary changes in lifestyles and personal morals, and the entry of the Baby Boom generation into the labor force. In fact, the same forces that were causing turbulence in the streets were contributing to the transformation of newspapers: the appearance of the better-educated offspring of the affluent in the newsroom, the growing power of the press in an era of instant communications, the questioning of authority in society at large, and the growth of the consumer movement. Many young reporters, filled with the idealism and crusading spirit of the era, found themselves working in newsrooms where, if they showed enterprise and initiative, they could find a ready market for aggressive journalism that challenged the power structure.

With the rise of journalism reviews and media criticism in many publications, the press also found itself the target, as well as the fomenter, of the antiestablishment mood. Edwin Diamond wrote in 1970: "As often as not, a good university-trained reporter who is now in his or her late twenties picketed for civil rights while in high school, spent a freshman summer in Mississippi or Appalachia, and sat in at the Dean's office during senior year—or covered these events for the school paper. Now they are turning reformist toward their own profession."[42]

Ron Dorfman, the editor of the now defunct *Chicago Journalism Review,* describes the "reporter power" movement that sprang up after the riot at the 1968 Democratic convention in Chicago, when many reporters felt their bosses were complicit in condoning police suppression of the demonstrations.

> In the early 1960s something else began to happen. People began coming out of the universities into journalism, people who had been marked by the characteristic stigmata of this generation. We were indelibly changed by the civil rights movement. We had begun what we now see is a movement, of which Ralph Nader is the highest expression, a movement for institutional responsibility—responsibility to a wider public and more particularly responsibility to the men and women who have to live and work within the institution.[43]

This was the heyday for reporters. For a brief spell, roughly from the mid-1960s to the late 1970s, reporters reached the peak of their power in newsrooms. It was widely perceived—by reporters, editors, and the public—that reporters in the trenches were largely responsible for bringing down the Nixon administration and helping to end the Vietnam War. Seymour Hersh, Woodward and Bernstein, and other top investigative reporters were folk heroes of young reporters. The push toward writer- and reporter-driven newspapers was given a boost from the "new" journalism—clever, colorfully textured, point-of-view writing that tried to capture the dramatic and cinematic experience of television, rock music, and the drug culture. "Advocacy" journalism and alternative newspapers spurred the establishment press on to re-think many of its news values. As Ed Lambeth put it in his book *Committed Journalism,* "Investigative reporting helped alter the ethos of American journalism in the 1960s and 1970s. While practiced, in fact, only by a few, its visibility cast a new, romantic aura over a profession whose entrepreneurial talents had lain largely dormant in the 1940s and 1950s."[44]

But the backlash was quick in coming. While the struggle was a muted one in most newsrooms, editors, skeptical of so much reporter freedom, began to reassert managerial control almost as soon as they had given it away. Boylan notes that the claim later made by editors that "they had been overrun by activists hostile to newspaper traditions is largely false." But, he said, there is no question that older journalists watched the new breed uneasily, worried that they seemed to believe the worst about authority. Boylan says that at the very apex of the press's triumph—Watergate—many news executives had come to be-lieve that the press's confrontation with government had become ex-cessive. The Janet Cooke scandal became a rallying cry for stronger editor supervision of newsrooms and added impetus to the trend toward ombudsmen, correction columns, and other tools to deal with press credibility. "Thus, the most recent generation of journalists, the one that grew up in the Vietnam and Watergate years, is now receiving the message from its elders that the heyday of autonomy has ended," Boylan said.[45] Michael J. O'Neill, former editor of the *New York Daily News,* summed up the views of many newspaper executives when he complained in a 1982 speech to ASNE that the press's "harshly adver-sarial posture toward government and its infatuation with investigative reporting" had contributed to the "disarray in government." He sug-gested the press adopt an editorial posture that is more "tolerant of the frailties of institutions," make peace with government, put less empha-sis on the downbeat, and refrain from "needlessly" hurting public figures.[46]

In a somewhat more temperate tone, in an article for the ASNE *Bulletin* in September 1983, O'Neill explained why the investigative wave that surged through American journalism after Watergate seemed to be ebbing. He speculated that times of great social conflict seem to be followed by periods of slack. And he traced the demise of investigative reporting to the general retreat in the 1980s from the extraordinary tensions of the 1960s and 1970s. O'Neill argued that investigative reporting was too reactive and had failed to anticipate society's problems. He called on the media instead to emphasize "preventive journalism," a new kind of reporting that puts the emphasis on insight and explanation in the search for the underlying social currents that threaten future problems.[47]

As it turned out, O'Neill gave up on investigative reporting just at the time it was most needed. Unlike the Nixon years, virtually all the scandals of the Reagan administration—at HUD, EPA, the Pentagon, the S & L crisis—were exposed, for the most part, by government investigative agencies and not by the U.S. press. In fact, the press, which was largely practicing the kind of explanatory journalism O'Neill was advocating, was extremely lax in scrutinizing Reagan's government and remarkably passive in allowing scandal after scandal to break without rekindling its investigative zeal.[48]

Somewhat surprisingly, the media spent much of the decade of the 1980s fighting off a campaign by industry groups unhappy with the kind of coverage business began to receive in the 1970s. The most notable of these attacks came from the Mobil Oil Corporation, whose ads chided the press for its "antibusiness" bias. At the same time, there was a proliferation of business "image-improvement" advertising, corporate forums to discuss media portrayal of business, business-backed programs to foster better understanding of business in journalism schools, and foundations endowed by corporations to make probusiness experts available to the press.[49]

Ironically, this all happened while almost every major newspaper expanded its business pages, increased business coverage, and launched special business sections. By and large, these sections were (and still are) filled with puffy profiles and consumer financial help that has done little to change the image of the business pages as soft on business. Even a close look at the scrutiny of business on the news pages seldom shows much aggressiveness on the part of most newspapers. Bagdikian, for example, has noted that of the 1,100 members of the Investigative Reporters and Editors organization, only six had corporate life as their beat.[50]

Peter Dreier argues that negative portrayals of business in the press have usually been the result of coverage of material presented by consumer organizations, public interest groups, or government agencies. Ralph Nader's people, for example, have been key sources for reporters trying to interpret the complex maneuverings of businesses to gain breaks for themselves in congressional tax legislation. "For many reasons, journalists tend to avoid the hard work required to investigate corporate behavior," Dreier says.[51]

People like Dreier and Bagdikian have long noted that the nation's major newspapers are heavily linked to its business establishment. Dreier documents 24 news organizations with 447 ties with business organizations, mostly outside directors brought onto newspaper boards. Dreier notes that the nation's four "top" newspapers—the *New York Times,* the *Washington Post,* the *Los Angeles Times,* and the *Wall Street Journal*—have the largest number of industry ties. At first glance, this may seem odd, since those newspapers have taken the lead in what little exposure of corporate wrongdoing has been provided in U.S. newspapers. But Dreier argues that it is exactly because of these ties that these newspapers can afford to adopt a liberal corporate outlook— an outlook that, Dreier notes, is likely to appeal to the upscale, affluent readers, who are the favorite target for both advertisers and opinion leaders.[52]

In *Media*Power*Politics,* David Paletz and Robert Entman argue that the media's routines, content, and impact on the public are deeply imbued with elite perceptions, which help bend into conformity any demands that threaten the economic status quo. According to Paletz and Entman, this is true even of the nation's prestige newspapers. "As long as income exceeds expenditures, a few newspaper owners with profitable properties sacrifice maximum profit in search of quality reporting," they say. "They value their fourth-estate tradition and the prestige and power that accompany it. But it depends upon the owner. With the growth of multipaper chains and conglomerates, noblesse oblige is succumbing to mercantilism."[53]

Leftists like Robert Cirino and Michael Parenti are even harsher in their assessment of the unspoken understanding between media and business. "To hide their role of serving the establishment, the agencies of mass media have used their propaganda tools to create in the public's mind myths about the news media," says Cirino. "It is these myths which persuade the people to accept a communication system prostituted to the special interests of a few."[54] Adds Parenti: "Behind the superficiality of the news there stands a whole configuration of power and interest that makes the lazy, conventional way of presenting things also the politically safer, less troublesome way."[55]

Right-wing critics, on the other hand, accuse the press of harboring a liberal bias that favors government activism to deal with domestic social problems. For example, Edith Efron's 1972 study, *The News Twisters,* in which she alleges the network news reports were biased against Richard Nixon in the 1968 presidential campaign, concludes that the "rationalized evasions" and "institutionalized mythologies" of the media serve to "cover up the existence of a liberal monopoly in the network news departments" run by an "entrenched" and "ruling" elite determined to hold on to its power.[56]

Ironically, at least one media critic, Austin Ranney, thinks that both the critics of the left and those of the right are not talking "total nonsense." Yet Ranney disputes the notion that bias stems from some conspiracy or cabal at the top of news organizations. Ranney argues that news organizations—and the television networks, in particular—tend to be biased against someone for "journalistic" and not partisan reasons. The bias, he says, stems not from a desire to promote a political cause but from the structural and economic imperatives in newscasting, such as entertainment needs, time limitations, and legal concerns.[57]

Marketing, in the minds of many of its advocates, is hardly a political activity. But it's hard not to see a lurking ideology, and ultimately a reshaped journalistic mission, in it. After all, Horace Greeley and William Allen White and Lincoln Steffens and Ida Tarbell and a long line of crusading editors and investigative reporters who followed them would certainly recognize the sound of a new battle cry for the press if they heard James Batten, Knight-Ridder's CEO, say, as he did in the 1989 Press-Enterprise Lecture, that newspapers need to develop a "new and fierce commitment to publishing newspapers that strain to please and satisfy our customers every day. The days when we could do newspapering *our* way, and tell the world to go to hell if it didn't like the results, are gone forever."[58]

CHAPTER FIVE

Imitations
of the Tube

You don't have to cut off all a dinosaur's food. You have to cut off five percent of its food, and it starts to get thin and panicky, and starts getting a little more hungry . . . and that spiral down occurs.
—Former NBC programming chief Paul Klein

That was the essence of the Sauter revolution at CBS News, the heart of the Sauter vision: CBS News was not the *New York Times,* but if it did its job right, it could be *USA Today.*
—Peter Boyer, *Who Killed CBS?*

Our impatience with television's view of politics represents, in part, a longing for an era when the news regularly achieved the depth, impartiality and seriousness of the civics lesson—an era that never was.
—Mitchell Stephens, *A History of News*

In fact, throughout every news organization it's as if a palace revolution has taken place, with the old king of the conventional hard-news story having been toppled from his granite throne, and with the chamberlains now running about the kingdom proclaiming first one leader and then another, apparently not yet quite willing to actually crown the charming Prince of Entertainment, but without the conviction to really crown anybody else instead, and with the general populace generally delighted at not being governed at all.
—Michael J. Arlen, *The Camera Age*

In Washington, D.C., there is a saying that the greatest service to America performed by the *Washington Post* and the *New York Times* is that they are read each morning by the television network correspondents. Austin Ranney has dubbed this the "two-step flow" of news in the age of television: the top newspapers tell the networks what is newsworthy, and the networks pass it on to the mass public.[1]

Even as they struggle with stagnant circulation and competition from their electronic competitors and a collapsing advertising base, daily newspapers continue to occupy the higher ground in today's media environment, providing the kind of depth and perspective and background in their reporting that television can't or won't deliver. At the nation's best newspapers—the *New York Times*, the *Washington Post*, the *Wall Street Journal*, the *Los Angeles Times*—journalists are on the frontlines of the Information Age. They are the diggers, the investigators, the analysts. Television follows behind—its power coming from the size of its audience, the vividness of the medium, and the instantaneousness of its communication.

So it has been with a mixture of resignation and sadness and even anger that daily newspaper journalists have watched the newspaper business—and the newspapers it produces—come to imitate television's audience-grabbing, visually fixated, and marketing-obsessed techniques. "More and more, newspapers are following television—aping its quick-brush, once-over-lightly style and giving increased space to celebrity coverage and gossip," says syndicated *Newsday* columnist Sydney Schanberg. "The primary strategy has been to copy and adapt all those television techniques in which success is founded on a very short American attention span."[2]

In fact, print journalists can no longer feel smug when they look at the practices of their broadcasting colleagues. Both in philosophy and in the way they run their news operations newspaper executives are moving closer to their television counterparts. While not in the iron grip of daily ratings to the extent of television executives, newspaper executives increasingly feel the inexorable press of the cold, hard, statistical "facts" that circumscribe their business: stagnant circulation figures, slipping advertising linage, "churn" (the constant turnover in newspaper readers), audience studies showing that young people ignore them and other Americans are too busy for them. The new pressures on newspaper reporters to think of their text in visual terms, to shorten their writing, to write with the market in mind, and to take responsibility for the overall packaging of the product are reminiscent of the television business. Although the practice is by no means as ingrained as it is in television, many of today's newspaper journalists are increasingly being asked to pander to what critics most lament about the broadcasting industry: its attraction to easily illustrated, superficial events, its eager response to fads and viewer tastes, and its appetite for predictable and planned events."The pervasiveness of the corporate mentality, the emphasis on marketing, the disinclination to look beyond the surface of a story—all are signs of a transformation almost unthinkable a decade ago: The values that shape newspapers are now the same values that shape TV news," says Bill Walker.[3]

The blending of the philosophy of the television and the newspaper business is happening because, to a great degree, the leaders of both industries are frightened by many of the same things. Much more publicized than daily newspapers' problems, the loss of audience by the networks was one of the biggest media stories of the 1980s. With the explosive growth of cable television, satellite systems, resource-sharing local news operations, independent television networks, and the home entertainment business eroding their audience, the prime time market share of the three major networks—CBS, NBC, and ABC—fell from 92 percent to less than 70 percent in just 10 years.[4]

During television's turbulent 1980s, all th ee networks changed ownership—General Electric purchasing NBC, Laurence Tisch of Loews Corporation purchasing CBS, and ABC acquired by Capital Cities. Led by CBS News, which slashed its work force by one-third in one fourteen-month period, the news staff at all three networks has been downsized, and the once lavish newsroom budgets have been trimmed mercilessly.[5] At the same time, local television affiliates—always known for their bottom-line mentality and their fixation with ratings—tightened news budgets even further, developed even more gimmicks to cater to the audience, and showed an ever greater avidness for letting show business values dictate the direction of their news operations.

All during the 1980s television executives wrung their hands over many of the same demographic, audience, and technological forces that have struck fear into the heart of their newspaper counterparts. While newspaper executives worry that newspapers are no longer read by the young and the busy and the easily distracted, television executives have had to worry about "zappers" and "grazers" and "trawlers"—viewers, instantly bored, who incessantly roam the television dial or snap off advertisements or use their video systems to record programs without commercial interruptions. While newspaper executives worry about churn, the transition to preprinted inserts, and the growth of target-marketed publications, network executives are confronted with the proliferation of cable stations and independent television networks and a multitude of news and entertainment shows that have expanded the television dial into a cornucopia of off-network programing. While newspaper executives worry about their future in the ever expanding Information Age, network news executives find themselves already facing a situation where satellite systems and local resource sharing consortia mean local affiliates have the wherewithal to abandon the networks and establish their own world and national newscasts anytime they want.

As if this weren't enough, television executives have begun to gird themselves for a time when computers and television and telephones merge into a single instrument, and the American home will be wired to a virtually infinite number of channels and be capable of capturing satellite signals directly in the living room.

While the development of technology and the tastes of the marketplace will have much to do with the exact shape of this future, television executives already find themselves traveling an increasingly crowded "video highway" that includes twenty-four-hour local news operations, pay-per-view channels, specialized information and educational services, interactive voice and video technology, and live coverage of everything from high profile court trials to Congress. As Jon Katz puts it, "new technological Godzillas" will lead to even more "evolutionary leaps for the box that dominates our living rooms. . . . News media already battered by recession, defecting youth, cable and VCR competition, and tabloid television have little relief in sight."[6] In fact, the possibilities of this new media tomorrow have led the handwringers, just as in the newspapers, to pronounce the coming death of over-the-airways television as we know it today. As Patrick Maines, the president of the Media Institute, a Washington-based think tank specializing in communications policy, says,

> To put it bluntly, the ultimate survival of local television stations [affiliates and independents alike] is in serious doubt. Over-the-air broadcasting is an utterly obsolete technology—and that fact, together with the commercial pressures imposed by a wildly proliferating video marketplace, does not bode well for local stations.[7]

In his 1988 article "The Future of Television," *Newsweek* magazine writer Harry F. Waters presents an equally pessimistic view of the networks' situation. He uses words like "bleak" and "catastrophic" to assess the future of the networks and network news in particular. "The nightly network newscast—perhaps the most ritualized manifestation of our teleculture—could be a mere memory by the century's end," he writes.[8]

This backdrop of future shock and near financial desperation provides the economic environment for today's television journalists. Both at the networks and the local affiliate level (where new owners are often saddled with heavy debt from mergers and acquisitions and determined to maximize revenues), television employees have weathered a decade of newsroom staffing cutbacks, reductions in overseas coverage, the near disappearance of the serious documentary, and the rise of "pseudonews" and "pseudohistory" in the form of docu-dramas, crime reenactments, tabloid talk shows, celebrity news, so-called reality television, and other hyped-up sensationalism that passes for standard programing these days.[9] At the same time, the local television executives—who developed audience pandering and ratings-grubbing to a fine art well before television fell on tough times—have only grown more feverish in their drive to turn local newscasting into entertainment fare.

These days, the distinction between news and entertainment has grown increasingly blurred as television executives happily reshape history or run crime reenactment shows or hype the bizarre and the amazing to appeal to the elusive viewing pleasure of their audience. Local news departments are particularly prone to breaking into the regular network programing to promote a feature on the late local news—maybe something on "satanism" or "Sasquatch" or "teen suicide"—or a news segment expanding on the theme of a prime time docudrama or a big special. "The television news business, having surrendered to the idea that its purpose is business and that news is just another product in the great American sellathon, is having a hard time figuring out how it is losing its business as well as its identity," writes former NBC correspondent John Hart.[10]

Seattle is a good example of the wasteland that is now local news. As the three major local stations battle it out for local news supremacy, the airways have become filled with the "Hook 'em and hold 'em. Whatever it takes. Or else" philosophy, as *Seattle Post-Intelligencer* television critic John Engstrom puts it. There is packaged news "spindled and mutilated to fit a formula," Engstrom says. There is "crime and fire news, scare news, cute-animals-doing-anything news." In an industry trying to survive in an economic jungle and flooded with research about who watches what, there are sexy, frightening, and warm-and-fuzzy stories, along with teases and "tie-ins" to popular prime time shows. Engstrom quotes one local news director as saying "we're not in the news business, we're in the audience business." A newcomer local TV reporter told Engstrom, "I'm not a journalist. I'm a ratings machine."[11]

All this has left television journalists almost nostalgic about the "good old days" when news marketing was viewed as the purchase of a station helicopter and "happy talk" was about how far most stations went to personalize their relationship with viewers. Julie Blacklow, a twenty-year veteran reporter at Seattle's KING-5, recently left the business saying it had become "all twinkies and no protein."[12] Blacklow (who said she rejected a sizable severance bonus if she'd agree not to talk about the station for three years) complains about ratings and advertisers and consultants holding sway over the television news business. "These realities explain why television news is the way it is today: A daily dose of mostly meaningless, poorly researched, irrelevant, and insubstantial 'filler,' pretending to be news," she says.[13]

At a 1990 Sigma Delta Chi gathering in Chicago, local broadcast personnel lamented that they were caught in a business undergoing a "historic amount of rapid change" and complained of:

- Newsroom budgets that are down to "nickels and dimes" and scrutinized "line by line."
- Cuts in staff that have led to the "one-day investigative" report "you start at 9 and put on the air at 6."
- A constant battle to make the news fit time constraints, with an ever greater emphasis on news briefs and headline reading services.
- Less original reporting and a greater reliance for material on morning newspapers, computer data bases, and the wire services.
- Oversensationalized "sweeps" pieces put on during those times when local television stations gain their ratings.
- Promotional spots that embarrass news personnel and violate professional standards.
- Pressures to market everything from the news "product" to the anchor people themselves.
- Anchor jobs that have turned into "white collar migrant" work, where people market-hop and are pushed to be pseudo-street reporters (often during the heavily promoted "sweeps" periods).
- Producers who have come to be the dominant force in news decisions and policy judgments in the broadcast news operation.
- A business where too many reporters all "dress the same, sound the same, even report the same" and where local stations all do the same news stories.[14]

Ironically, these television journalists sounded remarkably like their print counterparts in complaining about the tensions of newsroom economics, about being "packaged" for promotions, about the way original thinking is fast becoming an old-fashioned luxury, and about working for a business that, while less flush than in the old days, is still (for most broadcast television operations) very profitable.

In fact, both the newspaper and the broadcasting business are not just growing together in philosophy—they are growing together in reality. Over the last decade, a number of newspaper companies have become big forces in the broadcasting marketplace. In some cases, media organizations—like the Washington Post, the New York Times, Hearst, Capital Cities, Scripps Howard, the Tribune Corporation, the Providence Journal and about a half-dozen other smaller chains— already own both newspapers and television properties. The ones that didn't have a large number of broadcast properties, like Gannett, got them through merger. A company like Gannett, in particular, seems to operate under the principle that with the coming proliferation of elec- tronic competition the role of newspaper and broadcast properties will increasingly blend together. Not only was *USA Today* very consciously designed to be television on newsprint, but Gannett caused a stir when it put a television version of *USA Today* on the air. To the delight of its critics, Gannett discovered this merging of media forms to be trickier than expected. When it tried to imitate its televisionlike newspaper on television, it was a huge ratings failure.

Traditionally, television has been about a decade ahead of newspa- pers when it comes to pioneering new techniques in the areas of audience research and packaging of the product and treating the news as entertainment. Edward Jay Epstein pinpoints 1969 as the year the networks jumped feet first into the news-as-entertainment business.[15] That was a year when then vice-president Spiro Agnew began com- plaining that TV news was not being fair to the Nixon administration nor reflecting the values of middle-class Americans. And, as Epstein tells it, ABC-TV executives decided to do something about it.

As part of an effort to "restructure" its news operation, the network hired a consulting firm, invested in "attitudinal surveys" of its audi- ence, and "heightened the entertainment value" of its news shows. To do this, ABC news executives emphasized "constructive" human inter- est stories and downplayed stories that stressed the "problematic" na- ture of news; fashioned a set of highly graphic symbols and comic book-style bubbles as backdrops for its broadcasts; limited the length of every story to less than three minutes; instituted a system to "antici- pate" events; and established tight executive control over the entire news operation so correspondents would be sure to conform to the formula. "Stories—both film and anchorman's scripted on-camera ma- terial—are combined into a logical thread, leading the audience through the news so that their distracted minds do not have to make sharp twists and turns to follow what is going on," said then ABC news executive Avram Westin in explaining the network's philosophy.[16]

ABC's tactics were a precursor of what would happen—with a ven- geance—in both print and broadcast journalism in the 1980s. Enter- taining the audience and doing it with appealing visuals, ABC's executives divined, would be the method of operation for the news organizations of the future. And, whether it was a self-fulfilling prophecy or not, it has become the gospel in both television news and newspapers. Looking back on those moves at ABC news more than twenty years ago, all the elements of the news-as-entertainment craze that has swept through the print media during the 1980s are there: audience research, packaging, the creation of a compact and eye-catching news product, the development of newsroom management systems that keep a firm grip on newsroom personnel.

Today, it has become commonplace to find newspapers modifying their format and their content as acknowledgement that Americans now spend almost as many hours in front of their television sets (an estimated seven hours a day) as they do sleeping.[17] At first, these changes were subtle and halting and less visible, such as the addition of TV columns, the advent of less formal, television-style writing, and alterations in news coverage reflecting television's advantage in capturing breaking events. However, with the new press color capabilities, the computer graphics revolution, and the appearance of *USA Today,* newspapers in recent years have rushed headlong to turn themselves into a full-fledged visual experience. Sadly, the modern television newsroom—described by one critic as "the Gulag Archipelago of journalism"[18]—is also fast becoming the model for the newsroom of the modern daily newspaper. Today's local television reporters are overworked, overmanaged, and overstressed. The bottom-line efficiencies, the demands for producing a slickly packaged product, the pressures of producing two stories a day, the difficulties of dealing with news directors unprepared for handling personnel problems—all are part of the life of the typical local television news journalist. In a 1989 survey of twenty-five TV stations, Ted Dracos found none that had in-house research and development or formal stress management programs or systematic plans for rewarding performance.[19]

While the lack of these kinds of programs is not the only indicator of the livability of a newsroom environment (few newspaper newsrooms have them, either), it does point to the future for a newspaper business that is increasingly shaped by technology and the bottom line. Newspaper newsrooms can expect to function more and more like television newsrooms as portable communications equipment becomes ever more sophisticated; videotext and electronic newswires (with their instant news needs) become available to newspaper customers; customer phone-in services for news briefs, sports, and business updates become more widespread; electronic libraries and data base services are marketed; and newsroom editors are valued for the strength of their management and administrative styles as much as or more than for their journalistic skills.

Edwin Diamond's broadsides against television's fixation with taking the pulse of the audience and finicking with the news formula sound more and more applicable to print media: "In television news, as in any other art form, incessant fussing with manner, rather than matter, is usually clear evidence of sterility; it marks the exhaustion of a style."[20]

In years past, many television journalists might have objected to the characterization of television news as superficial and corrupted by entertainment values. Network news, they say, has a legacy of fine journalism, dating back to the days when Edward R. Murrow helped bring down the late Senator Joseph McCarthy and Daniel Schorr unearthed his Watergate scoops and Morley Safer filed some of the first vivid scenes of what was really happening in the Vietnam War.

Nevertheless, even in the prime of the medium, the notion of a golden era of television news was as much myth as reality. As far back as 1958, Murrow, the most legendary figure from that mythical period, complained about the need of television and radio news to make its content salable, packageable, and to select it so as not to antagonize sponsors.[21]

In the early 1970s Epstein noted that television news operations— at both the national and local level—did very little original reporting. The logistical problems of dispatching camera crews, the pressure to give every story a visual twist, the need for simple, understandable themes combined with the fact that entertainment-minded owners simply aren't willing to spend very much on newsgathering make it very difficult for small staffs of television news operations to tackle multifaceted topics or dig below the surface of events.[22] In fact, television news has always suffered from its superficiality and its encapsulation within an entertainment medium—a medium that, as former *Variety* television critic Les Brown once put it, is principally "in the business of delivering people to advertisers."[23] So it is almost with a sense of resignation that critics watched as television executives— increasingly treating the news departments as a profit center—have slowly dismantled what journalistic tradition existed within their news operations and remolded them in the image of the entertainment package that so dominates the rest of the broadcast schedule.

In 1982 *New York Times* television writer Tony Schwartz described the movement at the networks to make television news more popular and appealing. Schwartz said the emphasis was on the graphics, promotion, and overall design of the news product. Pacing was picking up and audience-grabbing stories were pushed to the front of the news-cast. "The result is an increasing emphasis on eye-catching graphics, slick packaging and alluring promotion of highly paid stars," Schwartz said. Schwartz goes on to quote CBS correspondent Charles Kuralt as saying, "At the networks today, there is an unseemly emphasis upon image and flash, and the tricks of electronics for the hard fact, arrived at by hard work."[24]

The hunger for ratings has pushed television news executives to become ever more commercial in their search for an audience. This has meant giving the public less of what it needs to know and more of what it wants to know, says John Weisman in a 1985 article for *TV Guide*. Television has become big business, says Weisman, run by people who "are not seat-of-the-pants journalists but managers, who utilize research, engage in product-testing and employ consultants. They say they are committed to journalistic excellence and the auton-omy of their news operations, and there is little reason to doubt their sincerity. But they are also, in effect, middle-level managers of huge corporations who are subject to pressure from above when their divi-sions do not show increased audience shares, or profits."[25]

The focus of the critics' wrath has been CBS TV News, where the journalistic tradition has been most celebrated—and where budget cuts and staff layoffs in the news division have been carried out in the most brutal fashion. Although top level network executives (such as CBS owner Laurence Tisch) have clearly been the ones responsible for the budget slashings, critics have focused on news executives like Van Gordon Sauter, the former CBS news president who emerges as the engaging, but clearly villainous, lead character in Peter Boyer's *Who Killed CBS?*[26]

In his book, Boyer describes how Sauter, who came out of local news operations in Chicago and Los Angeles, brought with him to CBS the kind of flashy, entertainment values that characterize local tele-vision news and a strong feeling that time had passed by the network of Murrow and Charles Collingwood and Walter Cronkite. With Sauter, new technical gadgets were introduced that could instantly create graphs and charts and make a picture shrink or expand or spin, Boyer says. Sauter pushed the instant, quick-hit, top-of-the-news, "instant documentary" while cutting back public affairs programing and tradi-tional documentary units. In the meantime, the finance people insin-uated their way into the news operation with weekly cost reports, and finance officers were once actually put into the field with journalists.

In this atmosphere, Boyer says correspondents were told that it was no longer just what they said that mattered, but the way they said it, how they performed as part of the entertainment package. After the budget and staff cutbacks, CBS correspondent Bill Leonard captured the anguish in the news division: "Something's happening here. They're destroying the fucking place. It is heartbreaking. It's not just the news division. The company, the company is destroyed."[27]

CBS wasn't the only place where the news divisions underwent major changes in the 1980s. Edwin Diamond describes how NBC executives tried a more subtle, less blunt axe approach to achieving a major cost savings in their news division. Diamond says that rather than going the way of Laurence Tisch at CBS, who chopped $50 million out of the news division budget by "brute-force" cuts, NBC executives decided to try an "MBA" approach. Soon after the network was acquired by the General Electric Corporation, NBC hired the consulting firm of McKinsey and Company, headed by John Stewart, a Harvard MBA and former Pershing missile manager for TRW (and, incidentally, the same company that helped the *New York Times* restructure its management operation). As part of the "GE-like budget exercise," Diamond says, the McKinsey people tried to put hard numbers on the entire news process—total assignments, managers involved in story selection, the rate of on-air appearances by correspondents, the cost differential between breaking stories and more expensive feature and investigative stories. "The McKinseyites have been applying their MBA skills and pocket calculators to the slippery, sprawling, booby-trapped entity known as the News," Diamond says. "They are trying to analyze news as they might any other product, attempting to quantify what journalists, innocent of business-school principles, have long held to be unquantifiable. What, after all, makes a 'good' story or an 'efficient' reporter, and how do you assign numbers to these qualities?"[28]

The loss of viewers by the networks continues to be one of the biggest media stories of the 1990s, and there are strong indications that economic pressures are making things even more perilous for news traditionalists at the networks. Cable television, VCRs, twenty-four hour news, sports networks, satellite systems, and other electronic competitors continue to make inroads into the once monolithic audience enjoyed by the networks. Not only has the audience erosion and ratings slide served as the justification for the slashing of news budgets, but it has also put heavy profit pressures on the news divisions— once places where the networks didn't look to make much money. With the discovery that news can serve as profitable, popular entertainment (a discovery, ironically, demonstrated initially by the success of CBS's "Sixty Minutes"), the news divisions find themselves under greater pressure to succeed in the field of entertainment. And as the syndicators and the networks' cable competitors use ever more aggressive marketing formulas, the television channels are filled with shows like "Entertainment Today," "Lifestyles of the Rich and Famous," "A Current Affair, "The Reporters," "This Evening," "Inside Edition," and "Unsolved Mysteries" (known as "trash television" by their critics) as the networks keep developing tabloid news programs of their own to try to keep their viewers.

Television historians like Brown and Erik Barnouw see an almost historical inevitability in this process as the television networks—watching the havoc technological change is wreaking upon their market—writhe to find ways to survive.[29] Journalistic principle has never had much place in an industry that defines itself almost exclusively by its ability to draw an audience, Barnouw says. He notes that long before the marketing frenzy had engulfed the news professionals at the networks, local news operations had hired consultants, adopted ratings-raising formulas, and "merged almost wholly into sponsored 'entertainment' " by the 1970s.[30]

According to Barnouw, for all intents and purposes, television *is* little more than a marketplace for the promotion of goods and services. The sponsor, he claims, has dictated the form and content of television since its very beginnings. Advertisements are the focal point of programing, protected by entertainment designed to fit sponsor needs and bordered by a fringe of successfully neutralized public service elements. "To manufacture a product without at the same time manufacturing a demand has become unthinkable. Today the manufacture of demand means, for most large companies, television," he says.[31]

The sad state of television news is amply illustrated in a 1988 study of 769 local television journalists by Conrad Smith. Some of the toughest critics of television news, it turns out, are television news employees themselves. Smith's study showed that in every case television reporters agree with most of what the critics of television news say—TV overdramatizes and depends too much on ratings, live shots, and "bang-bang" footage. Perhaps not unexpectedly, producers and news directors were less inclined to agree with critics. In fact, at each step higher up the chain of command, television employees became less critical of their craft, Smith said.[32]

However, the debate is not only about the content of television. Almost three decades ago, Marshall McLuhan argued that television's real contribution to the culture was how it changed the way we thought and communicated with each other, not just the content of television programing.[33] Although McLuhan is not now held in esteem in most academic circles, his thinking has influenced media theorists who believe that television has changed the very fabric of society and profoundly altered the course of modern events.

At its most fundamental level, television is blamed for reshaping our view of the world in the way it transmits reality. Almost forty years ago, researchers Gladys and Kurt Lang showed television's propensity to frame audience perception by conveying events in ways that largely fulfilled the expectations of viewers and broadcasters.[34] Epstein has demonstrated how the economic and organizational realities of television (such as the placement of personnel, the logistics of moving television equipment, and the need for visuals and predictable events to cover) shape the way television presents the news.[35]

At a deeper level, however, McLuhan and his followers argue that television doesn't just change the way we perceive the world—it changes us. In his book, *No Sense of Place,* Joshua Meyrowitz describes a society that has been turned upside down by the way television alters our sense of geographical place, exposes children to the secrets of the adult world, demystifies authority, opens up vistas to people with only "television literacy," publicly examines people's once private behavior, and generally breaks down the gender, age, and occupational stereotypes of the old print-dominated world. Meyrowitz sees the turmoil of the 1960s and the changes in morals and behavior that emerged from it as an outgrowth of television and the result of the coming of age of the Baby Boom generation, the first group to grow up on television.[36]

In general, Meyrowitz echoes the classic view of McLuhan (and Harold Innis, McLuhan's mentor) that the print culture is growing less important and being absorbed by the emerging age of instant electronic information transmission. The hostility toward print held by McLuhan and his followers is based largely on their belief that the traditional print world is less democratic than the coming electronic age. The traditional print world, in this view, has benefited elite groups who hold power, required a long and arduous initiation into knowledge, encouraged people to think in hierarchical, linear terms, kept people segregated by class and occupation, and generally taught people to "know their place," as Meyrowitz puts it.

Yet, in his analysis, Meyrowitz, like McLuhan, underestimates the role of newspapers in the culture. In fact, as Michael Schudson points out, mass media newspapers in the nineteenth century—the so-called penny press—performed many of the roles Meyrowitz now ascribes to television. Those included absorbing and shaping popular values, reflecting the values not of an elite but of a varied, middle- and working-class world, satisfying public curiosity about how the wealthy and successful live, demystifying the powerful, making sense of the urban landscape, and helping immigrants learn about the culture. Newspaper reading in this country—while certainly now a more elite activity than in the days of the penny press—is still the underpinning of our society's knowledge base. And newspapers are a vital link in the communications system by which television viewers—even if, in Ranney's terms, through the "two-step" flow of information—become educated about events.

Meyrowitz introduces one term that is particularly helpful for understanding the relationship between television and the print media. Dubbing it an "effect loop," Meyrowitz notes—as others have—that television's dominance in our society has led the print media to emulate it.[37] Television's natural intimacy—its ability to show people vividly and up close—has led to more "personality" journalism in books, newspapers, and magazines, he says. Writing styles, reflecting television's informality, are more personal and subjective. Events are now often defined by newspapers, Meyrowitz says, in terms of how they appeared on television.

Meyrowitz isn't as disturbed by this as Neil Postman is. Postman argues vehemently that we have been corrupted by the "entertainment" orientation of television. We can't do anything these days—become educated, engage in public dialogue, carry on the basic affairs of life—without feeling that we must be entertained in the process, he says. "I do not mean that the trivialization of public information is all accomplished on television," Postman says. "I mean that television is the paradigm for our conception of public information. . . . In presenting news to us packaged as vaudeville, television induces other media to do the same, so that the total information environment begins to mirror television."[38]

Two final thoughts—perhaps reassuring to those who worry about the power of television, perhaps not—close out this chapter. The first is the conclusion, reached long ago by researchers, that television is not necessarily the window to the world for most Americans. Researcher Lawrence Lichty points to a 1981 study by Simmons Market Research showing that the perception that the majority of Americans get their news from television is a false one.[39] Fewer than one-third of U.S. adults watch TV news (which is still lower than the percentage that read a newspaper each day). Other data, he says, indicate that TV is far from the dominant source of news. Overall, the TV audience is disproportionately older and less educated, with two types of people who watch a lot of TV news: people who watch a lot of TV (and who are predominantly less educated) and those younger, better-educated Americans who are heavy readers of news and watch lots of news and information but not much else on TV.

In fact, newspaper executives continually have been warned—by people ranging from Leo Bogart to Christine Urban to Philip Meyer—that they imitate television at their peril. The underlying reasons for the newspapers' readership stagnation are serious and complex. Yet research quite consistently shows that people are not abandoning newspapers for television.[40] It is true that young people—where newspapers' greatest readership problems lie—may be more visually oriented and less patient with the printed word. But it is also true that the better-educated, more affluent, upwardly mobile part of society—a group that still makes up the bulk of the newspaper reading audience—has a need for serious, in-depth, informative, and enterprising news. If those readers begin to find daily newspapers adopting television's superficial tactics for covering and displaying the news, they will search elsewhere for the information that is meaningful to them.

The second thought concerns the optimistic view of television held by media philosophers like McLuhan and Walter Ong, a McLuhan devotee. Ong, a Jesuit priest who teaches at St. Louis University, believes that the evolving electronic technology is expanding global contacts, increasing our cross-cultural sense of each other, promoting dialogue between peoples, and helping open us to each other in trust and love.[41] Television as a means to world brotherhood is an attractive message and one that, at first glance, we might all hope would prove true. And yet the philosophy of Ong's *The Presence of the Word* was tested not long ago by the events that grew out of the student demonstrations in the People's Republic of China.

It was apparent that Ong's optimism was intuitively shared by the U.S. television correspondents who covered the demonstrations as well as by most Americans who watched them. Television treated the protest much like it does any other big, important event—live feeds, constant updates, nightly special reports. And, in a fashion more profound than it often does, the televising of the event became a part of the event itself. The television people were caught up in the fervor of the students' calls for democracy. The students, in turn, were caught up in the heady sense that television was showing the world Chinese history in the making. The new global information order reinforced events: fax machines brought in supportive communications from Chinese students abroad, reports from the Voice of America repeated for the Chinese the message that was being broadcast in the free world.

And that message, communicated back and forth between the correspondents and the demonstrators, was: the whole world is watching, so how could anything bad happen.

In the end, many of those television performers—the students interviewed day after day by correspondents crowding the square—ended up dead or imprisoned after the massacre at Tiananmen Square. To the horror of television correspondents, video clips were used to identify many of the protesters. Political power, the TV people and the rest of us learned, was not automatically going to surrender to the power of the medium or the global reach of television.

Tragically, everyone involved—the TV people, the Chinese students and their supporters, and the world viewing audience—came to realize that we had been caught up in an event of television's own creation. In the political sense, Meyrowitz's "effect loop" closed around the necks of the Chinese students.

CHAPTER SIX

Managers and the Mind of the Computer

Having extended or translated our central nervous system into the electromagnetic technology, it is but a further stage to transfer our consciousness to the computer world as well.
—Marshall McLuhan, *Understanding Media*

Experience, as Nabokov describes it . . . is more like a stew than a filing system.
—Theodore Roszak, *The Cult of Information*

The real problem in applying computer science to the newspaper industry was that of breaking down habitual attitudes and methods within the newspaper organization itself.
—Anthony Smith, *Goodbye Gutenberg*

When the only tool you have is a hammer, everything begins to look like a nail.
—Abraham Maslow, quoted in David Burnham's *The Rise of the Computer State*

WHEN a Northwest Airlines jet crashed at the Detroit airport in 1987, Pegie Stark directed a newsroom exercise that ten years earlier would not even have been a part of a newspaper's coverage of a major disaster.[1]

Stark, then the graphics director of the *Detroit News,* was in charge of putting together the computer-generated graphics for a newspaper that, in Stark's words, views text and graphics as equally important in the news presentation process. Reporters were directed to spend time gathering information for the graphics—what the inside of the cockpit looked like, detailed drawings of the crash site, and other material on how an airplane works.

The *News*'s front page the next day reflected the priority the newspaper puts on computer graphics. A computer drawing showed a jet headed toward the ground with a large X marking the spot where it crashed. The *News*'s coverage, with its emphasis on computer-generated graphics, had a modern, visually arresting quality to it—but also a cold, technological feel compared to the more traditional, photo-oriented coverage of its competitor, the *Free Press.*

Stark has been in the forefront of a revolution that has now thoroughly taken hold at most of today's daily newspapers. The graphics revolution is occurring thanks to the "Mac" computer technology, a driving force in the trend toward emphasizing the layout and the design of the newspaper—at the expense, critics say, of the substance of writing and reporting.[2] In fact, computers and the computer graphics that have become key elements in the wave of newspaper redesigns have probably done more to homogenize the look and feel of newspapers than anything else since the advent of the steam-powered printing press in the 1800s.

And yet the burgeoning use of computer graphics is only the latest development in the ongoing transformation of the newsroom into a fully computerized operation where the reporting and editing of the news are integrated with the production and marketing of the newspaper. For almost forty years computers have played an ever larger role in putting out the daily news product. Large, centralized computer systems were introduced as the powerful, coordinating link between the newsroom and the backshop (where the printing and the production of the news pages take place) in the 1950s. Computerized phototypesetting equipment arrived with the advent of offset printing in the 1960s. Computer terminals came to the desks of reporters and editors in the 1970s. And in the 1980s ever smaller, more powerful, and more efficient computers began to replace the old, front-end computer systems and their accompanying phototypesetters as the "desktop" computer revolution turned the newsroom into a coordinated network of personal computers.

The new pagination technology, the latest development to come to the newsroom, puts editors to work at a computerized drawing board, where editing, page layout, and graphics are all designed directly on a computer screen. On pagination equipment, the layout can be sent directly, with the push of a single button, to a high-speed laser printer from which it emerges as camera-ready copy. The system is methodically eliminating the traditional backshop jobs of laying out pages, pasting up pages, and stripping in half-tones of photographs. At many smaller newspapers, which have been the fastest to adopt pagination technology, backshop employment has virtually disappeared. As pagination systems move into the newsrooms of larger newspapers, the newsroom has become a home for a new breed of graphics editors, computer systems managers, and computer-literate reporters who are expected to come up with graphics along with story ideas. In fact, demand has soared for a new kind of newsroom employee who can combine the job of copy editor, newspaper designer, and the video-version of a paste-up specialist—a hybrid journalist/artist/technician that is changing the old definition of journalist.[3]

The new newsroom computer systems have become the major force in helping newspaper executives "plan" and "package" the modern newspaper. On computers it is very easy to do the kind of aggressive management required of today's newspaper executives—updating and transferring lists of upcoming news stories, sending stories back to reporters, inserting comments, moving around blocks of text, trimming stories for space. Cruising computer files is an effective method for editors to oversee their reporters and survey their work. Sending electronic messages, exchanging computer data, or handing around computer printouts are efficient ways for editors at all levels of the newspaper hierarchy to coordinate the marketing, production, and news-gathering process.

Much of the chaos of the old city room—the clatter of wire machines, aides running back and forth with copy, reporters banging away on typewriters—has been reduced to a computer hum. With the changes in the physical environment, today's newspaper editors have been encouraged by computerization to clean up their own mental spaces and reorganize the work-life around them. Computers have done much to aid newsroom managers in their ongoing, but tough and tricky, task of requiring a group of hard-driving, egocentric, and often antiauthoritarian souls, on a daily basis, to meet the demands of a mass-produced commodity manufactured and merchandised on tight deadlines. The proliferation of the computer terminal has allowed quietness, efficiency, planning—and firm control—to become the watchwords of the modern editor.

"Computers are logical, while people are very illogical at times. Also, when you give a computer the correct command, it will do what you want. People aren't always like that," says Mary Lipscomb, the news/systems manager for the *Enquirer* in Battle Creek, Michigan.[4]

In fact, the computer is playing a key role in newsrooms—as it is in many other fields—in the automation of white collar professionals. Newspaper executives eliminated a major barrier between white collar and blue collar work when pagination technology allowed them to assign to newsroom personnel many of the old backshop functions of page makeup and layout. As reporters and editors find themselves spending more and more time designing news pages, updating electronic files, exchanging electronic memos, helping to prepare computer graphics, and working off computer lists of preplanned and packaged stories, they slowly (if unconsciously) become captives of their computers—rather than the other way around. In a job that has always been considered a "semiprofessional" one, many newsroom employees are likely to find their jobs looking more like those of data entry workers or information processing clerks rather than the fully professional roles that they have always aspired to.

In her book, *The Electronic Sweatshop,* Barbara Garson argues that computer automation is making white collar workers cheaper to train, easier to replace, less skilled, less expensive—and therefore less special.[5] She compares the process to the one that occurred in nineteenth century industrial management when craftsmen were transformed into factory hands. Rather than improving efficiency, she claims that the real motivation of managers is to use computers to centralize control—with themselves in charge.[6] "The important element isn't the computer program but the management determination to centralize decision making," she says. "However it's implemented, the result is more clerks, whatever their titles, and fewer full-fledged professionals."[7]

It is ironic that newspaper people—so interested in change elsewhere in the world—have treated with cheerful disinterest the technological revolution going on within their own newsroom. The coming of the computer to the newspaper business has been accepted virtually without protest by newsroom employees.[8] Except for a small debate about the safety of video display terminals (which, perhaps not surprisingly, has been given only nominal coverage by newspapers), most reporters and editors have made the transition to composing and editing on computers with remarkable ease.[9] To be sure, the flexibility of the computer terminal—where corrections can be made instantly, type moved around at will, and stories transmitted with the push of a button—has clear advantages to newsworkers over the type-it-up-and-paste-it-onto-copy-paper system of the past.

Researchers have generally found that newsroom employees liked the new computer systems. Shipley, Gentry, and Clarke (1978) reported that the vast majority of editors prefer VDT editing to editing with pencil and paper.[10] Ogan (1982) found that most newsroom managers had a positive attitude about the use of computers,[11] and the Burgoons and Atkin (1981) found in a survey of 489 newsroom people that the majority agreed that they were comfortable with VDTs.[12] Researchers like Ullmann (1983), Miller (1983), and Ruth (1985) have concluded that use of electronic data bases has grown at newspapers, and electronic information retrieval systems are generally viewed as valuable by newsworkers.[13]

Yet beneath the optimism some signs of discontent have been noted.

In their nationwide survey of journalists in the early 1980s, Weaver and Wilhoit found that virtually all the journalists indicated that the new technology had improved the quality of their work. But they also showed an ambivalence toward the new computers, with many reporting such negative effects as eye strain, more tedious work, a "dehumanizing" environment, regret at the loss of the "old atmosphere," an increase in competition in the newsroom, and more emphasis on technology than on the news.[14] Weaver and Wilhoit's concerns have been echoed by researcher John Shipman, Jr., who said computers appear to be a tempting tool for newspaper managers who are asserting more management control of newsrooms.[15] "Most of the literature about computerization, when coupled with what is known about newsroom employees, indicates autonomy, and less control, is called for," Shipman says. "However, that approach might be impractical in a time when more control is being seen in newsrooms."[16]

One of the few aspects of computers that has grown into a controversy is the violation of the privacy of computer files. In a 1984 article in the *Columbia Journalism Review*, Richard Cunningham described such abuses as private password "log-ons" becoming known in the newsroom, newsroom "hackers" outsmarting the computer security system, and editors who insist they must be able to get into reporter files.[17] There have also been instances of other dubious uses of the computer in the newsroom, such as the retrieval by an editor of a reporter's notes and their insertion in a story without the reporter's knowledge; the printing out of correspondence from personal, supposedly safeguarded files and its posting on bulletin boards; or a computer cruiser's breaking into the files of a competing news organization.[18]

Computers also have the ability to quantify the output and production of a work force, which several newspapers already use to monitor the productivity of workers in their classified and circulation departments. At most newspapers, a computer check can be run to calculate the number of stories produced by a reporter, the number of column inches, and the placement in the newspaper. Even though most newspaper managers would probably insist they'd never use such a crude measurement to calculate a reporter's value to the company, the computer is capable of performing the task—and that means someone has enough interest in the measurement to program it into the system.

Newspaper managers and their computer systems specialists are quick to note that it is not the computer but how people use it that can be bad or good. The *Columbia Journalism Review* has paid homage to the newspapers—including the *Seattle Times*, the Atlanta *Journal and Constitution*, *Newsday*, the *Providence Journal-Bulletin*, and the *New*

York Times—that have used computer-assisted programs to help with their investigative projects.[19] In fact, computers have been used effectively by reporters at places like the *Philadelphia Inquirer* and the *Dallas Morning News* and the *Wall Street Journal,* which have won Pulitzer prizes for complex investigations of things like court corruption and federal housing programs and the stock market crash, investigations that would have been virtually impossible without a computer system to process reams of data.

But reporters who praise computers as investigative tools are the first to acknowledge that their efforts are only scratching the surface of the mountains of data produced by a society that is advancing into the Information Age at a mind-boggling speed. If the computer were not so profoundly revolutionizing the rest of society, it would not take a computer to keep abreast with the changes. The few newspapers that even employ investigative reporters (let alone, computer-oriented investigative reporters) are far outnumbered by the newspapers with overworked, undertrained journalists who simply don't have the time, the technical knowledge, the computer resources, or the interpretative skills to keep up with the technicians who are building, and in some cases abusing, the information society.

Sadly, the model for the newspaper of tomorrow is more likely to reflect the surface appeal of information as a commodity rather than the depth appeal of information as a tool to better comprehend a complex world. The notion of information as a product to be marketed is becoming more and more common in the unfolding Information Age, and for many news organizations "information" has become the byword of the future. It is no surprise to find *USA Today*—with its slick, colorful look, its emphasis on readers and market research, and its treatment of text as something to illustrate the graphics—proudly touting itself as a pioneering product of the Information Age. In fact, the executives at *USA Today,* which was made possible by the newest advances in computer and satellite technologies, have become some of the most aggressive experimenters with computer technology, including working with Apple and the Associated Press to develop a multimedia news system (combining text, video, and special effects) via the personal computer.

Yet, while *USA Today* has promoted itself as the prototypical newspaper for the busy modern reader, its theories for producing the information of the Information Age leave much to be desired. The newspaper is known for its rip-and-read approach to news, with most of its staff-produced copy drawn from big events, press releases, census data, government reports, and other predictable and superficial sources of material. With its emphasis on "factoids" and televisionlike coverage, the newspaper represents the triumph of packaging and presentation over substance. John Quinn, the former *USA Today* editor, captured the spirit of the newspaper's news-as-information-as-commodity philosophy when he wrote that the paper must "sell news/info at a fast, hard pace. Every page one inch must be packed with news/info in easiest-to-read, most comfortable, quick-glance style. No repetition, no word waste, no nonfunctioning white space. . . . Every above-fold item must work to catch reader-on-run."[20]

However, despite their ceaseless talk about the coming Information Age, newspaper executives have been very slow to adopt truly innovative approaches to computerized news delivery. In fact, there are probably no more "future shocked" people in America than today's newspaper executives. The prospects of an electronic tomorrow have had a paralyzing impact on an industry that, encouraged by the proliferation of newspaper chains and one-newspaper towns, has operated with all the monopolist's habits of complacency and self-protection. The newspaper industry's reaction to an environment of constant technological change—which is so familiar to high tech firms, for example—is to talk lots about innovation but to do very little of it. In fact, most of today's newspaper executives, raised in an environment of monopoly and corporate careerism, know very little about surviving and thriving in a truly competitive media marketplace.

Join a typical group of newspaper executives at a typical industry gathering, and you'll be surrounded by lots of handwringing and worried talk about the future. The comments of Norman Pearlstine, executive editor of the *Wall Street Journal*, at a 1987 ASNE-sponsored panel entitled "The Future of Newspapers," are typical:

> When I look at kids who are going to schools today and how they spend their time, and I see kids who are 12 or 13 years old who spend five hours a night playing with their computer—not watching television and not reading, but playing with their games—I try to figure out how that person is going to be attracted to a newspaper 20 years from now. No matter how much you focus on quality and all the things we do in our daily jobs, because that is what the audience wants right now, if you are looking to the future for mass media, I think it is going to be very tough for newspapers.[21]

Nevertheless, one of the few places in the newspaper business where the entrepreneurial spirit is still alive is at the smaller daily and weekly newspapers—and the computer is largely the reason why. The advent of computer-driven desktop publishing has galvanized the small end of the newspaper business and has led to a surge of optimism about the future of the small newspaper publisher. Desktop systems are, in essence, small-scale, extremely cost efficient versions of the pagination systems that are making their way into larger newspapers. For desktop advocates, the evolution of computer publishing technology from centralized, mainframe computer phototypesetting systems to networks of small personal computers is putting a new, populist twist on A. J. Liebling's declaration that, "Freedom of the press is guaranteed only to those who own one."[22]

"This is the industrial revolution in the newspaper field," enthuses Blake Kellogg, a journalism professor in the outreach division of the University of Wisconsin at Madison, about the rush of small newspaper owners to desktop publishing. "And it's happening right before our eyes."[23]

More sober observers of the media scene aren't ready to predict that desktop publishing will produce a flowering of competition or to hail computers as a democratizing force in the industry. As most media scholars will point out, new information technologies have always seemed to hold the potential for two developments at the same time—for greater centralization as well as for decentralization. With ever greater concentration among the major media companies and the explosion of new, small publishers, advances in computer communications seem to be fulfilling this dual prophesy. While it would be nice to believe that the desktop revolution is stimulating a grassroots movement of new, intelligent, populist voices, it cannot be denied that it is also producing lots of shoppers and public relations newsletters and target-marketed magazines and throwaway publications that litter our consciousness and, in the process, help to erode the market for serious, daily newspapers. As Paul Brainerd, a former newspaper executive and the founder of Aldus Corporation, a pioneer in the field of desktop publishing, points out: "These tools have the potential for democratizing the industry. But they are just tools. And it really depends on the people and their use of the tools."[24]

In fact, as with most debates about new technology, the bottom line about desktop publishing is not a more humanized publishing world but economics. Whether it's new desktop publishers, like Eric Kramer who founded the *Falcon* in Lakeside, Arizona ("Before 1984, you'd need about $400,000 to buy [a system like this]. Now it's under $20,000. And the technology is only going to get cheaper."),[25] or old publishers who have converted, like Albert Scott, III, editor of the Carrollton (Ill.) *Gazette-Patriot*, who says his desktop system has saved him about $25,000 a year ("For us, it's been like finding money."),[26] the underlying issue is how much money the technology will put into their pockets. In this respect the discussion is no different than it has been for the last twenty years as computers have spread through the newsroom and the backshop. The cost savings of computer automation have always been a key to its popularity with publishers and in recent years have played a big role in the immense profitability of the newspaper industry. William Rinehart of *Presstime,* for example, estimates that since 1960 computer automation has cut newspaper labor costs in the backshop by 40 to 50 percent.[27]

As it has in the past, computer automation will continue to be tied inextricably to improved newspaper profitability. As newspaper executives head into an uncertain future, computer technology also will continue to be the key to the daily newspaper of tomorrow. In some respects, it is only the limitations of computer technology that have constrained newspapers from developing such things as the "tailored" newspaper—where newspapers can even more specifically target particular readers and advertisers by delivering them portions of the newspaper (like sports or business or police news). In fact, the daily newspaper of the future is likely to be reshaped along the lines of computer advances not only in the newsroom, but in the mailroom, the circulation department, and the printing plant.

It is also clear that it will be financial pressures—and the marketing demands that go with it—that will drive newspapers into the electronic information delivery business. The temptations will be enormous for newspaper editors who will find it cheaper and easier to be the "repackagers" of information rather than the producers of original, enterprise journalism. Unfortunately, if this philosophy prevails, it won't bode well for our data-dependent tomorrow. At this early stage of what futurologists say is going to be an information-rich future, we rely heavily on newspapers—and the information produced by the digging and the investigating and the analyzing of newspaper workers—as the base of the information pyramid that undergirds society. Electronic library systems, marketed data bases, and information search firms depend greatly on newspaper-generated material as the underpinning of their services. But if those newspapers begin to think of information as simply a commodity to be produced and packaged and marketed—and spend less on its original creation—we are in trouble. After all, it is the production of original information that is going to insure that our Information Age is one where people will have access to data that is illuminating and significant and empowering—and not just what has been marketed as information. It is worrisome to realize that the merchants of information are already giving a new, mercantile meaning to the concept of the "marketplace of ideas." The danger, of course, is that if the marketing model prevails, newspaper companies may decide it is the marketing of data, rather than the digging up of original news, that is their primary role. And that could leave the news as just another alluring but insubstantial product to be disseminated in the electronic marketplace. As Gary Gumpert warns us, "The rise of the 'information broker' indicates a shift of priorities and a change of attitude toward knowledge and information. The 'information broker' is a specialist bartering data; he is neither teacher nor student, but a salesman."[28]

Theodore Roszak worries that we may have already reached a point where computers and the people who market them have us in an inexorable grip. For Roszak, the author of *The Cult of Information,* the danger of computers is that we will begin to believe their wonderfully efficient, but programmed and linear, system of reasoning is superior to ours—and, in time, our embrace of the computer's capacities will dictate the way we think. The tendency to celebrate the computer mind at the expense of our own is particularly worrisome, Roszak believes, when we remember that at the bottom of the computer revolution is a powerful corporate system devoted to the marketing of computers and their use to maximize profits.

"Depth, originality, excellence, which have always been factors in the evaluation of knowledge, have somewhere been lost in the fast, futurological shuffle. . . . This is a liability that dogs every effort to inflate the cultural value of information," Roszak says.[29]

Other media theorists, such as Harold Innis, Marshall McLuhan, Walter Ong, and Joshua Meyrowitz, express many of the same thoughts about the potential of the computer—although with different levels of concern. All believe that new media reshape the old information order and, while retaining some aspects of it, create a transformed communications environment that, in turn, will transform the people who communicate within it. And all see the media as extensions of the human senses and suggest that the use of different technologies affects the organization of the human senses and, ultimately, the organization of civilization. As Ong says of the computer: "Electronic computers will never eliminate writing or print—they will simply change the kinds of things we put into these earlier media."[30]

On one level, the emergence of the computer culture looks like a resurgence of the power of the printed word. The demands upon computer users—specialized knowledge, a step-by-step initiation into the rites of learning, a dependence on abstract thought, the ability to make sense of proliferating data bases, the requirement that the isolated individual spend great amounts of time in front of a screen—

seem to be bringing us a new variation of the old print order. In this view, the requirements of the computer are creating an even more extreme version of the print world that both Innis and McLuhan lamented had led to our individualized, specialized, hierarchical, technocratic, and elitist culture.

However, on another level, computers can be seen as another of the great leveling machines. Teachers already agonize over whether they should bother to force students to learn to do mathematical calculations or memorize material or learn to spell when the information is available from a computer with the push of a button. Voice-activated computers are becoming more common, and in time computers will be as easy to use as (and blended with) the telephone and television and the electronic calculator. Computer graphics and multimedia software offer us the ability to be "creative"—but only within the confines of the preprogrammed and formulaic data packages. On computers, the use or knowledge of words promises to serve less as a pathway to an appreciation of true knowledge than as a key to the easy retrieval of specialized information. Increasingly, literacy and computer literacy are growing apart. As with other dualisms of the computer age, computers offer us the potential of becoming much smarter—but they also make it a lot easier to stay dumb.

The skeptics say that, like the loss of the epic poets to the world of the printed page, the computer is leading to a world where people are losing the long-valued skills of memorization, complex reasoning, and mathematical calculation. And they note that—as much as the proponents of the Information Age talk about easy access and democracy—the cost of entry to electronic data bases is increasingly high and controlled by private data marketing firms that have made the ability to pay the price of access. While some software programs seem to stay cheap, these are usually entertainment programs, computer games, and simple word processing systems. The major data retrieval services are increasingly specialized and more and more available only to the well-heeled and the well-trained. In the future, the cost of access to information—and the knowledge necessary to make sense of the data—are likely to become more critical questions than the capability of new technologies to deliver new forms of information.

Still, the computer optimists seem to outweigh the pessimists, at least in the world of communications scholars. Meyrowitz, for example, dismisses George Orwell's "gloomy" vision of *1984* and maintains that computer technology is taking us in the direction away from surveillance devices and a decline in privacy. Electronic communications, says Meyrowitz, allow people "low on the ladder of hierarchy" to gain access to vast stores of information previously limited to "experts" and to communicate with each other horizontally through electronic channels.[31] The growth of computer networks—and the obvious desire of people to use computers to "interact" with each other rather than just to retrieve information—would seem to buttress Meyrowitz's point.

Anthony Smith, like Meyrowitz, believes that electronic technology has been a boon to the consumer of information and swung the power from the producer to the consumer of news.[32] But this, he says, may not necessarily be a good thing for the future business prospects of the newspaper industry. The 1970s were a period of internal reorganization of the newspaper product, the 1980s a period of consolidation (when chains grew and companies diversified), and the next decade, he predicts, will lead to the "cold blasts of the 1990s" when electronic systems begin to undermine the traditional printed press.[33]

It is this "cold blast" that has begun to be felt by the daily newspaper industry and that is driving the industry to reinvent itself in somewhat desperate, and in many cases, painful ways.

CHAPTER SEVEN

The Think Tanks Spread the Word

Every year, thousands of journalists take part in midcareer education programs, ranging from how-to-seminars on laying out the newspaper to brainstorming on the future of the industry. The proliferation proves that newspapers finally have realized the need for formalized programs to nurture editors, writers, and photographers.

—Cindy Rose Stiff in the *Newsroom Management Handbook*

I blame all this on APME and ASNE and their panels and all these kind of industry things. They drive you that way. All they want to do is tell you how to get readers. It's all this marketing stuff. I'm not sure I'll go anymore.

—David Burgin, then editor of the *Dallas Times-Herald*

Over the years, Harless and his colleagues put together a management development system unlike anything ever seen in the newspaper world—complete with a training institute where managers took classes and an assessment center to give them feedback. Virtually every important Knight-Ridder executive was subjected to the process—a method of quality control that, as Harless saw it, could "provide a continuity of management with the same or similar value systems for years."   —Ellis Cose, *The Press*

It's a gray flannel suit atmosphere. It has a very sterile atmosphere. When they opened the plant, they made sure it looked like an IBM office. It used to be seat-of-the-pants journalism. It was Class B, 1930s movie-style journalism. It was a fun place. Now they take themselves super-seriously. Unbelievably seriously. It's a very humorless place.

—William Davis, Guild officer at the *San Jose Mercury News* describing the newspaper after its merger into Knight-Ridder, Inc.

As they gathered under the clouds of recession in cloudy, gray Vancouver, B.C., the attendees of the 1991 annual convention of the American Newspaper Publishers Association were treated to a lot of talk about how the daily newspaper must be "reinvented" in a time of slipping advertising revenues, financially troubled retailers, sagging circulation, and a continuing decline in readership rates.[1]

At different sessions at the Vancouver Trade and Convention Centre, the conventioneers found themselves listening to or participating in:

- A simulated video game—using a Nintendo-like cartoon character, Ned the Newsboy, who presented the options facing newspaper managers who want to customize new products for a changing media marketplace.
- A Harvard business school professor who said retail advertisers, facing their own recessionary pressures and excess debt from leveraged buy-outs, weren't ever going to return to their prerecession advertising levels in daily newspapers.
- A department store executive who said he wanted to see newspapers develop editorial formats that enhance advertising content and feature retailers that give top value.
- A number of speakers predicting that staff downsizing and reduced newspaper profits—both products of the recession of the early 1990s—are likely to stay even after the recession.
- Praise for a range of new special sections target-marketed for a particular audience—aimed, for example, at college and high school students, ethnic groups, farmers, auto buyers, health-care consumers, and diners—that have been unveiled by daily newspapers around the country.
- A newspaper executive speculating that before the end of the decade the phone company and the postal service will become key allies as daily newspapers complement and supplement their information delivery systems.

"Newspapers face two worlds: the world of our memories and the new world of our future," said Lloyd G. Schermer, chairman of Lee Enterprises, in the keynote address. "We will reinvent ourselves. Otherwise, change will dictate to us, and we will lose control of our future."[2]

Although the recession has intensified matters, this handwringing about finances and fretting about the future have long been standard fare for daily newspaper executives as they travel the circuit of events hosted each year by the top officials of the daily newspaper industry. In fact, the ANPA gathering is just one of a multitude of conventions, workshops, and training sessions that play key roles in the industry's network of organizations established to proselytize and promote the word about the latest business problems facing newspapers—and the industry's latest approaches to dealing with them.

Newspaper officials can choose what organizations to join and what conventions to attend from a broad range of acronym-laden groups— ANPA, American Society of Newspaper Editors (ASNE), Associated Press Managing Editors (APME), Newspaper Advertising Bureau (NAB), International Circulation Managers Association (ICMA), International Newspaper Advertising and Marketing Executives (INAME), International Newspaper Financial Executives (INFE), International Newspaper Marketing Association (INMA)—designed to match their duties within their respective news organization. All in all, daily newspaper associations spend about $40 million a year trying to harness the collective power of the industry to attract advertisers, share ideas about marketing and finance, and to improve the professional skills of members of the industry.[3]

The hub of this web of organizations is the American Press Institute, a $2.6 million industry-sponsored training center in Reston, Virginia, which sits beside a complex of other newspaper industry offices (including ANPA, ASNE, ICMA, INAME, INFE, and INMA). API, which built its new quarters in 1974 with contributions from more than 700 newspapers, is a veritable mecca for editors and other newspaper executives seeking immersion in the latest industry management techniques. For example, its menu of seminars in 1988—the year the marketing and management revolution was beginning to be felt in the furthest corners of the industry—included ones dealing with newspaper design and graphics, the development of management skills, marketing the daily newspaper, management and costs, newspaper production and new technology, human resources management, and cross-training programs for nonnews executives in news-editorial management.[4]

In recent years, API's twin in the training of newspaper journalists has become the Poynter Institute for Media Studies in St. Petersburg, Florida, established by the former publisher of the *St. Petersburg Times* in 1975 and devoted to raising journalism standards through training and research. More than API, Poynter stresses programs aimed at the content of newspapers, and its Writing Center plays a big role in trying to improve the quality of newspaper writing.[5] But the institute's Management Center also concerns itself with developing the broad skills of the modern editor who must know how to prepare budgets, shape stories by talking to reporters, master the diplomatic skills needed to deal with prima donna employees, and maneuver through office politics.[6] At the same time, Poynter also stresses the importance of the looks of the newspaper in its Graphics and Design Center. Mario Garcia, the institute's graphic design specialist and a promoter of newspaper redesign within the industry, works at getting reporters and editors involved in the graphics process by pushing ideas that, in his words, will lead to the "marriage" between words and visual images in newspapers.[7]

The growth of journalism management and training programs is largely a phenomenon of the last fifteen years when—not coincidentally—the newspaper industry began to fret seriously about how to improve its long-term financial prospects. With newsrooms known for their seat-of-the-pants management, it became almost a cliché within industry circles that newspaper editors didn't have the training to be newsroom "managers" or "administrators." And top newspaper executives—with prodding from their industry organizations—figured they needed a way to process their mid- and upper-level managers through marketing seminars, management training institutes, business school programs, or whatever it took to quickly inculcate them with "modern" business management skills. The pace of this management revolution can be measured by two studies—one, done in 1978, showed that few managing editors had received any special training in administration or coordinated their work with other departments of the newspaper,[8] another, done in 1983, showed that 90 percent of male and 83 percent of female newspaper managers had participated in some form of management training.[9]

In a 1985 article for *Presstime,* Frank Quine (then API director) said strategic and long-range planning have become mainstays of modern industry management skills programs. "Managerial and supervisory development seminars and workshops have sprouted everywhere," Quine said, adding, "We, as an industry, have only begun to focus on modern management and supervisory techniques. The entire field of human behavior in the workplace, internal communications, disciplining, performance evaluation, goal-setting, strategic planning and the plain old-fashioned art of listening will receive even broader attention."[10]

In fact, the burgeoning interest in research and management training is really just an extension of a long history of newspaper industry efforts at keeping its members up to speed on the latest developments in technology and the social sciences. ANPA was founded in 1887 as an industrywide means of collecting the newly developing national advertising for newspapers and to create a forum for the discussion of industrywide problems. In 1926 the ANPA founded its Mechanical Department which, Anthony Smith says, has been a strong impetus behind technical solutions to organizational and marketing problems. Smith says the industry took to the computer faster because of the proselytizing influence of ANPA. And the annual production conference has become, he says, a massive jamboree celebrating technical achievement.[11]

In fact, ANPA's efforts became just one prong in an expanded newspaper industry marketing and management improvement campaign during the 1980s and 1990s. Organizations like ASNE, APME, ICMA, INAME, INFE, INMA, and the NAB have spread the word about the financial threats to newspapers and the trends within the industry to counteract them. These organizations have mounted educational campaigns both in regular publications, such as *Presstime* and the *Bulletin* of the ASNE, and in a whole host of special publications, many summarizing the work of special conferences or committees, such as ASNE's *The Next Newspapers* and *The Future of Newspapers* and the *Newsroom Management Handbook* and *Constructing the Future: A Self-Test for Editors*; ANPA's *Success Stories: What 28 Newspapers are Doing to Gain and Retain Readers* and *Keys to Success: Strategies for Newspaper Marketing in the '90s*; and INPA's *Promoting the Total Newspaper*.

Special industry projects—most notably the Newspaper Readership project—have spawned hundreds of studies, many farmed out to academic researchers, on readership, demographics, circulation, and other crucial economic and social issues facing the industry. Newspaper foundations—such as the Gannett Foundation (now called the Freedom Forum) and the Knight Foundation—sponsor a variety of programs to improve journalism education and professionalism and to study advanced communications and technological change. Grants from the industry have helped university journalism programs keep up with the changing technology—particularly (in an effort spearheaded by Gannett) in the area of installing computerized news laboratories. The Knight Foundation sponsors a variety of midcareer programs—including recently founding the Newspaper Management Institute, a midcareer training program, at Northwestern University. Industry-sponsored midcareer and management training programs for journalists have flourished. A recent publication of the Gannett Center for Media Studies (now the Freedom Forum Media Studies Center), which was itself founded at Columbia University in 1985, lists five media studies centers, twenty-two midcareer fellowship programs, nine midcareer journalism skills training programs, and seven writing fellowships and other seminars.[12]

The industry's most recent effort at rethinking the solutions to its problems is the New Direction for News, set up in 1987 at the University of Missouri. With a membership of editors and publishers from around the country, the organization has sponsored a number of brainstorming sessions for newspaper executives and is trying to develop an "inventory of innovations" that will show newspapers the way out of the financial wilderness.[13] Despite their much-touted campaigns, editors and publishers are well aware that they have not arrested the decline in newspaper readership nor solved the financial, social, and demographic problems facing daily newspapers. And that's why they hope—despite having been unsuccessful in the past—to still find new and imaginative, yet collective, ways to solve their problems.

There is, of course, a strong irony in newspaper industry organizations trying to promote entrepreneurial thinking by compiling lists of innovative strategies for their members. Few "risk-takers" within the industry will try new and experimental approaches, complains Ted Natt, publisher of the *Daily News* in Longview, Washington, and one of the founders of the New Direction for News. "The industry has changed so much—it's been a corporate mentality rather than an independent enterprise mentality," he says. With chains owning three-quarters of the newspapers, the attitude has been "you've got to serve the corporate purpose first," and that doesn't mean "getting out on the cutting edge," he adds.[14]

Yet critics of the newspaper business point out that new ideas don't come cheaply. The daily newspaper industry, they say, hasn't been spending the kind of money on research and development that it should. In an article entitled "Technology, Fear, and Tomorrow's Newspaper," Joe Logan criticizes the newspaper industry for spending only an estimated .0005 percent of its sales on research and development at a time when the auto industry spends 2.4 percent of its profits on research and development and the computer industry 8.3 percent.[15] This lack of support, Logan says, is no way for an industry that has seen a big drop in newspaper penetration and a slump in national advertising to be acting.

Like Logan, other critics of the newspaper industry complain that despite all their talk about innovation and the future, newspaper executives behave like classic monopolists who don't respond to the dangers, or the opportunities, in the new technologies. The industry receives a particularly strong tongue-lashing from John Diebold, a communications consultant, who complains that newspaper companies have spent too much time trying to keep the telephone companies out of the electronic information delivery business instead of moving into the field themselves. "I believe that you have behaved the way most industries do when they have successfully practiced protectionism," Diebold said. "You have enjoyed the protection but have done little to provide new services using the technology you so fear in the hands of others."[16]

There is almost an inherent contradiction in the pleas for innovation coming from newspaper circles and the nature of the newspaper industry's training, research, and communications structure. Newspaper executives claim they have been turning away from "cookie-cutter" answers to the industry's financial problems and have emphasized the need for newspapers to develop unique solutions within the context of their own particular markets. However, the daily newspaper industry's approach to training and research encourages imitation, conformity, group-thinking, and bottom-line analysis.

On virtually every front, the newspaper industry's approach has been to get its members to adapt the corporate "marketing" and "management" solutions to handling their difficulties. Take for example the class and workshop offerings of industry training institutes. Some samples, taken from API's 1988 brochure (a typical year for management seminars at the height of the marketing and management revolution), illustrate the "modern" management thrust of API's training.[17] In its seminar for executive editors and managing editors, API emphasized newsroom management (hiring and training, effective management styles, communications, and human relations); organization of the newsroom (defining duties and responsibilities, interdepartmental cooperation, the budgeting process, pagination, and new technology); the role of research (attracting and maintaining readership, achieving variety and balance in content selection); pictures and graphics (planning, use of photos, charts, and information graphics); and newspaper design and packaging (quality color and reproduction).

Issues of journalistic principle, as well as some discussion of the content of newspapers, received only passing treatment in API's training of top newsroom executives, with only a small portion of the program devoted to improving writing and editing quality, ethics, and legal concerns for the newsroom. Seminars geared toward entrepreneurship, risk-taking, or creative approaches to the industry's troubles were missing (as they still are, for the most part, in today's API programs).

Then there is the tendency of newspaper associations to push tactics that, critics say, have led to newspapers that are derivative and suffer from the feel of sameness. Even members of the Society of Newspaper Design (SND), founded in 1979, have launched this criticism against their own organization. The organization, for example, took some tough shots at its tenth anniversary conference in Louisville, Kentucky, in 1988. "Probably the Society of Newspaper Design has done as much to cause the homogenization of design in American newspapers as anything else could have," complained Chris Anderson of the *Orange County Register,* in a special desktop-published newspaper issued by the group at the convention.[18]

"The last few years there's been a backlash in graphics and design," added Tony Majeri, former SND president and senior editor of special projects for the *Chicago Tribune.* "And there's a whole new school of designers creeping into newspapers who really scare me. I call them the Pee-wee Herman School. They're decorating. They have to have their fingerprints all over the newspaper."[19]

Moreover, agendas at industry association conferences have been filled with the latest marketing and reader-friendly suggestions—almost to the point where it is hard to distinguish convention from convention and one year from the previous one. For example, at the 1987 APME convention in Seattle, conferees could select from such topics as: "Technology: What's Off-the-Shelf and State-of-the-Art, and How it Affects Newsroom Life"; "Circulation: Why Readers Are Deserting Us"; and "Covering Our Changing Lifestyles: Tracking Trends and Editing for Special Readers."[20] These same panels (in roughly the same form) have been offered at most of the major industry conventions in the years since then.

Journalism education programs, if funded by the newspaper industry, reflect the industry's concerns with technology and marketing. For example, at a 1988 teaching fellowship program sponsored by the Gannett Foundation at the University of Indiana, the university journalism educators were exposed to an array of ideas about how ex-journalists can better teach journalism to undergraduates. But packaged with it was a slew of industry propagandizing about the need to teach graphics, make greater use of computers, and emphasize the need for teamwork in the newsroom in university journalism programs. The program, like most sponsored by the newspaper industry, was designed to sell university journalism educators on the skills needed in the high tech journalism business—to make them better programmers, as it were, for a rapidly transforming industry.[21]

In fact, the newspaper industry doesn't need to directly underwrite programs to encourage university efforts to teach technology or management skills in the classroom. University journalism educators—dependent on the newspaper business for internships and financial support and eager to help students enter the work force—are quick to pick up on the latest management trends in the journalism world and carry them into the classroom.

Ron Dorfman, the former editor of the now defunct *Chicago Journalism Review,* has complained that university journalism education has been corrupted by the "modern corporate publisher's credo" that emphasizes finances over journalism. Dorfman criticized the magazine writing program at Northwestern's Medill School of Journalism for teaching students how to put out slick, upscale, "target-marketed" magazines designed mostly with advertisers in mind. In an article entitled "Learning Cashbox Journalism," Dorfman said,

> It's disquieting that students and faculty go so gently into that good night. . . . One of the functions of the university ought to be to stand as a bastion against the corruptions of ordinary business in the "real world.". . . Let them teach that heresy in the Kellogg School of Management. In the Medill School of Journalism, they should stick to One True Faith: You write for readers, not for consumers, and you want as many readers as you can get, and you don't care whether they drive a BMW or a broken-down Beetle.[22]

With all the emphasis on marketing and long-range planning and newsroom budgeting, newspapers have begun to put a special emphasis on management training—which may, or may not, be the same as journalism training. More and more, newspapers are promoting people into management positions whose strengths are viewed as administrative. This trend has been accelerated by the push in the newspaper industry to open more management jobs for women and minorities. Many women and minority newsworkers have found themselves on a fast track to the top, and management training has been viewed as one way of overcoming a lack of journalistic experience.

Kathy Kozdemba, the former managing editor at the *News-Leader* in Springfield, Missouri, who is now an executive in Gannett's News Division, says this was a key reason why she returned to school to earn her MBA. Kozdemba says that when she was named a department head at age twenty-three, she felt she needed to learn more about management, motivation, finance, and supervisory skills. "I felt hesitant in my leadership skills to manage people much older than I was," she said. "I just didn't have the confidence."[23]

This fixation on management training—and the desire to spread its benefits throughout the business—is reflected in ASNE's *Newsroom Management Handbook.* The handbook, which was written by editors from all over the country, is filled with the kind of managementese and executive lingo that would have seemed foreign to the old breed of blunt-speaking journalists. For example, in the *Handbook,* Bill Pukmel, the former managing editor of Gannett's *Poughkeepsie (N.Y.) Journal,* writes euphemistically about the often painful newsroom budgeting process (particularly during recessions) in his essay "Budget Building:" "Budgets are simply tools, tools that help us set priorities. ... A newsroom budget, then, is simply a monitoring device to help the editor take the action he or she wants to take on behalf of readers."[24]

To a surprising degree, the marketing and management-oriented programs offered by these industry training groups have changed little since they were launched at the onset of the marketing revolution. The recession of the 1990s, continued readership stagnation, and other financial troubles have not much altered the agenda of the industry's approach to management training even though they have cut down on the wherewithal of newspaper companies to finance training for their executives. API's 1991 and 1992 catalogs, for example, show the program still consists largely of seminars in newspaper design and graphics, management costs, developing management skills, and marketing the newspaper. Only a couple of programs focusing on the substance of journalism—such as one promoting effective writing and editing—are sprinkled throughout the catalog. Interestingly, API added a new seminar in 1992 (consistent with the industry's emphasis on "reinvented newspapers") on new product development.[25]

So what do reporters have as a counterweight to management's training and propaganda programs? Not very much. Like other unions, the Newspaper Guild, which represents only about 10 percent of daily newspapers in the U.S. and Canada (about 150 out of 1,600), has seen its difficulties in management negotiations increase and its prospects decline during the last decade. The financially struggling Society of Professional Journalists, the oldest national reporters organization, has seen a dip in membership and is in decline. Probably the most viable and active organization is that of Investigative Reporters and Editors, which was set up in the wake of the death of Arizona investigative reporter Don Bolles. IRE, which meets nationally and regionally to promote the cause of investigative reporting, operates a data bank and resource center at Columbia, Missouri, and generally serves a worthy goal of trying to keep alive a craft that's traditionally had only nominal, sporadic support from publishers and editors.

However, like other reporters' organizations, IRE has not developed any programs to help good journalists survive in the package-and-market-the-news business of today. At a 1988 regional convention in

Portland, Oregon, participants heard mostly "war stories" detailing the big investigative successes of panelists. When one panelist was asked what to do if your organization does not give you the time or the resources to investigate (an endemic problem for reporters around the country), the only advice offered was, "Look for another job."[26]

In a country where people love to attend conferences and to set up training institutes and to organize professional gatherings, it may seem unfair to single out the newspaper business for promoting its interests this way. But newspapers are, after all, a special business with responsibilities that (at least in theory) go beyond the bottom line. And propaganda is something journalists are supposed to probe and expose—not propagate. There is no question that many of the organizations and institutions mentioned here do much more than worry about the industry's financial prospects. They wrestle with important professional issues, foster personal and professional development among journalists, and promote the improvement of the finer elements of the journalistic craft. Yet they also teach a buzz-word communication style that obscures the real meaning of things, puts an upbeat corporate face on the often downbeat message of budget cuts, and sounds downright fatuous to old-fashioned, straight-talking journalists.

Five years of attending Gannett corporate conferences taught me that careers were built on espousing all the higher principles of journalism at company meetings while very often doing something much less inspiring back home at the newspaper. It can seem baffling to hear so much talk about good journalism and newspaper quality at gatherings of Gannett executives and to see so little of it in the Gannett newspapers. Yet that is the formula. From a business standpoint, it is cheaper to create a foundation, to fund a few university and midcareer education programs, to train managers to say the right things, and to send around corporate publications advocating high-sounding principles than to adopt truly creative, innovative, risk-taking solutions—or do the expensive job of really upgrading the quality of news operations.

Even at Knight-Ridder—a company that has been identified by its commitment to spending money in pursuit of journalistic quality—there prevails an undertone of bitterness at the "managerialism" and the "MBO-thinking" that dominates the executive levels of the company. In a 1987 article in the *Washington Monthly*, Matthew Cooper praises the company for whipping a number of mediocre newspapers into shape, enlarging staffs, and winning a bundle of Pulitzer prizes at its newspapers.[27] But Cooper also describes a "corpocracy" of management-by-objective systems, prospective employee testing, and lavish corporate training headquarters specializing in the teaching of newspaper production skills, interpersonal and organizational skills, face-to-face communication techniques, and other "touchy-feely" programs. "I hate the fuckers," Cooper quotes one California editor as saying. "The part I don't like about them is that they can lead to someone becoming a bureaucratic manager. As long as you hold X number of meetings on a topic or meet with 'community leaders' Y number of times you're okay."[28]

Yet, as with the newspaper business in general, it seems that hard times are forcing the newspaper industry to rethink its industrywide research, communications, and management training strategy. The recession and declining memberships have spurred a move to merge the Newspaper Advertising Bureau (NAB) and six smaller groups— INAME, INMA, ICMA, the Association of Newspaper Classified Advertising Managers, the Newspaper Advertising Co-op Network, the Newspaper Research Council—into a new Newspaper Marketing Association that will focus on revenue and business matters.[29] Since June 1990 the NAB has lost over one hundred newspaper members, and the consolidation effort is expected to save the newspaper industry $2 million annually.[30] *Presstime* also reported that ANPA membership in 1991 was 1,358, a decrease of 63 members from the year before, and only 1,401 people registered for the 1991 ANPA convention in Vancouver, the smallest number in recent years.[31]

Although the recession is the real culprit, the shake-up of the industry groups was prompted by a 1991 report—as one might expect, from consultants Booz, Allen and Hamilton—that concluded that the newspaper industry lacks strong, visible leadership and wastes millions on duplicate services. Publishers were also said to be unhappy about an NAB national advertising campaign that reaped only a paltry $16 million in new national advertising over three years.[32]

At the Vancouver convention, the news executives repeatedly called the recession a blessing in disguise and promised that the daily newspaper business will emerge from it as a very different industry. But there are others who believe the shake-up of the trade groups is simply a symptom of an industry that did not know how to deal with the economic and technological threats on the horizon—and still doesn't. "There is not a true strategic thinker in the newspaper business," one former trade group executive lamented to *NewsInc.* magazine. "It's a collection of the shortest-thinking ad hoc people I can think of."[33]

CHAPTER EIGHT

The Cult of Colorful Tidbits

I'm convinced that because of our tiredness and exhaustion, and in some cases blind ambition, we are all brainwashed and intimidated.
—Sheryl Bills in describing the early days of *USA Today*

Ferried about in limousines and personalized jets, enveloped in Gatsby-like glitter, Neuharth glides comfortably through the world of privilege, a conquering potentate enjoying the spoils of war.
—Ellis Cose, *The Press*

Gannett editing strives for a nobody's home feeling.
—Philip Weiss in "Invasion of the Gannettoids"

That's business. I don't think it has anything at all to do with the First Amendment.
—Al Neuharth, recently retired chairman of the Gannett Corporation

VISITORS to *USA Today*'s headquarters in Rosslyn, Virginia, often feel as though they have entered a shrine, self-consciously constructed and unapologetically self-promotional, of the gauche new corporate culture of today's big media. The twin, high-rise towers have a hermetically sealed feel, an ersatz atmosphere of manmade waterfalls and indoor palms mixed with service shops selling yuppy goods from designer clothes to IRAs. Near the first floor bank of elevators sits the famous bust of Al Neuharth—a solipsistic honor for the self-anointed, conglomerate-era version of a press baron. Inside the corporate offices television sets hang soundlessly from the ceiling; there are nouveau art, ellipsoid tables and bathrooms of brown marble and floor-to-ceiling mirrors.

Ironically, Gannett, a corporation that gave Wall Street its first sweet rush of addictive, upward-spiraling record earnings from a newspaper company, only burst into the national consciousness when it founded *USA Today,* the nation's first general circulation national newspaper— and a project that still has not earned any money for Gannett. But while *USA Today* is still a financial liability, the company's pay-back has come from its elevated corporate profile, its enhanced influence within media circles, the ego gratification (of Neuharth, for sure), and the impact it has had on other daily newspapers, which are now awash in color, filled with computer graphics, and ready to give the readers whatever they want to read.

In fact, *USA Today* is the quintessential product of modern corporate media engineering. It symbolizes the fixation on reader research, the fascination with the marketplace, and the possibilities of computer and satellite technology that had been percolating in the industry for more than a decade before Gannett launched its bold venture in 1982. And the newspaper's orientation—or "editing with the reader always first in mind," as Neuharth put it—has been paid homage to by the country's newspaper marketing executives, who recognized a pure product of their profession. "*USA Today* wasn't born until marketing had become a major management concern," explained one newspaper industry publication. "Its very name, format and choice of contents obviously came from a marketing perspective."[1]

Critics of *USA Today* complain that the only vision at the heart of the newspaper is a marketer's vision. They condemn the newspaper for its overemphasis on packaging, graphics, brief text, factoids, flashy color, and news summaries in lieu of in-depth reporting. But editors en masse have followed the newspaper's lead in appealing to busy Americans who (their research tells them) aren't taking the time to read. In a report for APME in 1983, more than one hundred newspapers reported a variety of changes in news editing, reporting, and production as a result of competition from *USA Today*.[2]

Robert Logan acknowledges all the epithets that have been used to describe *USA Today,* the newspaper, and its contents—"comic book" journalism, "the journalistic equivalent of junk food," "television in print." But he says *USA Today*'s heavy use of color, its information graphics, its use of maps and lists, its promotion techniques, and its sports coverage justify calling it "radically innovative" within the newspaper industry.

While most of journalism's heavy-hitters have little good to say about the newspaper (the *Washington Post*'s Ben Bradlee once said that if *USA Today* is judged as one of the country's top newspapers, "then I'm in the wrong business")[3], *USA Today* has been a big hit with readers all over the country and, it seems, with many heartland editors. "All of us in the newspaper business have to tip our hats to the people at *USA Today* for the way they pioneered the use of infographics for newspapers," says Dan Baumann, president and editor of the *Daily*

Herald in Arlington Heights, Illinois. "They provide color and zest . . . and tell some stories that are difficult to tell using the more traditional methods."[4]

Andrew Brimmer, a member of Gannett's board of directors, once said that he felt the company had taken a classic Harvard Business School approach to introducing a new product.[5] In the *Making of McPaper*, Peter Prichard points out that two of the three key Gannett executives who planned the prototype of the newspaper (Tom Curley and Paul Kessinger) held master's degrees in business.[6] It was their research, Prichard indicates, that convinced Gannett executives that *USA Today* should seek a mobile, active, well-paid, well-educated, largely male audience—a target-marketing approach that, like much else of what the newspaper represents, has taken a trend within the industry and stretched it to the extreme.[7]

The newspaper was launched after extensive planning and months of product research. Prototypes were distributed in homes and reader reactions were studied in markets across the country. Everything involved in the venture—the satellites, the installation of expensive color presses, the designing of new, space-age vending boxes—was part of a massive logistical effort to take advantage of all the latest trends in marketing and communications technology.[8] It's no coincidence that *USA Today*—probably the first major daily newspaper ever founded almost solely on the basis of exhaustive market surveys—was created during a period of financial self-seeking and personal self-indulgence when the nation was, in one of the newspaper's early front-page headlines, "beachbound bumper-to-bumper."

USA Today's appeal is closely parallel to Ronald Reagan's own appeal, says Daniel Hallin—a journalism not of issues but of symbols and everyday life, presenting an upbeat picture of the country as defined primarily by the mass culture of leisure and consumption. "*USA Today* gives the answer to 'where' that national advertisers want to hear," Hallin says. "Its America is their America—happy, homogeneous, prosperous, and overwhelmingly concerned with the affairs of private life."[9]

For those who see Neuharth's personality behind the developments at Gannett in the 1980s, *USA Today* represents his values—a "journalism of hope" based on Neuharth's South Dakota background, his up-from-the-roots philosophy, his us-versus-them mentality, his nouveau-riche love of the trappings of success, his fervent loyalty to the corporate ethic, and his lack of any principle or personal vision independent of Gannett.

Neuharth used the new newspaper not only to raise the company's profile but also to market a Gannett corporate value system that was passed off as an American cultural ethic. Neuharth's formula was to combine the company's long-standing interest in the latest communications and marketing technology with a heavy emphasis on the fast-track, yuppy values of the 1980s—all revolving around himself as a self-styled svengali whose motivational campaigns and outrageous tastelessness (Gannett robots, company "Last Suppers," GO! Teams and Project S Squads) seemed to fall somewhere between corporate hucksterism and self-parody.

For folks in the daily newspaper business, chuckling at the garish self-promotions, the "Bus-capades," the travels to meet world leaders, and the vapid corporate proselytizing of Neuharth wasn't a whole lot different from the headshaking prompted by Ronald Reagan. In fact, Neuharth emerged in the 1980s as the media counterpart to a president who didn't seem to know what was going on but could be dubbed the "Great Communicator." Like Reagan, who couched his espousal of corporate causes behind a veil of conservative populist rhetoric, Neuharth sold his corporate franchiser's philosophy and his reader-friendly formulas as something reflecting the concerns of folks in the heartland. And while Ronald Reagan's charms launched a conservative revolution, Neuharth, an utterly uncharming man, put an indelible mark on American journalism before retiring from Gannett in 1989 to head the Gannett Foundation (which he renamed the Freedom Forum).

What Neuharth left behind was a company and a newspaper that pretend to speak for the nation, that reflect an amalgam of the chamber-of-commerce values of Gannett's many smalltown journalists with the sophisticated financial and marketing concerns of a corporation that has come to set the pace for newspaper profit making. That, to Gannett's and *USA Today*'s critics, has meant the "Babbittizing" of the American newspaper scene on a grand corporate scale. In his article "The Invasion of the Gannettoids," Philip Weiss wrote,

> The problem with Gannett isn't simply its formula or its chairman, but the company's corporate culture. The product is the company—cheerful, superficial, self-promoting, suspicious of ideas, conformist, and implicitly authoritarian. Gannett's story is part of the familiar American pattern of executive indulgence, in which more glory surrounds corporate ascension than a good product, in which quality need not be earned, merely purchased.[10]

At the same time, Neuharth probably deserves less credit than he has received for revolutionizing the content of newspapers. It is true that *USA Today*'s characteristics—its relentlessly upbeat tone, its focus on fads and lifestyle information, its glossy graphics and design, its friendly text, its view of America as one homogenized "we" out there— epitomize a newspaper world reinventing itself around marketing principles and advances in communications technology. Yet it is a mistake to think of Neuharth as a great innovator. What he did was simply distill everything that's been happening in newspapers for the past fifteen years and then give it to the nation with a special Gannett flourish.

Gannett's ultimate financial success with *USA Today,* of course, is problematical, and the newspaper's enormous losses hang over any claims of triumph by the company. Much as they say they like the newspaper's formula, national advertisers have been reluctant to advertise in *USA Today,* and the newspaper has shown only a small profit during one quarter of its existence. While circulation has grown to almost two million, it is estimated that *USA Today* had a whopping $800 million in pretax losses in its first nine years.[11]

In many respects Gannett's willingness to forge ahead with the newspaper mirrors the determination of the newspaper industry to press on with reader-driven formulas despite evidence that they have not solved the industry's problems. Gannett's "News 2000" program, for example, has been advertised by the company as an effort to better respond to community issues and reader needs. But at Gannett's newspaper in Olympia, Washington, where editors have replaced traditional beats with "hot topics" teams, slapped limits on story lengths and jumps, added extensive reader service lists, and replaced some reporters with news assistants who gather "news-you-can-use" data from local agencies, reporters claim the company is trying to turn its newspapers into local versions of *USA Today.*[12]

"It's a sad, sad day," says one veteran Gannett reporter. "Journalism is dead. . . . We're dinosaurs. It's going to be data collectors instead of reporters. They'll go out and get marriage licenses and job openings and anything you can put on lists. It's labels and lists."

In a much less celebrated way, *USA Today* has left its mark on newsroom management as much as it has on newspaper content. The way Gannett set up the management system at *USA Today* can be seen as a model for strapping today's journalists into a corporately controlled structure for celebrating the status quo. Working at *USA Today*—with its banks of editors and endless rewriting of copy—can be a grinding experience for serious journalists who have known something better. Yet the *USA Today* approach, with its rigid editorial bureaucracies, the heavy involvement of financial people in product decisions, the emphasis on packaging over the product, and an editing system that enforces formula journalism, is an increasingly tempting model for newspaper organizations both inside and outside Gannett.

"At a managed newspaper, it beats you down . . . it's a degrading experience," says Eric Brazil, a former *USA Today* bureau chief who is now a reporter for the *San Francisco Examiner*. "They tell you what news is. They have to put their fingerprints on everything."[13]

Not surprisingly, the managers at *USA Today* have adopted the language of "teamwork" and "goals and directions" and staff "involvement" that has become the trend with newspaper managers in the 1990s. Paul McMaster, associate editor of *USA Today*'s editorial page, puts a sunny, humanistic interpretation on *USA Today*'s "team" approach to newsroom management. "Experts in the management field talk about 'team play,' 'participatory management,' and 'Theory Y,' " writes McMaster in the *Newsroom Management Handbook*. "Put simply—and ideally—this approach to management draws subeditors and their staff members into the decision-making process, improves communication in all directions and enlists the enthusiastic support of the whole staff in striving to achieve objectives mutually agreed on."[14]

However, Gannett journalists complain that much of the upbeat talk about collaboration at Gannett is corporate doublespeak and simply doesn't square with their experience. Many of Gannett's best journalists have taken a fling at *USA Today*-style journalism—and quickly fled back to their jobs at the Gannett News Service or left the company. The only people who can survive within *USA Today*'s rigid management system, they say, are journalists who, by and large, have come from smaller Gannett newspapers and have had little exposure to more sophisticated journalistic practices. "At *USA Today*, the only way to get people to go along with a paper where everybody changes everything you do is to get people who are young, with no journalistic values," says one former Gannett News Service reporter who is still with the company. "They're all clones. They look like they've been cut out with the same cookie cutter."

Nevertheless, one thing is certain—*USA Today* now dominates the corporation's philosophy, its approach to newsgathering, and Gannett's presence in the American media family. It wasn't always that way. In the pre-*USA Today* days, the Gannett News Service—with its Washington, D.C., and state house bureaus, in particular—was the company's showcase operation. Many fine journalists worked for Gannett, and many of the best were promoted to the news service. Still, Gannett has always been a curious place as far as the practice of serious journalism is concerned. While Gannett was generous in supporting the efforts of its top news service reporters, the company seemed largely indifferent to their work, except perhaps for the prizes and the recognition it occasionally brought the company. Gannett was so large and the news service's relationship with the local newspapers such a distant one, no one—with the possible exception of a handful of Gannett officials in the news bureaus themselves—seemed to care what the news service staff did. Even in the pre-*USA Today* days, the impression was that as long as the copy was flowing to the company's newspapers and the sophisticated computer systems and transmissions networks were up and working, the top Gannett executives were satisfied that the corporate mission was being fulfilled.

The survival of a serious news ethic within this corporate climate has always been a fragile thing. The company's response to an article in the 1982 *Gannetteer* by John McMillan, then the publisher at the Salem, Oregon, *Statesman-Journal,* illustrates the point. In the article, McMillan suggested that the corporate demands had grown so great that Gannett risked the disaffection of the company's reporters. McMillan said that industry publications portrayed reporters as "production workers," that consultants were urging editors to get rid of troublemakers in the newsroom, and that top reporters from a variety of Gannett newspapers had complained to him that they were tired of low pay, overwork, small newsholes, lack of respect and feedback, and bosses who knew less than they did.[15]

The *Gannetteer* asked a number of Gannett executives to respond to McMillan's concerns, which they did in good company fashion. For example, Barbara Henry, then managing editor of the *Nevada State Journal,* said of the reporters' complaints about small newsholes and understaffing: "I don't think there's an editor around—Gannett or not—who doesn't want more money for reporters, more staff and more newshole. Reporters need to be told of the economic realities we face." If reporters believe there is a rising level of frustration, anxiety, and cynicism in the newsroom, she said, they are overstating the case. "If it is the case, there is a giant lack of communication from the reporters," she said.[16]

Consistent with a theme so popular with Gannett executives—do more with less—Sheryl Bills, then the managing editor of the *Cincinnati Enquirer,* praised a reporter at her newspaper for his concerns that tight budgeting, space cuts, and staff shortages were affecting the quality of the newspaper but offered him little more than consolation. "The feelings he expressed about our newspaper in this meeting were emotional and his questions thoughtful, and I relate this incident simply to show that good reporters are deeply concerned about the degree of quality and excellence they see in the newspapers they work for," she said.[17]

Finally, Larry Fuller, then publisher of the Sioux Falls, South Dakota, *Argus Leader,* suggested to McMillan a variety of management solutions that are familiar themes within the company and the industry. They included: set newsroom goals that are clearly identified for the staff and be sure your MBO (management-by-objective) forms have real meaning; make certain newsroom goals are consistent with the work of other departments and the marketing efforts of the newspaper; insure your city editor works within his or her area and doesn't overstep the limits of the job; study your newsroom and operate it efficiently; make training a top priority; use staff evaluations as a tool and weed out nonproducers; communicate effectively; motivate yourself and your staff; plan, plan, plan.[18]

In *The Buying and Selling of America's Newspapers,* Peter Katel explains why local Gannett editors are forced to substitute "management-speak" solutions for real dollar improvements in staffing, news coverage, and the news product. In his profile of the Santa Fe *New Mexican,* Katel points out that Gannett executives were quoted in 1977 as saying that the *New Mexican's* pretax profits should be in the 36 to 38 percent range—up from a profit margin of 22 to 23 percent when Gannett purchased the newspaper. Katel noted that under Gannett, fewer words and news stories appeared in the newspaper than under the old regime, the staff outside Santa Fe was trimmed, and advertising rates climbed 77 percent between 1975 and 1980. He also said that under Gannett there was little aggressive coverage of the city, and the newspaper was usually the follower, rather than the leader, on capitol coverage.[19]

Gannett's treatment of its local newspapers has long been a subject of debate, with editors at its more prestigious purchases, like the *Des Moines Register* and the *Courier-Journal* in Louisville, claiming that Gannett hasn't cut back news resources; in fact, the *Detroit News* (in anticipation of a joint operating agreement) initially saw an infusion of money pumped into the newspaper after Gannett acquired it.[20] However, the recession has hit Gannett's local newspapers hard with staff and other cutbacks as the company struggles to maintain its high profit margins in bad times. At the same time, editors of some Gannett newspapers still complain that they have had to absorb a loss of staffers loaned to *USA Today.*

In *The Media Monopoly,* Ben Bagdikian paints the picture of a company that is forever trying to impress Wall Street by adding to its string of ever increasing earnings reports while pretending this doesn't come at the cost of news quality. Gannett, he says, tends to hire younger, cheaper, less qualified reporters; pressures its local news executives to meet profit margins of 30 to 50 percent a year; jumps ad rates substantially at its monopoly newspapers; sacrifices circulation for more revenue; and substitutes cosmetic changes in its newspapers for serious local news coverage.[21] In 1966, before Gannett began its drive to create its international empire, its local newspapers averaged about forty-five employees per newspaper. By 1980, while average circulation held steady, this was down to twenty-six employees per Gannett newspaper, Bagdikian says. Even the company's vaunted efforts to hire and promote minorities and women, he says, are mostly an effort at corporate public relations and are part of a $1.5 million campaign by the firm of Young and Rubicam to build a "heroic" image for the company—a view confirmed in the minds of many by the furor over a 1989 Neuharth column in *USA Today* where he complained about aging female flight attendants and urged the airlines to bring back the "sky girls."[22] "Many of Gannett's four thousand reporters and editors produce individual pieces of admirable journalism," Bagdikian says. "These become the stuff of the full-page ads. But most of the empire consists of vast silent domains where ruthless demands for ever increasing profits crush journalistic enterprise and block adequate coverage of the news in their communities."[23]

With the retirement of Neuharth, there are some signs indicating that the cause of serious journalism is making a comeback within Gannett, albeit only slightly. Many Gannett employees, including top executives, have always viewed Neuharth as a figure of ridicule and simply went along with his stunts to pacify him. Now that the reins have been passed on to John Curley, the new chairman and president of Gannett, the company has charted a more modest course. Curley doesn't conduct business in Neuharth's lavish manner nor is he interested in promoting his own cult of personality. And he and Neuharth have squabbled over efforts by Neuharth to use the threatened sale of Gannett stock held by the Freedom Forum as leverage to control the company's future from afar.

In recent years, *USA Today* has also taken on a harder edge in its coverage and played down the fluffier pieces that brought it such reproach in its early years. Howard Kurtz reported in the *Washington Post* that *USA Today*'s executives have made a deliberate decision to emphasize important political and issue-oriented stories, add veteran big-city reporters to the staff, and play down the McNuggets and "silly and superficial crap," as one editor put it. Kurtz noted that the newspaper still does little investigative reporting, runs lots of celebrity and life-style features, and covers major stories by slicing them into small, digestible chunks. However, he says the emphasis on hard news appears to be paying off in added circulation. "It's become a much more substantial newspaper just at the time when all the apes are aping the thing that didn't work," said Bill Kovach, now curator of the Nieman Foundation at Harvard University.[24]

Sadly, Gannett executives still view themselves as pioneers in treating their various media properties as tools to be refashioned or repositioned or blended together in any way that will insure marketplace success in the coming Information Age. Gannett's mergers, which brought it television stations, a billboard company, and a polling firm, have encouraged the company to think in multimedia terms that take advantage of the company's marketing power and its wide range of information services. *USA Today* and the ill-fated effort to transfer its formula to television have pushed the company to think even more about new mixes of media that may be a success. And Gannett—with its "Gannett New Media" and "Gannett New Business" arms—has expanded into such areas as *USA Today* brandname sportswear, men's and women's apparel, accessories (like watches, hats, umbrellas, and calendars), a *USA Today* radio service, a *USA Today* baseball weekly, a news and graphics network for college newspapers, hot lines for worldwide weather reports and sports news, and electronic delivery of business news.[25] Gannett appears determined to insure that in the future the world of media and the world of marketing will grow even more blurred.

I would like to close this chapter with a piece of scholarship that—to me, at least—has much to say about both the "nation's newspaper" and Gannett's philosophy of news-as-marketable-information. While reading James Carey's *Communication as Culture*, I was struck by his two-fold definition of our culture's view of communication. The most common view, he said, was the "transmission" view where people treat the act of communication as simply the sending and receiving of information, a largely practical and pragmatic view that has come to serve the commercial purposes of the society. He contrasts this with the "ritual" view of communication, which he says draws people together as a community—where movement in space can be an act of "communion," where the use of words can be a spiritual experience, and where we see the problems of communication linked to the problems of community.[26]

What I believe is so vexing about *USA Today*—to borrow from Carey's theory—is that Gannett executives have confused a "transmission" view of communication with a "ritual" one. That's why *USA Today*'s constant use of "us" and "we" rings so wrong. Those of us who believe that newspapers do play a powerful role in creating community rebel because we see the purpose of *USA Today* as a crassly commercial one. We see its underpinnings of marketing and market research, and we know its vision for the nation is a happy-face reflection of how corporate America would like the country to be. For most of us—at least, those of us who don't fly around in corporate jets and live in a futuristic beachfront palace like Neuharth's "Pumpkin Center"—this isn't our view of the nation as a community. *USA Today,* we sense, has held up a mirror to itself and not to us. No matter how much its executives tell us they are interested in "us" as readers and Americans, we know they are interested in "us" mostly as members of a market.

I can't help but think of Neuharth and how far his newspaper falls short of satisfying our deeper needs for a journalism that reflects true community when Carey writes, "We recognize, as with religious rituals, that news changes little and yet is intrinsically satisfying; it performs few functions yet is habitually consumed. Newspapers do not operate as a source of effects or functions but as dramatically satisfying, which is not to say pleasing, presentations of what the world at root is."[27]

PART TWO

CHAPTER NINE

What Newspapers— and Newspaper Researchers— Don't Tell Us About Newspapers

"Quality" is almost immune to the investigative techniques of social science.

—Anthony Smith, *Goodbye Gutenberg*

I have witnessed meetings of editors and broadcasters where the table of contents of leading academic journals were read aloud for their comical effect.

—Everette Dennis, executive director of the Freedom Forum Media Studies Center

We use research like a drunk uses a street lamp, for support, not for illumination.

—Milton Gossett, president and CEO of Compton Advertising

In the past, I was uncertain whether to laugh at the ludicrous titles, bizarre organization, and the dreadful writing of the articles, or whether to cry at the waste of brainpower and trees.

—Steve Weinberg, a journalist-turned-academic commenting on communications scholarship

NEWSPAPERS, A. J. Liebling once commented acerbicly, cover themselves rarely and then only with "awe."[1] So it was with some surprise that I received a call from a *Wall Street Journal* reporter in 1989 who told me he was preparing a story about newspapers that were editing the news based on readership surveys.[2]

The trend toward managing newspapers with the market in mind is a subject newspapers seldom discuss in their news columns. In any case, they certainly tell their readers little, if anything, about their own in-house research efforts that have come to dictate what is in the news columns.

It was no secret that the *Wall Street Journal* had gone through a major remodeling of its format in 1988, much of it based on the results of focus groups and research about its readers.[3] So I was looking forward to seeing how one of the nation's most astute and insightful newspapers would analyze its own foray into the world of reader-driven journalism.

Well, it turned out that the tradition of newspapers keeping their internal business matters to themselves held true again. The story never appeared in the *Journal*. And efforts to find out why did not elicit a particularly satisfactory explanation.

In a 1991 interview, Lawrence Rout, the editor who I understood was handling the story, said he simply didn't remember such a story.[4] Many stories produced by *Journal* reporters aren't used by the newspaper, he said. And if it didn't make the newspaper, it wasn't because of any special sensitivities about readership research on the part of *Journal* editors, he assured me. "I guarantee no one will remember that story," Rout said. "If it was killed, it was because it wasn't a good story."

The marketing and readership revolution that has transformed the daily newspaper industry has been a story that, for the most part, the reading public has not been let in on. However, that doesn't mean that marketing research has not boomed into a big business for newspapers. *Presstime* reports that in 1988 the industry spent $35 to $40 million on polling, focus groups, and other research; large newspapers generally have their own in-house research capacity; and membership in the Newspaper Research Council multiplied more than three-fold between 1977 and 1989.[5]

Yet, except for occasional comments in industry publications like *Presstime,* newspapers have maintained a virtual blackout of information they have gathered from their readers. Like the editors at the *Journal,* newspaper industry executives act very skittishly anytime there is any discussion of the public pulse taking that has become such a big part of the business.

Virtually all of the marketing data collected by newspapers is held as proprietary material, which means that it is unavailable for scrutiny by the public or other researchers. Newspapers say they do this to avoid giving a boost to the competition. But this has meant that very little is known about the reaction of the public to the give-the-readers-what-they-want movement. The few newspapers that do research in the newsroom are equally close-mouthed about the reaction of their staffs to the marketing changes around them.[6]

This situation has left the job of scrutinizing the newspaper industry (at least, from the standpoint of social science research) to a handful of academic communications scholars around the country. To some degree, communications researchers have played their own role in the move toward market-oriented newspapering, and, in some cases, they have directly participated in the industry's proprietary research projects. However, most of the research on newspapers ends up in scholarly publications—such as *Journalism Quarterly* and the *Newspaper Research Journal*—that circulate largely among communications researchers on the campuses.

Before embarking on the following study of the marketing phenomenon at newspapers, I examined the academic literature to see what it said about reader-driven journalism. Surprisingly, there was little reference to the changes that were so dramatically altering the professional lives of my former newspaper colleagues. This is not to say that some of the studies didn't hint at the phenomenon. Still, to a remarkable degree the move toward market-oriented, research-driven newspapering has gone unnoticed—or, at best, not very deeply examined—in the academic journals.

Take, for example, an intriguing sounding study entitled, "Running Newspapers or Building Empires: Analysis of Gannett's Ideology."[7] Its title promised to analyze something that critics of Gannett have sometimes accused the company of doing, namely, using its commitment to press freedom issues and the promotion of women and minorities as a public relations device to deflect attention from the company's crasser economic motives.

Instead the article by Carol Smith in the *Newspaper Research Journal* turned out to be less ambitious than that. What it did was present a content analysis of Gannett's corporate publications. The conclusion? That in the company magazine, the *Gannetteer*, annual reports, and its corporate advertising, Gannett most often used such terms as "editorial excellence," "group" (as opposed to "chain"), "business excellence," and "autonomy." She concluded that those terms received greater or lesser emphasis depending on whether the audience was the public, Gannett employees, board members, or other members of the industry.

In one respect, Smith's study made a point that was worth making, namely, that Gannett reshapes its corporate message depending on the audience. But Smith's research stopped short of pursuing such larger questions as the role of public relations firms in the development of Gannett's corporate strategy or the motives behind the company's efforts to put a positive face on its public image.[8] Her study, like much of the academic research on newspapers and newspaper companies, made a point that was measurable and quantifiable and verifiable but that told only a very small part of a much bigger and more interesting story.

The point here is not to fault Smith's research. Her study was actually one of the more interesting examples of the communications research scholarship that appears in countless academic publications every year. She cannot necessarily be faulted for failing to pursue a more ambitious examination of Gannett that would have taken a good deal of time and money—and probably more company cooperation than may be available.[9] Yet, because of these limitations, Smith's study, like much social science research, focused on the product of media organizations, which can be empirically measured and systematically analyzed, and not on the more elusive organizational process inside the companies, which is harder to quantify.

Perhaps it is this narrowness of scope, the shortage of resources, and the difficulties of access that explain why social science research by academics has largely overlooked the marketing and newsroom management revolution—the so-called "give-the-readers-what-they-want" movement—that has swept the newspaper industry in recent years. This doesn't mean that researchers haven't paid a good deal of attention to many of the elements that have transformed newspapering, such as the introduction of computers, the increased use of graphics and color, the emphasis on readability, the greater role of management training. However, as in Smith's study, researchers have focused on what can be demonstrated within the methodological confines of social science inquiry. They have tended to avoid making connections, seeking larger truths, or examining the broader implications for the quality of newspapers or the future of the journalism profession.

In his book *Examining Newspapers,* Gerald Stone summarizes much of the social science research in the field, and he points to a dichotomy that goes a long way toward explaining why newspaper researchers have paid so little attention to the marketing, planning, and packaging phenomenon. In his chapter on newspaper management, Stone laments that so little research has been done on the way newspapers are managed.[10] Yet, later in the book, he concludes that communications researchers have been unable, based on the empirical evidence, to make a case for chain ownership being either a blessing or a threat for the newspaper industry.[11] If studying the management of newsrooms isn't the basis of this conclusion, what is?

Most of the studies about chains arrive at their conclusion by examining the use of wire material, the news content, the price of ads, and other measurable aspects of newspapers produced by chain and independent owners.[12] And yet, if the issue is the quality of newspapers, not only the product that ends up on the news pages but the way a news organization operates internally—the management practices, the control systems imposed by corporate ownership, the treatment received by newsroom staffers, the latitude given to reporters to dig below the surface of events, the encouragement to do enterprise journalism, the commitment to staffing levels, the resources invested in the newsroom—are also truly important. As likely as not, this will point to what *isn't* in the newspaper rather than to what is in it. And that, as any working journalist knows, is the best way to measure the kind of job the newspaper—or the newspaper chain—is doing.

A number of factors appear to explain why academic researchers—like newspapers themselves—have not much noted the trend toward MBA journalism.[13] First, social science methodology and the need for quantifiable and verifiable data put an inordinate emphasis on the material gained from surveys and other forms of data collection. Yet the logistics of distributing and collecting large numbers of surveys often limit the scope of the people sampled. As a result, the kind of multidimensional analysis that could bring a deeper perspective to the topic often isn't undertaken.

For example, a 1986 study by Sharon H. Polansky and Douglas W. W. Hughes purports to measure "Managerial Innovation in Newspaper Organizations."[14] The study, a survey of 493 newspaper editors and publishers, concludes that managers of large newspapers showed the highest degree of innovation, followed by small and medium-sized newspapers. It appears, the authors say, that larger newspapers overcome the bureaucratic constraints that Polansky and Hughes had originally speculated would hinder innovation.

However, only editors and publishers are queried in the study. Do reporters, midlevel editors, and other newsroom staffers agree? Quite frequently, newspaper researchers seem to take the respondents in their surveys at their word—or at least base their conclusions on data from newspaper executives alone—without cross-checking with those who might have a less vested interest in the matter.

Academic research projects are also generally limited by the money and resources available to researchers. With federal research money going mostly to the hard and medical sciences and with scant resources available from private sources, there are few places where newspaper researchers can turn for support. As a result, many of the studies draw their conclusions from a very limited sample—usually one or two news organizations or at most a small cluster of newspapers.

For example, Mark Fishman's well-regarded study, *Manufacturing the News*—in which he concludes that the world is "bureaucratically organized for reporters" and that "news consumers are led to see the world . . . through the eyes of the existing authority structure"—is based on his observations while working as a reporter at one midsized newspaper in California.[15] True as his conclusions appear to be, given the limited sample size, they can hardly be viewed as universal.

Another article by Cecilie Gaziano and David C. Coulson—which concludes that journalists show an overwhelming desire to be free of organizational restraints in their work—was based on a survey of the management policies at only two daily newspapers.[16] A study by Steve Pasternack and Sandra Utt, which concludes that readers approve of modern techniques and color in newspapers, was based on showing slides of twenty daily newspapers to ninety-one students from New Mexico State and Memphis State universities.[17] Ruth C. Flegel and Steven H. Chaffee's study, in which they concluded that reporters are strongly directed by their opinions in their reporting, was based on a sample of reporters at two dailies in Madison, Wisconsin.[18]

Even if a source of funding is found, it often comes with strings attached. For example, in noting that a comprehensive study of the impact of chain ownership on quality of news hasn't been done, F. Dennis Hale asks where the money for such an expensive project would come from. He notes that most sources—media foundations, university journalism programs, and the federal government—are beholden to chain affiliates in one way or another.[19]

The few extensive research projects that touch upon newspaper management practices have been funded by foundations related to the newspaper industry or by the industry itself. For example, the Weaver and Wilhoit studies, which involved nationwide samples of more than one thousand journalists, were underwritten by the Gannett Foundation and the Freedom Forum. *The Changing Face of the Newsroom,* a 1988 survey of 1,200 newspaper journalists across the nation, was conducted by the American Society of Newspaper Editors.

Researchers also face a major hurdle in gaining access to newsrooms. Even if newspaper executives are inclined to open their newsrooms to scrutiny (and they often aren't), they usually want to know what is in it for them, and they are reluctant to cooperate if they feel threatened by a research project's aims. It is interesting to note, for example, that of the roughly forty research projects subsidized by ANPA as part of the industry's Readership Project between 1977 and 1982, none involved any direct examination of newsrooms.[20] The studies (many performed by some of the country's top communications scholars) focused mostly on the audience and readership worries of the publishers. Even when researchers do gain access to a newspaper's inner operations, they usually must agree not to identify the newspaper in the subsequent publication of the research—an anonymity that, interestingly, newspaper organizations are less and less willing to grant to other sources in their own reporting.

In fact, academics have played their own role in promoting reader-driven journalism. Ernest F. Larkin and Gerald L. Grotta, for example, argued as early as 1974 that publishers and editors must learn to define their products in relationship to the market.[21] Other communications researchers have gone to work helping newspapers analyze their readers' interests and their market needs. Yet, when researchers go to work for newspapers—as many do—the studies, which are generally held as proprietary material anyway, are invariably used to analyze the newspaper's market situation, rather than to probe the nature or effectiveness of adopting a market-oriented approach to the newspaper business or other issues of news philosophy or ethics.[22]

There are other reasons for the limitations in academic studies of newspaper economics. Until a couple of years ago, there was no journalism faculty trained in the economics of the industry; now there are maybe one or two. Ex-journalists who move to academia aren't trained in economics, either, and few have the appetite to teach or do research in the area of newspaper marketing or management. Management schools, for whatever reason, also have not decided that newspapers are a fruitful object of study. The recent rush to start courses in newspaper management reflects a desire to teach how to manage newspapers—not how to study the consequences of this management.

Finally, the few studies of newspapers that have been done seem to contradict each other, and it is difficult to know what to make of them. For example, a 1987 survey by David Pearce Demers and Daniel B. Wackman of nine hundred daily newspaper publishers, top editors, and advertising managers (with 101 responses) concluded that slightly more than two-thirds of the editors at chain-owned newspapers (69 percent) mentioned profit as a driving force behind their operation, compared with slightly more than a third of those (38 percent) at independent newspapers.[23] Their study contradicts the findings of a 1985 study by C. N. Olien, P. J. Tichenor, and G. A. Donohue of the editors of 78 Minnesota newspapers.[24] Olien and her colleagues concluded that editors at independent newspapers are more likely to mention profit as a goal than chain editors and less likely to mention product quality. So what is one to think? On the one hand, the Demers-Wackman study, by surveying news executives nationally, seemed more extensive. But with only 101 responses, was it? These are the kinds of difficulties that confront anyone who tries to find large truths in the often conflicting survey research on newsroom management.[25]

Most surveys—limited in scope as they often are—don't pretend to be scientific samplings of the selected population. And survey researchers will acknowledge that their results can seldom be extrapolated beyond the specific group that has been studied. However, are the results any more significant than a similar inquiry by a journalist using professional judgment to determine whom to interview and what to emphasize? Social scientists say they are. Journalists, as you might expect, aren't so sure. These questions, of course, go to the heart of a rivalry over the best way to determine the "truth" about the world.

Steve Weinberg, a journalist-turned-academic, discussed this dilemma in a piece he wrote for the *Quill* after his attendance at the 1990 convention of the Association for Education in Journalism and Mass Communication (AEJMC)—the principal organization for journalism academics. Weinberg described sorting through dozens of studies—most of which he described as "obscure" or "thumbsucking"—before finding a few that he felt would be useful to working professionals. Weinberg lamented that journalism departments have become so dominated by research-oriented Ph.D.s; then he went on to make a plea for better cooperation between academics and journalists as a way to produce research of value to both fields.[26]

With this in mind, it must be noted that the study that follows suffers from some of the same limitations as earlier examinations of newspaper management practices. Keith Stamm and I had hoped, for example, to visit the newsrooms of a broad range of newspapers in the Northwest, but we were denied access at least as often as we were welcomed. As a result, our sample of journalists in the Northwest—while extensive by the standards of most communications research—isn't as reflective of what is happening within the industry as we might have liked. We also hoped to expand our study into a nationwide one, but we received little encouragement from media foundations or other sources.

However, modest as our effort may be, we believe it still offers some illuminating insights into the inroads that market thinking has made into the newsrooms of daily newspapers and the way today's journalists feel about it.

CHAPTER TEN

The "New" Daily Newspaper Newsroom— and What Our Research Tells Us About It

More shock/schlock stories on the front page, such as, and I kid you not, "Your Lawn Can Kill You.". . . I like my job, but I'm scared shitless about the future of this paper and this industry.
—Anonymous journalist responding to our survey of newsrooms of twelve West Coast daily newspapers

We are trying harder to listen to our readers. Research is highly valued. Company mission and vision are key shared concerns. We are attempting to involve all workers in more decisions.   —Anonymous survey respondent

Management wears a mask here. It pretends to do all the right things, progressive things, says all the right things . . . but in practice, there is an iron hand in the soft glove. . . . There is no future here for anyone who doesn't buy into the hypocrisy.   —Anonymous survey respondent

We have a plague of micromanagers, but no leaders.   —Anonymous survey respondent

I love this paper, I love this job.
—Anonymous survey respondent

IN a recent survey of twenty-four top newspaper editors, the staff of *NewsInc.* magazine found that more than three-quarters of the editors indicated an "overwhelming willingness" to get more involved in the strategic marketing of their newspapers.[1] In fact, the results of the survey, done as part of the magazine's 1991 "State of the Industry" report, wouldn't have come as a complete surprise to the 429 journalists (including top and midlevel editors, copy editors, reporters, and photojournalists) who participated in our own survey of daily newspaper newsrooms.[2]

The purpose of our study was to see what, if any, impact the pressures of market-driven journalism were having on the management policies in today's newsrooms. Even though I had already written extensively as a journalist and a media critic on the phenomenon I dubbed "MBA journalism,"[3] my partnership with Keith Stamm gave us an opportunity to test the hypothesis through the use of traditional social science survey methods.

We conducted our study by visiting twelve different daily newspapers in California, Idaho, and Washington in the summer and fall of 1990.[4] Our sample included four small (under 100,000 circulation) family-owned newspapers, four small chain-owned newspapers, two large (over 100,000 circulation) family-owned newspapers, and two large chain-owned newspapers. Permission for the site visits was requested from the senior editors, and anonymity for the newspaper and participating staffers was promised in exchange for their cooperation. A copy of the questionnaire, which included a series of both open-ended and closed questions, was sent to the senior editor in advance of our visit.[5] The sampling frame for the survey was official staff lists provided by each newspaper. On the whole, 429 staffers were surveyed from a total of 713 listed, amounting to an overall completion rate of 60 percent.[6]

It must be noted that in about a dozen cases our request for a site visit was refused. There was a tendency for news executives, particularly at larger papers, to refuse access to their newsrooms, especially if they perceived they were experiencing management difficulties, and/or were engaged in difficult Guild negotiations.[7] In fact, many of the newspapers that turned us down are known (based on the accounts of news staffers we have talked to there) to be engaged in market-oriented journalism to an even greater degree than many of the newspapers we did survey. As a result, our study probably understates this trend.[8]

The journalists we surveyed confirmed what many newspaper industry analysts have noted, namely, that newspapers are becoming more reader-oriented and market-driven.[9] This is borne out by journalists at newspapers of all types and sizes who reported changes in newsroom policies that reflect a greater orientation toward marketing and business concerns. This is particularly true at chain-owned newspapers, which on almost every level of measurement showed a stronger predilection toward market-oriented management.

Two areas of policy seem to stand out most strongly in the eyes of the journalists we surveyed. First, they see lots of management changes occurring in the newsrooms where they work, which is consistent with the move toward more aggressive newsroom management noted by analysts.[10] Second, they identified market-oriented, reader-friendly journalism as the policy that receives the most emphasis from their newsroom managers. Clearly, journalists are aware of the trend toward treating readers as customers at their newspapers.

However, this phenomenon is happening at the same time as journalists see their newspapers still stressing many of the time-honored journalistic values. At both chain- and family-owned newspapers, traditional news values, such as preserving editorial autonomy, treating readers as citizens, and serving the community, received more emphasis than policies emphasizing marketing and tighter management. Once again the chain-owned newspapers showed a greater propensity to emphasize business values—particularly in their profit emphasis—than did the independently owned newspapers.

In the face of this, staffers indicated that the management changes adopted at their newspapers had skewed the balance between business and journalism in favor of business policies.[11] This was evident in staffers' perceptions that a number of recent policy changes had worsened the balance between the pursuit of business and journalistic principles in their newsrooms. It was also evident in reports of cutbacks in coverage, softening of news content, loss of depth, and reductions in news staff. From the journalists' perspective, business policies are clearly an intrusion into the journalistic domain.

In the job satisfaction portion of the study, we also found that the journalists we surveyed reported lower levels of job satisfaction when business and marketing-oriented policies were being emphasized in their newsrooms and higher levels of satisfaction when the cause of journalism was emphasized.[12]

As a result of these changes, have newspapers grown better or worse? The views of our journalists were split. Over 70 percent of staffers at large independently owned newspapers saw their newspapers as improved. But of the newsworkers at large and small chain newspapers as well as at small independent newspapers only slightly more felt their newspapers had improved than said they had grown worse. By and large, newsroom staffers felt that changes motivated by marketing considerations, such as tightening up of management reins, staff cutbacks, and changes in content at their newspapers, had contributed to a decline in quality.

Here, in more detail, are the results of our findings:

- Change, much of it driven by the forces of market-oriented journalism, has come to today's newsrooms (see table 1 in the appendix). Management changes were most commonly reported by staffers in answer to our open-ended questions, showing that efforts to reorganize newsrooms have become a top priority. With editors' emphasis on packaging the newspaper to appeal to readers, it was also no surprise to find design changes in the newspaper near the top of the list. We might have expected content changes to be more prominent given the push toward reader-oriented journalism, but instead changes in coverage (usually meaning cutbacks) were more often mentioned. Staffers also reported that their newspapers were putting a strong emphasis on marketing the newspaper and increasing profits although not as prominently as we might have expected. However, note the emphasis on staff changes (once again, usually meaning cutbacks) at the small family-owned newspapers and the greater emphasis on marketing, content changes, and profits at the large chain newspapers.

· Most of the recent changes in newsroom policies reported by the newsroom staffers fell into the category of "business-oriented" as opposed to "journalism-oriented" policies, most notably at the chain-owned newspapers (see tables 2 and 3). It is interesting to note, however, that journalists at small chain and large independently owned newspapers were in agreement in seeing journalistic motivations behind the changes in news coverage at their newspapers while identifying design changes as primarily business-motivated. Journalists at small independent and large chain newspapers saw it the opposite way—design changes were seen as adopted for journalistic reasons, and changes in coverage were viewed as largely undertaken for business reasons. Changes in staffing patterns at the large newspapers were also seen as a journalistic plus by the journalists there while staff changes at the small newspapers were viewed by our respondents as undertaken for business purposes.

· Newsroom staffers were about evenly split in their analysis of whether recent management changes had improved or harmed their newspapers (see tables 4 and 5). In fact, staffers at large family-owned newspapers were the only group that clearly viewed the changes at their newspapers as improvements. Those who reported improvements cited staffing (hiring more and better journalists), improved design and appearance of the newspaper, and changes in management practices (more flexible and employee-sensitive practices) as the principal reasons why their newspapers were better. Despite the grumbling by critics that market-minded editors have become obsessed with the look of the newspaper, more staffers viewed design and appearance changes as a positive rather than a negative development. Those who felt the quality of their newspaper had deteriorated put changes in management practices (that is, tougher and more authoritarian practices), staff cutbacks, and adjustments to content at the top of their lists.

- Many of the journalists we surveyed felt the policy changes at their newspapers have intruded into the journalist's traditional domain and skewed newsroom activities toward the business aims of the newspaper (see table 6). The majority of policy changes mentioned by staffers were identified as worsening the balance between business and journalistic pursuits in their newsrooms. They blamed an increased profit and marketing emphasis at their newspapers, a reduction in ethical standards, changes in news content, and staff reductions for this shift. On the other hand, changes in design/appearance, news coverage, and management practices were cited as the principal evidence by staffers who believed that the cause of journalism, rather than the newspaper's bottom line, benefited most from the new policies.

- In answer to our closed questions, journalists reported the emphasis they felt was given to different management policies in their newsrooms, and we were thus able to quantify this emphasis.[13] Our respondents reacted negatively—and strongly—to the notion that greater profit emphasis is compatible with the pursuit of journalistic values, such as editorial autonomy, reader as citizen, and service to the community in the newsroom (see table 7). At the same time, there were weaker correlations—some slightly negative, some slightly positive—between the emphasis on those journalistic values and the pursuit of other business policies, such as treating the reader as customer, exercising management control, and integrating the editorial and business sides of the newspaper. The emphasis on journalistic pursuits in the newsroom received the strongest positive endorsements, which is supported by our findings throughout our study.

- According to staffers, the greatest emphasis in their newsrooms is given to treating the reader as a customer (see table 8). This emphasis on creating "reader-friendly" newspapers is consistent with the trend toward market-oriented journalism we found throughout our research. But it should be noted that this was the only business-oriented policy to receive stronger emphasis than journalistic policies. The least overall emphasis was given to profits, editorial/business integration, and management control—all business-oriented policies.

- Journalists told us that the newsroom policy emphasis varies, at least to some degree, with the kind of newspaper they work for (see table 9). Each type of newspaper seemed to have its own distinctive policy "signature." Large chain newspapers stood out with their emphasis on treating the reader as a customer. The "signature" of small chains is found in their strong emphasis on profits. Independently owned newspapers (both small and large) stood out with their emphasis on journalistic values. The major factor distinguishing small from large family newspapers, staffers reported, was the greater emphasis on management control at the large family-owned newspapers.

The strongest difference in newsroom policy emphasis, according to our respondents, was between chain and family-owned newspapers. Compared to family-owned newspapers, chains were, for the most part, perceived as giving more emphasis to business-oriented policies, particularly in the profits area.

· This trend is just as pronounced if we categorize the newspapers we surveyed by whether they were in a competitive situation or not (see table 10). Many of the trends toward market-oriented management are even stronger at newspapers facing competition from other daily newspapers in their major market area. This is particularly true for chain-owned newspapers in competitive situations. Note that staffers of chain-owned newspapers facing competition reported the highest levels of management emphasis on most of the business policy areas (i.e., profit emphasis, treating readers as customers, and management control). In contrast, family-owned newspapers, whether they were in a competitive situation or not, put the strongest emphasis on journalistic policies.

· In the job satisfaction portion of our study, we came up with results showing that for the most part market-oriented journalism has had a negative impact on journalists' satisfaction with their work. To measure morale among the journalists we surveyed, we included a series of scales for different kinds of job satisfaction.[14] After examining other job satisfaction research,[15] we decided to distinguish between two kinds of employee morale, "intrinsic" and "extrinsic" morale.[16] We defined "intrinsic" or "internal" morale as the satisfaction journalists gain (largely internal to themselves) from the substance of their work within the newsroom and "extrinsic" or "external" morale as the rewards gained (largely in relationship with others) from recognition outside the newspaper. We sorted each of the scales into an internal and external category of job satisfaction (see table 11). We then analyzed the relationship of job satisfaction to each specific policy change and policy emphasis identified in our open-ended and closed questions.

· On first examination, it appeared that the kinds of management policy changes reported by journalists in response to our open-ended questions didn't have much relationship to job satisfaction (see table 12). Regardless of the kind of new policies that they see being implemented in their newsrooms, our respondents' job satisfaction seemed to be moderate and relatively unvarying. Policy changes made some difference in our measures of internal and external job satisfaction, but not much.

However, we found that while changes in policy themselves may have minimal impact on job satisfaction, the way those changes are implemented in the newsroom has a big impact (see table 13). In response to our closed questions, the journalists we surveyed reported lower levels of both internal and external job satisfaction the stronger the profit emphasis was at their newspapers. At the same time, job satisfaction increased to the extent that journalistic causes—serving the community, preserving editorial autonomy, and treating readers as citizens—were emphasized in their newsrooms. However, job satisfaction proved to be largely unrelated to emphasis on other business-oriented policies, such as reader as customer, editorial/business integration, and management control.

· Even though job satisfaction was not directly related to changes in management policies themselves, we decided to pursue this further by examining the impact of those changes on the newspaper and the journalists who work there. We reasoned that job satisfaction may be related to policy changes to the extent that those changes have an impact on newspaper quality, journalists' comfort with newsroom policy, their perception of the management style at their newspaper, and the perceived balance between the pursuit of business and journalism goals in the newsroom. Here we found that policy changes did have an effect on job satisfaction in a number of areas, particularly in the perception of newspaper quality and the balance between business and journalism goals in the newsroom (see table 14). Note that such business-oriented policies as profit emphasis, marketing, and staff changes (i.e., cutbacks) were viewed as contributing to reduced newspaper quality and to a worsening balance between business and journalistic aims in the newsroom.

· Analyzing our data further, we were able to confirm a strong connection between job satisfaction and the way staffers perceived the quality of their newspaper, the style of management in their newsroom, and their comfort with this management style (see table 15). The more staffers felt their newspaper had improved, the happier in their work they were. The same relationship held true concerning staffers' comfort with management policies at their newspaper. At the same time, our respondents reported lower levels of job satisfaction if they identified the management style at their newspaper as authoritarian and higher job satisfaction levels if the management style was more democratic.[17]

· The journalists we surveyed were also less happy if they perceived the balance between journalistic and business goals in their newsroom had tilted in favor of business (see table 16). In every measure where our respondents reported the business-journalism balance had grown worse, they also reported lower levels of job satisfaction.

· Analyzing the relationship between the size of the newspapers we surveyed and the job satisfaction of the newsroom employees there, we found that the size of the newspaper did not make much difference. However, the ownership of the newspaper did (see table 17). Internal job satisfaction was higher at family-owned newspapers (both small and large) than at chain-owned newspapers, and external job satisfaction was higher at small independently owned newspapers than at the other three types. By this measurement, the employees of chain newspapers once again seemed to be feeling the brunt of the changes taking place at newspapers.

· Finally, we analyzed job satisfaction by the position held in the news organization (see table 18). Perhaps not surprisingly (because they set policy), top managers reported the highest levels of both internal and external job satisfaction as well as the greatest degree of comfort with management policies. Again not unexpectedly, midlevel editors reported the next highest levels of external job satisfaction and comfort with newsroom policy. Job satisfaction, it appears, tends to follow the organization chart with top managers happiest, midlevel editors next happiest, and the morale of the rest of the newsroom following behind.

Our survey confirms what many newspaper staffers—and even some of their top editors—have been saying, namely, that market-driven journalism has not made for happier newsrooms. In virtually every category, journalists' job satisfaction appears to be inextricably tied to the pursuit of journalistic, as opposed to business, goals in the newsroom. While newsroom morale has not necessarily been a top priority among today's marketing-minded managers,[18] our study confirms that it is a problem and that the trend toward market-driven journalism appears to be making the problem worse.

It is hardly remarkable to discover that journalists are happier when they are about the business of journalism rather than the business of business. Journalists, for the most part, take jobs in the newsroom because they are interested in—and believe in the values of—the profession of journalism. Journalists have traditionally been led to believe that many of the profession's most cherished principles—the right of independent inquiry, the protection from advertiser pressure, the freedom to put the public's business ahead of private business—were preserved by maintaining a barrier between the news and business departments of the newspaper. Publishers being what they are, this separation has largely been a fiction, more honored as a principle than as something that existed in practice. However, the open advocacy of incorporating marketing policy into the mission of the newsroom does not sit well with journalists, at least not if measured by its impact on levels of job satisfaction.

The advocates of market-oriented journalism say that today's turbulent media environment is forcing them to remind their staffs of a timeless truth: every employee's fate is tied to the newspaper's success in the marketplace. They claim that there is no reason why journalism can't flourish—and everybody be happy in his or her work—in an atmosphere where everyone keeps an eye on the marketplace. Still, at least from the results of our survey, they haven't yet convinced their staffs.

There are also those who will take heart in the fact that the majority of journalists we surveyed believe that the quality of their newspaper has improved in recent years and that improvements in staffing, newspaper design and appearance, and management have had much to do with this improvement. Since it is likely that newspaper executives implemented most of these policy changes to please readers (and not newsroom staffers), this could be viewed as a real plus.

However, it can hardly be comforting for newspaper executives to look at the flip side of the coin, namely, that almost half of our respondents feel that the quality of their newspapers has declined in recent years. These staffers saw this decline in quality even in a decade when newspapers were rolling in profits and advertising revenue and when many of these market-driven changes were implemented for the sake of improving the product.[19] It should also be troubling (even to many editors) that the journalists we surveyed felt that most of the new policy changes in their newsrooms have tilted the balance in favor of the economic, as opposed to the journalistic, interests of the newspaper. This may be a warning sign that the claim of market-oriented editors that they can insulate their staffs from the pressures of the financial side simply isn't proving to be true.

The recession and the continued decline in daily newspaper readership rates have led some newspaper executives to wonder whether all the market surveying of the last decade and the market-oriented journalism it inspired have really done the industry much good.[20] If it can be presumed that today's market-oriented newspapers are really what readers want—and some editors have begun to question that they are—our study may point to a worrisome split in the attitudes of newsworkers and their readers. Many of our respondents are clearly uncomfortable with marketing values having penetrated so strongly into the newsroom. It seems evident that newsroom staffers we surveyed for the most part do not endorse the course daily newspapers have been steering in recent years.

Newspaper executives, of course, are free to believe that it doesn't matter if what readers want in their newspaper—and what newsroom staffers want—are not the same. But it's important to remember that newspaper staffers are newspaper readers, too. While newsworkers' professionalism surely fosters higher expectations of newspapers than those held by readers, newspaper executives shouldn't ignore how many of their employees feel their newspaper has slipped in quality. It's a judgment industry leaders can only hope is not shared by many readers.

PART THREE

CHAPTER ELEVEN

How Much News Is News?

When the newspaper is owned by a stock company, when its directors meet but to shave this year's expenses and increase next year's dividends, commercialism usually binds it. The height of its policy is then enlightened selfishness. If it approximate free journalism, it usually does so only because freedom may pay in the long run.

—Will Irwin, "The American Newspaper"

Since the press publishes the news, true or false or half-way, about everything in the world except itself, the American public knows nothing about what the rulers of public opinion annually decide for it.

—George Seldes, *Lords of the Press*

Newspaper proprietors, a notoriously timid bunch, weighed their various alternative strategies for the Nineties and came to the near-unanimous conclusion: time to hunker down. Boat-rocking is definitely out. Pulling in your journalistic horns is definitely in.

—David Nyhan, *Boston Globe* columnist

I have never seen and heard as much professional unhappiness as there seems to be these days among reporters and editors, correspondents and producers. . . . We are being defeated, and our values discarded, by accountants and management consultants and salesmen—the "managers," the bottom-line guys.

—Newspaper columnist Richard Reeves

IT sounded like worrisome stuff for anyone who flies around the skies in jets built by the Boeing Company. In April 1988 the *Seattle Times* printed an article, based on complaints from British Airways that were leaked to the newspaper, citing "a raft of problems" with new Boeing jets, including instances of missing parts, cracks, improperly fitted fasteners, and a bent cabin floor.[1] The story came just a few days after wire service accounts—summarized in both the *Times* and the *Seattle*

Post-Intelligencer—of a letter from the president of Japan Airlines criticizing defects in new Boeing aircraft that had been provided to the Japanese press.[2]

This was obviously the beginning of a big story, right? Wrong. In fact, it was part of a brief spate of coverage about quality control problems on Boeing's assembly lines that flashed across the pages of Seattle's daily newspapers, only to be submerged by a deluge of articles about a subsequent burst of new Boeing jet orders.

Boeing officials, as it turned out, were able to put the story largely to rest in the Seattle dailies simply by holding a press conference and telling reporters that airline complaints about quality control were part of the normal business relationship between Boeing and its customers. Boeing officials conceded that stepped-up production rates and the hiring of thousands of new workers to handle the boom of new jet orders had led to some defects in new jets. But, as the *P-I* quoted then Boeing vice-president Phil Condit, the company's tradition of finding a problem and then fixing it would keep Boeing on its course toward building "a perfect airplane."[3]

In fact, the quality control stories were a rare departure for the two Seattle newspapers, which seldom take a hard look at a company that dominates the Puget Sound economy. For the most part, business reporters at the Seattle dailies have followed a basic pattern typical of daily newspaper coverage of local business: stories about airplane sales, the development of new aircraft, new government contracts, and employment fluctuations at Boeing are covered eagerly by local reporters. Investigations of airplane crashes, scandals, and government probes at Boeing are usually left to national or specialty publications—if they are unearthed at all.[4]

Yet the marketing-minded editors at the *Seattle Times* can point— like most other newspaper editors during the booming probusiness years of the 1980s—to a business page that bulges with stories about local business developments, brims with features on stock market investment and personal finance management, and boasts a substantially bigger staff than it ever did in the past. So what is going on here?

In noting that virtually every major newspaper has expanded its business coverage since 1978, Peter Dreier says that much of the coverage is "simply boosterism—glowing stories of new investment plans, fawning profiles of corporate executives, summaries of quarterly and annual reports. . . . There is almost no investigative reporting on these pages and little good to say about unions or consumer groups. Their focus is on 'upscale readers.' "[5]

Dreier has hit upon a basic principle in this era of the planning, packaging, and marketing of newspapers. Business people—and the upscale readers who are most interested in business—are at the top of the target market sought by newspaper executives eager to match up affluent readers and advertisers. Increasingly the coverage of the news is being shaped by the desire of news executives for upscale readers, easy to plan-and-package material, and content that reflects what readership studies say interests readers most—in other words, the same type of marketing interests that concern most other businesses.

The organization of a newsroom around corporate marketing and management principles is a wonderful way to insure that troublesome stories don't get into the newspaper, says David Johnston, an investigative reporter formerly with the *Detroit Free Press* and the *Los Angeles Times* and now with the *Philadelphia Inquirer*. "Good reporters are like good detectives," he says. "You leave them alone. They don't work 9 to 5. They don't think bureaucratically. You can't manage them like accountants. . . . If you want to tame a newsroom so people aren't going to go out and dig up things that stir up controversy and may get you into litigation, then applying these corporate business techniques is a brilliant strategy."[6]

It's a commentary on our times that this marketing of the news, rather than the improvement of the news product, has so strongly held the fancy of today's editors. In the reams of marketing information produced by the newspaper industry about how to "remake" the daily newspapers, there is little reference to improving newspaper quality— to the substance of what's in the news columns and how to make it better, deeper, richer, truer, more meaningful. Even in the *Next Newspapers,* ASNE's publication put together by some of the industry's top editors, the marketing propaganda overwhelms any serious discussion of the quality of the news. For example, the suggestions from Richard Oppel and Ken Gepfert, the editor and former assistant managing editor, respectively, of Knight-Ridder's *Charlotte Observer,* include "tailoring" local news to reader interests, writing more about suburban lifestyles and less about government, editing "like TV producers think," becoming "more aggressive marketers," and assigning reporters to determine the biggest reader interests. They don't say anything about the use of investigative or enterprise reporting techniques to build reader loyalty—techniques that, ironically, helped the newspaper win the Pulitzer prize in 1988 for its coverage of the PTL scandal.[7]

The evolution of the business section at the *Seattle Times* illustrates how the marketing of the newspaper can dictate the way news is presented. In 1983 the *Times'* business section was redesigned with the help of a readership study that showed that many business page readers were intimidated by much business news and preferred articles about personal finances and money management.[8] Then in 1987 a major expansion of the business staff occurred when the *Times* began a Business Monday section, an unabashed effort to appeal to the insider interests of the business community.[9] Finally, as part of its strategy to attract affluent suburban readers, the *Times* added business staffers to its suburban zone bureaus in 1991.[10]

The result has been a substantially increased business staff and a bulkier business section that features a business gossip column, splashy features on local and national business trends, and regular profiles on local business people. At the same time, the *Times's* business section (or the *P-I's*, for that matter) does virtually no investigative reporting of local business, and virtually none of the major businesses in the Seattle area receive aggressive scrutiny. In recent years, both the *Times* and the *P-I* have doubled their manpower covering Boeing—from one to two reporters—but this has not resulted in any substantial increase in aggressive coverage of Boeing. In fact, when the quality control issue surfaced again in 1991, Boeing was able to limit the newspaper coverage to another press conference.[11]

While other newspapers have not been quite so obvious in their marketing intentions as the *Times,* the trend toward more sports, business, and suburban coverage, more target marketing, and more specialized coverage based on the perceived interests of upscale readers is apparent throughout the industry. For the most part, newspapers in this country—and business pages in particular—have done very little investigative or aggressive reporting to examine the businesses in their midst.[12]

Daily newspapers, of course, have a long history of adopting a chamber-of-commerce mentality when they cover business news. However, the 1970s saw a toughening up of business coverage, inspired in part by Watergate, the consumer and environmental movements, and the antiauthority mood of the times. However, for the most part, the Reagan-Bush years have seen a return to the days of quashed stories about corporate wrongdoing, deference to large corporate interests in the community, and boosteristic accounts of business activity.

The traditional treatment of business with kid gloves has been reinforced by the campaigns of newspaper executives to fit their newsrooms more efficiently into the marketing mission of the newspaper. As the walls between the news and marketing departments have come down, the news judgment required of today's marketing-minded news-paper executives has grown more complicated and, in some cases, more compromised. Not only is big media a big and ever bigger story in the global village and the expanding Information Age; the growth of the media conglomerates has made the big media's coverage of themselves as well as their coverage of their growing entanglements with other sectors of the economy an ever more critical issue for a society bound by the spreading web of electronic information networks.

Sadly, there are no signs that newspaper executives—fixated on their own market surveys, financial plans, and budgeting problems—are showing much inclination to scrutinize their counterparts in other industries, let alone the affairs of the media themselves. A closer look at a few examples of what passes as business and media coverage in the go-go 1980s and 1990s follows.

Retail Advertising

Since the midnineteenth century, big city newspapers and their big retail advertisers have coexisted in a comfortable, symbiotic relationship, two industries that grew up together and have needed each other ever since. But serious stresses have developed in this old partnership. The recession of the 1990s and the leveraged buy-out binge of the 1980s have left many big retail department stores struggling with enormous debt loads, managed from afar by conglomerate owners, and threatened with bankruptcy. This has prompted many retailers to re-evaluate their strategy of advertising so heavily in daily newspapers. Ominously for daily newspapers, a key reason for this shift in strategy has been that big retailers have begun to pay attention to the declining rates of newspaper readership, and they are questioning whether they are getting the best bargain for their advertising dollar.[13]

This development, however, leaves newspapers in a bind. If there is one industry that newspapers have tended to treat as a sacred cow (besides themselves, of course), it has been their big retail advertisers. Needless to say, newspapers' coverage of the plight of their big retail advertisers—let alone the latter's relationship to the financial dilemma of newspapers themselves—has been spotty, to say the least.

Typical of newspapers' reluctant approach to dealing with their retail advertisers' financial problems was the *St. Louis Post-Dispatch*'s tardiness in reporting that May Department Stores, headquartered in St. Louis, had paid over $1 million to settle lawsuits charging subsidiary stores in California, Maryland, and New York with deceptive advertising practices. As reported in the *St. Louis Journalism Review,* the *Post-Dispatch* had been alerted more than once to the company's habit of advertising big savings on items that were seldom sold at the higher price. Newspaper executives denied that the lack of coverage had anything to do with the fact that a local May chain is a big advertiser in the *Post-Dispatch;* however, they caught up with the story only after they were contacted by the *Columbia Journalism Review.* [14]

The Portland *Oregonian* showed how this deference to retailers can be extended to powerful figures connected with major advertisers. As reported in *Willamette Week,* an *Oregonian* reporter had developed a story in late 1989 about how an influential Oregon businessman connected to the company that controls the Fred Meyer retail stores, a major advertiser in the newspaper, may have profited from the connection. As a long-time member of Oregon's state pension board, Roger Meier was instrumental in steering hundreds of millions of dollars in state pension investments to Kohlberg Kravis Roberts and Co., a New York investment house that also controls the Fred Meyer Corporation. A few months after leaving the board, the investment house reportedly let Meier, who served on the boards of two companies owned by Kohlberg Kravis Roberts while also serving on the state pension board, in on a lucrative business deal that netted him a reported $900,000 paper profit. According to *Willamette Week,* the *Oregonian* didn't publish the story until the spring of 1991 and then only after *Oregonian* editors learned that an article detailing the affair and the *Oregonian's* decision not to publish the story was scheduled to appear in the *New York Times* magazine. *Oregonian* editors said the delay in publishing the story had to do with problems in the story and had nothing to do with the fact that Fred Meyer is one of the newspaper's largest advertisers. [15]

In fact, the Newhouse-owned *Oregonian* has developed a reputation as a place where advertiser interests are of paramount concern to editors. The *Wall Street Journal* (which seems to do a better job of covering other newspaper's internal compromises than it does of reporting its own) reported that the *Oregonian* once pulled a business page column because the writer criticized Fred Meyer for closing two neighborhood stores to boost profits. And in 1989 the newspaper demoted an editor and destroyed tens of thousands of copies of editions containing an article that offended real estate advertisers by suggesting a home can be purchased without the help of a broker. The *Journal* concluded that tough financial times have made daily newspapers all over the country pull their punches when covering major advertisers.

"I haven't seen a negative article written about auto dealers," one

Connecticut auto dealer was quoted as saying. "Consumer reporting is virtually nonexistent now." Added a spokesman for the National Automobile Dealers Association: "There used to be a very thick line between advertising and editorial. That's no longer the case. It's a thin line now." [16]

Unfortunately for newspaper readers, the kinds of stories about retail advertisers that do make it into the columns of the daily newspapers often cannot be distinguished from advertising. Typical in this era of market-savvy editors are stories like the nine thousand word, four-part series in the *Washington Post* celebrating the glories of Safeway Stores, one of the newspaper's largest advertisers [17]; or the *Arkansas Democrat*'s eight-page, four-color "special report" celebrating William T. Dillard, head of the Little-Rock based department store chain that advertises heavily in the *Democrat* [18]; or the *New York Daily News* edition that contained in selected areas a page-one headline (replacing the "Panama Coup Fails" in other editions) reading: "Gala Grand Opening Of J. C. Penney At Newport Centre." [19]

Even when newspapers do cover the troubles of the retail industry, they discover that retailers, accustomed to the soft, promotional treatment of the past, can become bitter. The *Seattle Times* and the *Seattle Post-Intelligencer* learned just such a lesson in 1990 after the Seattle-based Nordstrom, Inc., unhappy with the two newspapers' coverage of labor problems at the retail clothing chain, pulled most of its advertising from the two newspapers. While complaining about the coverage, Nordstrom executives claimed that the real reason they cut back their advertising was that they felt the two Seattle newspapers, which had jacked up advertising rates in recent years despite stagnant circulation, were no longer a good advertising buy. [20] To their credit, both Seattle dailies did cover Nordstrom's decision to pull its advertising from the newspapers. Perhaps the most interesting coverage of the controversy came from one *Times* columnist who speculated that the reason for Nordstrom's unhappiness was that the rapidly growing company, used to gushing press in the Seattle newspapers for so many years, simply did not know how to deal with the fact that its labor controversies were handled like any other news story. [21]

Real Estate Advertising

The real estate industry, which does an inordinate amount of advertising in daily newspapers, has traditionally received the same kind of kid-glove-treatment as retailers. The hot and cold real estate market of the 1980s and 1990s has led to more real estate coverage by newspapers—but not necessarily in ways that have been of benefit to readers. In recent decades, "advertorial" real estate sections, which look like a news section but whose columns are filled with copy written by the newspapers' advertising department, have proliferated. Even the staff-generated copy in the real estate sections of many daily newspapers often reads like recycled press releases. The millions of dollars in advertising that are poured into real estate sections help insure that this is one place where, as Mary Ellen Schoonmaker puts it, "papers are most tempted to sell their soul."[22]

Schoonmaker's 1987 article in the *Columbia Journalism Review* details the efforts at a number of newspapers to deepen and toughen up their real estate coverage and the obstacles they faced. The now-defunct *Dallas Times-Herald,* for example, tried to do away with its "advertorial" real estate section (for which the ad department wrote the copy) and improve its real estate coverage around 1980, but it went back to the "advertorial" format after a boycott cost the newspaper millions of dollars a year in real estate advertising. The *Times-Herald* was never able to convince the competing *Dallas Morning News* to go along with the move. The *News's* "wise marketing" but bad journalistic judgment, as one former *Times-Herald* executive put it, insured the continuation of the puffy, positive real estate coverage in both newspapers. While Schoonmaker praises the real estate coverage in some newspapers, she also notes that even some of the country's best dailies, like the *New York Times,* are known for their deference to developers. At the *Times,* for example, Sydney Schanberg, the Pulitzer prize winner who now works for *Newsday,* lost his city affairs column after he wrote a number of tough columns about New York real estate and related housing issues.

In a similar article in the *Washington Journalism Review,* Elizabeth Lesly details the "advertorial" coverage of real estate in newspapers like Knight-Ridder's reader-driven Boca Raton *News* where real estate editor Stephanie Murphy acknowledges that the news staff doesn't pay much attention to real estate and that most stories in her section have a pronounced industry spin; still, the primary purpose of the section (functioning as "an excellent profit center," as she put it) is served.[23] In the same issue of the magazine, Wendy Swallow Williams, a journalism professor at American University, describes her in-depth study of real estate sections in eight major U.S. dailies. Her conclusion is that "many contain little more than sanctified ad copy."[24] Much the same thing can be said about newspapers' other industry-oriented special sections, in particular, about automobile sections. How many times have newspapers been boycotted by automobile dealers after reporting something unfavorable about auto dealers—or been intimidated and kept from doing aggressive automobile journalism in the first place? [25]

Coverage of Large Companies by Town Newspapers

Newspaper editors in cities with large, dominating companies seldom choose to live with the tension of truly scrutinizing their powerful local employers. The *Flint (Mich.) Journal,* for example, returned to its booster traditions after a brief period in the late 1970s and early 1980s of experimenting with aggressive coverage of the local business community, including the town's extensive General Motors operations. In 1981 an editor was fired after the newspaper, which is part of the Newhouse-owned Booth chain, ran stories about G. M. shipping out cars with cast-iron shavings in the engines, speed-ups on G. M. assembly lines, and automobile brokers from Detroit who were underselling Flint dealers. He was replaced with another editor who made it his mission to provide positive coverage of community news and to put the best face on efforts to lift the economically crippled auto making community from its financial woes. [26]

The Flint newspaper's approach was mirrored by another Booth newspaper in Michigan's auto country, the *Grand Rapids Press,* where editors decided to change a critical headline about Chrysler's new Imperial model. The original headline reflected the criticism of the Imperial's roadworthiness by a syndicated automobile critic. However, after Booth's president intervened, the new headline in later editions praised the Imperial as "still a traditional American luxury car." [27]

Tobacco companies, like automobile companies, can cast a long shadow over their local newspapers, too. A few years ago, the *Winston-Salem (N.C.) Journal,* located in the hometown of the R. J. Reynolds tobacco company, decided to pull a Doonesbury comic strip in which an applicant for a job with Reynolds is asked to say, with a straight face, that cigarettes don't cause cancer. As noted in a story by the Associated Press, it was the first time the controversial strip has been pulled from a newspaper in deference to a corporation. [28]

The reverse happens, too. Take the fawning story in the *Journal and Constitution* of Atlanta about the popularity of Coca Cola in Brazil, a story that is typical of so many that are written about major hometown companies. The front-page story mentioned the local product by name some fifteen times and included a large color picture of a Brazilian vendor seated next to a cooler full of clearly labeled cans. [29]

Telecommunications and Electronic Competition

Many newspapers have reacted in a downright paranoid fashion to the intrusions into their territory of electronic information competitors. The *Seattle Times,* for example, has refused to take advertising from Prodigy, the IBM-Sears consortium that is marketing an electronic news and data delivery service for computer users.[30] Indeed, newspapers' willingness to touch on government media regulation issues in their editorials without signaling a conflict of interest is disturbing. A case in point was a 1990 editorial in the *News-Sentinel* in Knoxville, Tennessee, against South Central Bell's proposal to develop a fiber optic information and programming network. The editorial never told readers that South Central Bell's proposal might directly compete with cable systems, including the Knoxville cable system owned by Scripps Howard, the *News-Sentinel's* parent company.[31]

The complexities of newspaper coverage of the myriad issues of the unfolding Information Age is a fascinating spectacle as publishers struggle with their self-interest and the traditional demands of news reporting. The battle between the newspaper industry and the Baby Bell telephone companies, which want to get into the electronic information delivery business, has been a particularly taxing issue for newspaper companies. State regulators are being asked to settle these highly complex issues, and newspapers' coverage has been "spotty at best," according to Mark Silk, an editorial writer for the Atlanta *Constitution.*[32]

Silk bases his views in part on his own newspaper's efforts to cover Southern Bell's campaign to convince the Georgia Public Service Commission to let the company accelerate depreciation on a range of plants and equipment and prepare the way for the installation of new, high technology wiring into homes and businesses. This issue is of considerable consequence to Cox Enterprises, the owner of the *Constitution* and the seventh-largest cable operator in the country, including one franchise in Georgia. Cox has intervened in the dispute by opposing Bell South's moves at the same time that the *Constitution* has editorialized against the efforts by the telephone company. While the newspaper has clearly told readers of its self-interest in the matter, Southern Bell has accused Cox of using its editorial privileges to further its economic interests.

Silk highlights the difficulties newspapers face if they do (as many don't) cover the unfolding telecommunications controversies surrounding their business. Newspaper editors delude themselves if they think the issue is too technical and remote to interest readers, Silk says.

"Corporate executives never find it easy to acknowledge that the public interest may not be identical to their company's," as Silk puts it. "This has come particularly hard to newspaper publishers, accustomed as they are to consider themselves tribunes of the people. . . . What could be more in the public interest than for publishers to do everything in their power to protect newspapers' profitability?"[33]

Joint "News" and Marketing Promotions

Today's marketing-minded editors often join with their marketing departments to promote "news" that aids a joint newspaper/newspaper advertiser marketing campaign. Needless to say, newspaper readers haven't learned the inside story in the news columns when newspapers engage in such promotions. An example is the Knight-Ridder-owned *St. Paul Pioneer Press*'s partnership with the Minneapolis-based Dayton Hudson department store (the newspaper's largest advertiser) in promoting "Santabear," a purchase-with-purchase holiday item offered at Dayton Hudson stores. The newspaper publicized the promotion by treating readers to a flurry of pieces on Santabear costumes and accessories, full-page posters for collectors, and a sixteen-page special "educational supplement" using the animal in stories and games.[34] Similarly, a page one story in the *New York Daily News* headlined "Banking Made Better" with a subhead "Chase Introduces A Whole New Way of Banking! See Details On Pages MP10 and 11" directed readers to a two-page advertising spread.[35] And the *Arkansas Democrat* celebrated the opening of a new car dealership by local basketball star Sidney Moncrief with an eight-page section, complete with four by-lined tributes by *Democrat* staffers and decorated with eleven photos.[36] *USA Today* also has the habit of touting inside ads—such as a November 7, 1985, entry "Special Ad Report: Chrysler's new Plymouth - 'The Pride is Back.' 6–9A"—in its front-page "newsline."[37]

In fact, the trend toward marrying news and marketing in the news columns is likely to get worse if newspapers take their cue from magazines, which have exploited their editorial columns for commercial purposes to a degree only beginning to be seen in newspapers. In a 1989 article in the *Columbia Journalism Review,* the magazine chastised former *Vanity Fair* editor Tina Brown for running a series of puffed personality pieces on celebrities and fashion figures who advertise heavily in the magazine's pages. It was noted that in *Vanity Fair*'s March 1989 issue alone, fashion figures who received the celebrity treatment in the magazine's editorial columns accounted for twenty-one pages of advertising.[38]

In a follow-up piece *Columbia Journalism Review* associate editor Michael Hoyt blamed the revolution in marketing of the 1970s and 1980s—combined with the proliferation of "niche market" magazines offering advertisers "compatible" editorial philosophies—for blurring the line between advertising and editorial content and putting pressure on magazine editors to provide editorial coverage in return for advertising. Hoyt noted instances of the blurring of the lines in such magazines as *Lear's* (which featured on its cover the public relations director of a perfume maker who advertised heavily in the same issue), *Esquire* (which joined with a vodka advertiser in sponsoring a short story contest, judged by *Esquire* editors and printed in the magazine, that required the writers to mention the vodka in the story), and *Family Circle* (which joined forces with a major retailer-advertiser in sponsoring the reconstruction of the country home of a contributing editor, then covering the reconstruction and surrounding it with ads from the retailer for products useful for renovating homes).[39]

Unfortunately, the flap over the use of news columns for marketing purposes is only a somewhat more subtle twist to what has long been standard fare in the media. Magazines have long been willing to sell space for advertiser-produced "special supplements" that read like editorial copy and are probably indistinguishable from it for many readers. Newspapers—even the best ones—have traditionally been big promoters of "progress" editions and other copy produced by advertising departments that (even if properly labeled) is hardly untainted by commercialism. Television stations are running lots of paid programing these days where commercial interests buy big blocks of time to present their "newslike" message. And, of course, the public relations firms continue to get lots of "free" promotional material onto television and into newspapers. Video news releases are a booming business as newscasters, dealing with tight budgets, look for free video productions to fill out newscasts. According to *CJR*, industry produced video "news" programs on such subjects as "dolphin-safe" tuna and McDonald's move into Russia and Disneyland's thirty-fifth anniversary have reached anywhere from 20 to 80 million viewers.[40] Even such a well-respected stalwart of the daily newspaper industry as the *Wall Street Journal* is, according to a study by *CJR*, largely a bulletin board for company press releases. In an analysis of a typical *Wall Street Journal* edition in October 1979, the magazine determined by contacting the companies involved that 72 percent of the 70 stories examined were based solely on press releases.[41]

There are signs that as news departments get on board the marketing bandwagon the business concerns of newspapers have become paramount even in the newsroom. Recession-wracked advertising departments, under pressure to come up with "new products" to counter the loss of traditional advertising, are pushing for coverage (some in the form of "advertorials," some not) to please real estate, travel, auto, and entertainment advertisers. Ronald K. L. Collins of the Center for the Study of Commercialism recently issued a report detailing numerous instances where advertising pressure has corrupted news content. In a world where the walls between the news and advertising departments have come down, Collins quotes one hiring editor at the *Los Angeles Times* who says: "I get calls from reporters across the country who are . . . fearful . . . about the increasing pressure to do stories pleasing to advertisers. They've questioned the journalistic value of these 'stories' and have been told simply to find a way to make the 'stories' work. They're panicked that their careers are in jeopardy, that they have only one choice—do the advertiser-friendly stories or join the burgeoning ranks of the journalistic unemployed."[42]

The impact of advertiser pressure on the media is likewise a very old but also very underpublicized story. The instances of newspapers giving in to pressure, or shaping their coverage to satisfy advertiser needs, are so widespread that in 1977 the School of Journalism at the University of Missouri as part of its Freedom of Information Center reports issued a study listing dozens of examples of journalists punished for upsetting advertisers and of media coverage that was bent to suit advertiser needs.[43]

A few newspaper executives may maintain with a straight face that things are actually better than they were in the days before newsrooms became professionalized, when the news columns were often maintained in rigid service to advertisers and other powers-that-be in the community. In fact, however, the move among newspapers to bring marketing principles to the newsroom is just an updated version of the same old story. It is true that in the more sophisticated environment of today's journalism, many daily newspapers (now owned by chains with a savvy public relations outlook) are proud of the fact that they don't engage in the blatant self-promotions, the self-serving use of the news columns, or the boosterism of earlier periods.[44] However, as is always the case when it comes to media self-examination, it is the untold stories that tell a truer tale of the ties between the daily newspaper, major advertisers, and other powerful business interests in the community.

Modesty, editors believe, suggests that readers don't buy the newspaper to read about the newspaper's own financial dealings. However,

spaper executives' reluctance to cover their newspapers'
siness matters or their connections to advertisers and other
moneyed interests in the community is rooted in their percep-
it isn't in their self-interest to do so. Reporters can't always be
d and, if left to their own devices, may come back with a less
helpful story about the web of financial connections that surround
newspapers in any community.[45] Attempts to kill embarrassing
tories or to lay down heavy-handed rules about stories connected to
the newspaper can give a top newspaper executive a bad reputation in
the newsroom—or, worse, lead to embarrassing mentions in a media
review. Better to let the news staff know, in informal ways or through
the marketing-oriented structure of the news coverage, that it is safer
simply to write about the news in ways that are pleasing to readers—or
to advertisers or powerful people in the community or the publisher, to
be more exact.

This Catch-22 of the news business—namely, that the business of
the media isn't news unless the media decide it is—has long been with
us. One of the most telling accounts was written more than twenty
years ago by James Aronson who noted that the Newspaper Preservation Act—lobbied vigorously by an industry that wanted government
sanction for the merging of the business and circulation functions of
competitive but struggling daily newspapers—was little covered by the
nation's press. Despite more than two million words of testimony before the Senate Antitrust and Monopoly subcommittee and exhibits
filling 3,462 pages in seven volumes, some newspapers (including the
two Tucson newspapers, whose joint-operating agreement had been
struck down by the U.S. Supreme Court) carried nothing on the hearings, Aronson said. Even the *New York Times,* which sent an attorney
to testify against the measure, did not publish an editorial until more
than a week after the Senate approved the measure.[46]

Both journalists and academics have long noted the connection of
the business philosophy of newspaper owners, the application of management principles to newsroom organization, and the expectations
placed on reporters in producing the content of newspapers. A long
line of studies shows that editors and publishers have many, largely
informal, ways to impose their management philosophy on the journalist and the journalist's work. In 1955 Warren Breed first noted that
journalists learn newspaper policy through the unspoken conventions
of newsroom activity. Most newsroom managers are careful not to
tamper with the image that reporters entertain of their profession—the
reporter as the intrepid investigator rooting out graft and corruption,
the reporter as the lonely individualist loyal only to principle and the

reader. However, newsworkers soon learn by "osmosis," as Breed put it, the boundaries of their freedom and the rewards of performing their tasks in a routine manner.[47]

Breed's views have been buttressed by a number of other studies.[48] Todd Gitlin, a media critic at the University of California-Berkeley, says that this newsroom socialization translates into "news" through the use of "frames" that enable journalists to select, emphasize, and transmit large amounts of information under tight corporate control. "Day-to-day political and corporate pressures have not changed much: they go on setting unspoken outer limits for the routines that journalists are trained for and believe in," Gitlin says.[49] In fact, many journalists—at least, those who are aware of the restrictions under which they work—will confirm what academics have found in their studies. As Carlin Romano, a book reviewer for the *Philadelphia Inquirer,* puts it: "As a matter of philosophical and intellectual principle, the American journalist can pretty much cover what he wishes. As a matter of tradition and convention, he currently performs like a skater signed on for familiar routines."[50]

In his 1980 classic, *Deciding What's News,* Herbert Gans observed the activities of journalists at *Time, Newsweek,* CBS, and NBC and concluded that the "enduring values" of journalists are "blind to possible structural flaws within the system" and seldom stray from the fundamental views of the establishment.[51] This includes journalists' belief in "responsible capitalism," as Gans puts it, and a general affirmation of the free enterprise ownership of the news systems in America.[52] Gans, of course, wrote in the era before newspaper executives had tightened their grip on the newsroom and put in place the kinds of planning and packaging systems that have produced the reader-driven publication. Nevertheless, in a prophetic passage, he points toward the coming era of market thinking and corporate control of the newsroom: "News judgment is resistant to change, and journalists will fight hard to preserve their autonomy; but if corporate economic well-being is threatened, executives may insist that their news organizations adapt."[53]

The theme of the journalist as a foot soldier of the establishment is a common one in academic literature. For example, Leon Sigal, in his study of the *Washington Post* and the *New York Times,* concludes that newsmen, like most of the people they cover, are "organization men" and that the government bureaucracies they cover are programed to meet the needs of the newspaper bureaucracies they work for.[54] In many government agencies, public relations people vastly outnumber the reporters covering the beat, Sigal notes.[55] And one way public relations people do their job is by busying reporters with a steady stream of information through channels that keeps them from poking around elsewhere. "To appreciate the effect of organizational processes and politics on newsmaking, then, it helps to view newsmen as they but seldom view themselves—as bureaucrats," Sigal says.[56]

As these public relations people do the work for reporters, the implications for the news—or at least the news that gets into newspapers—are considerable. Gerald Stone, for example, points to studies that show how large amounts of the material in newspapers originate with public relations sources.[57] Sigal, in his study, determined that of a sample of about three thousand stories that appeared in the *Post* and the *Times*, about two-thirds came through "routine channels"—meaning that, for the most part, they are derived from public relations sources or staged, predicted events.[58] Michael Schudson says this means that newsgatherers—despite their lofty self-image—must be seen as "representatives of one bureaucracy picking up prefabricated news items from representatives of another bureaucracy."[59]

As far back as 1961, Daniel Boorstin outlined the dilemma of a society—led by its journalists and their news organizations—that so willingly plays into the hands of the public relations wizards, government flacks, and corporate image makers. In coining the phrase "pseudo-event," Boorstin complained of the "mirror effect" of a society that has become trapped in a world of contrived events.[60] In journalism, Boorstin said, reporting has become a problem of packaging. "Fact or fantasy, the image becomes the thing," Boorstin says. "Its very purpose is to overshadow reality. American life becomes a showcase for images. For frozen pseudo-events."[61]

This, as Boorstin anticipates, is the difficulty facing many reporters at the new marketing-oriented, corporate newspapers—how to deal with an increasingly contrived and packaged "pseudoproduct" that fits in so well with the needs of planned and packaged newspapers. When newspaper editors think about the news in packaging terms, it's difficult for them to maintain a level of outrage (or even skepticism) at the institutions that are more than happy to package the news for them. As this happens, news is slowly shaped into "pseudonews," to use Boorstin's term. The mission of reporters becomes less to look behind the appearance of things and unearth deeper truths but to collect material designed to fit into the package. In time, what is said becomes less important than how it is presented, how it can be planned by the managers of the newsroom to blend into the news package and the newspaper's marketing program. Not only do the promoters and the corporate image makers succeed in planting their version of the news into newspapers, but the obvious, the predictable, the safe-and-so-what becomes the news. Even the prettiest packages that promise in-depth examination of important issues can be deceptive. Often they are simply more of what the well-informed newspaper reader already knows or suspects.

Bill Walker, who recently left his job with the *Sacramento Bee,* describes what life is like in this world where editors are fixated on shaping the substance of the news to fit into the newspaper's marketing strategy.

> The result is newspapers in which content is secondary to packaging—the manufacture of a product carefully calculated, on the basis of the same kind of market research used by political candidates, to hit as many of the audience's emotional hot buttons as possible. . . . Editors know by the mid-morning meeting what the stories will say; the reporters' task is to fill in the blanks. That's not journalism, it's word processing. A reporter once was, at the most basic level, a writer communicating with an audience. But in today's high-concept journalism, where the most complex of ideas must fit neatly into a black-and-white box, reporters are no more than assembly-line workers packaging information.[62]

Needless to say, this kind of journalism is unlikely to produce much to threaten the status quo or closely examine what is really happening inside important institutions. Good reporters know that while they run around covering the safe and predictable stories, they are not paying attention to the hidden agenda of society's power brokers, the subterranean world within the government bureaucracy and the business community where a tangled mix of policy, promotion of self-interest, and the preservation of position makes up real decision making. As business people and public officials (and their public relations minions) figure out the changing internal rules that now operate at many newspapers (and they have, be sure), they know enough to give the newspapers a steady diet of news conferences, press releases, committee hearings, and other staged and easy-to-cover events. A good reporter senses that when he or she is elbow to elbow with other reporters at those events, somebody, somewhere, is getting away with something that is not being examined. This means that readers are deprived of finding out what's really going on in the community.

In this market-driven world of easy-to-digest events, news increasingly becomes almost a parody of the term. News is no longer something "new" but instead becomes a commodity that can be passed off as something interesting or original. Unfortunately, the lack of real news in the newspaper—news that gives a sense of depth and insight and context to surface events—is the one solution market-minded managers won't consider when they analyze why readers are abandoning newspapers. "Corporate managers want predictability," says David Johnston. "Readers don't want predictability. Newspapers print old news. They spend all their time printing what people already know."[63]

Newspapers, in fact, are only following television's lead in their obsession to become "friendlier" with their readers. Television viewers have long been witness to what happens when the package—the coverage of easy, predictable "pseudo-events," the audience appeal of the newscasters, the efforts to reflect back what researchers say the public wants—dominates news judgment. Researchers, like Fowler and Showalter, have measured how the networks, fearing nothing more than deviating from the safe, corporate formula, have become look-alikes in their news judgment and their treatment of stories.[64] Even worse, television's approach has forced other media to adapt to a world where television's needs dictate the production of so much of the "pseudonews" that surrounds us. Newspaper executives are "increasingly editing the paper for people who think life is a beer commercial," says Donald Kaul, a columnist for the Des Moines Register. "We are on the same path that TV followed," he adds. "And we've seen what happened there."[65]

Mark Hertsgaard has documented the way the Reagan administration, led by top aides Michael Deaver and David Gergen, built the president's public image by manipulating television's needs for a daily news line and lots of visual shots of Reagan. Print journalists covering the White House saw this for the cynical strategy it was, and they both protested and wrote about it—but to little avail. Even the few protesting television reporters found that they were hamstrung in convincing the public, or their news executives, of the dangers of media manipulation by the White House. "Central to Deaver's success was his recognition of something journalists were loath to admit about their business: that news was, to the corporations that produced it, primarily a commodity to be bought and sold," Hertsgaard says.[66]

Newspapers can hardly claim that, throughout history, they have not printed a uniform version of the news or that they have not traditionally been subject to manipulation by news sources. But the plan-design-and-package-the-news philosophy is only exacerbating the long tradition of newspaper owners thinking of the news as simply a commodity to fill the space between advertisements. In their rush to imitate their electronic competitors and embrace the latest marketing techniques, today's newspaper executives risk the abandonment of their vital role in the information order. By tradition (albeit, a shaky one), daily newspapers do much of the work of extracting the information on which our Information Age depends—at least, the information that is *hard* to extract. At the same time, legions of public relations agents and corporate and government image makers are standing by eager to be the brokers of information that is *easy* to gather. Sadly, all that stands between them and the public, in many cases, are the marketing-minded editors who—working for media corporations that share many of the values of their corporate counterparts—are cheerfully participating in the corporate reshaping of the news.[67]

As it happened, David Halberstam made a Seattle appearance shortly after the stories about Boeing's quality control problems appeared in the Seattle dailies. In *The Reckoning,* Halberstam's book about the troubles of the U.S. auto industry, he suggests that American business needs to retool to cope with the industrial competition from Japan.[68] During a talk to business journalists in the Northwest, he suggested that they—and the daily press in general—could use some retooling too. A deeper probing of U.S. business is vital, Halberstam said, if we are to avoid letting the troubles of major industries, such as the decline in the quality of autos made in the U.S., go unexamined until it is too late. Newspapers, Halberstam warned, must begin to cover business with the same tough-mindedness they've reserved for government and politics.[69]

But what happens, Halberstam was asked, if newspapers—plagued by monopoly habits, an emphasis on product packaging over product quality, and a fixation on the bottom line—suffer from the same ills as the rest of American industry? Halberstam didn't have a ready answer. But he did challenge the gathering of journalists to remember that a nation that is slipping in the world economic order deserves a press that is more probing of that and other issues. As he told the business editors, "the nation demands it."

CHAPTER TWELVE

Fear and the Future of Newspapers

> The content of news and the terms in which it is written are undergoing changes similar to the old theological upheavals.
> —Ben Bagdikian, *The Information Machines*

> The electric technology is within the gates, and we are numb, deaf, blind, and mute about its encounter with the Gutenberg technology.
> —Marshall McLuhan, *Understanding Media*

> Technology opens doors, and oligopoly marches in just behind, slamming them.
> —Todd Gitlin, *Inside Prime Time*

> Journalists see change nowhere as evident as in journalism itself.
> —Mitchell Stephens, *A History of News*

RECENTLY, the readers of the *Kansas City Star* were treated to an intriguing new audio-electronic feature. In a box above a six-paragraph feature story about a rock band headed by Chicago White Sox pitcher Jack McDowell, readers were invited to dial a number to hear some of the band's music. Thirteen hundred people dialed into the *Star*'s audio "StarTouch" system to hear the brief samples of McDowell's songwriting, singing, and guitar playing.

These days boxed invitations abound as reporters at the *Star* strive to turn the newspaper into a "navigational tool" for readers using their telephones and computer modems to gain access to the *Star*'s new audio- and videotext systems. "We're turning this technology over to the newsroom," says Scott Whiteside, until recently the *Star*'s vice-president for new product development. "We've told them, 'You have the privilege of redefining journalism. Nobody has done this before.' "[1]

After decades of wringing their hands about the coming of the Information Age but doing little about it, daily newspaper executives are embarking on the "reinvention" of the daily newspaper, the newest buzzword in industry circles. The depth of the recession, the persistence of daily newspaper circulation problems, and the setbacks in their fight to keep the Bell companies out of the information delivery business have frightened newspaper executives and led to a new willingness to revamp the traditional mission of the daily newspaper that has remained virtually unchanged since the nineteenth century.

Thus far, the moves toward creating the newspaper of the future have been few and tentative. Newspapers' financial crisis has turned into a crisis of identity for the newspaper industry. While words like "innovation" and "entrepreneurship" have become the cry of today's newspaper executives, the reshaping of the traditional newspaper product is being accompanied by much confusion, uncertainty, and very little investment by an industry known for spending little money on research and development. However, newspaper companies are now moving, cautiously and tentatively, albeit with more and more enthusiasm every year, into a world where, media futurists predict, newspapers will become subsumed in multimedia communications systems, two-way interactive information networks, reader- and viewer-driven news, fiber optics and digital electronic information transmission, and tailored data bases.

Gannett's "News 2000" program is a case in point. As part of a plan to get Gannett's local newspapers to pay more attention to reader interests and community issues, Gannett editors are remaking their beat structures and restructuring their newsrooms to respond to perceived reader interests—a move some see as a transitional step between the reader-driven journalism of the 1980s and the electronic newspapering of the future.[2] Gannett has taken its cue from the *Orange County Register,* which shook up newspaper traditionalists with its switch to reader-friendly beats and its New Age approach to newsroom management, and from Knight-Ridder's experimental newspaper in Boca Raton, Florida, which demonstrated that even a company that had built its reputation on the winning of Pulitzer Prizes and the slogan that quality pays sees the future in reader-driven news formulas.[3] Newspapers are also experimenting once again with electronic newspapering—a field many journalists thought was dead when Knight-Ridder shut down its pioneering Viewtron videotext program in the early 1980s. Telephone info-lines have become so popular that syndicates are marketing them to newspapers, and more sophisticated telephone-access audiotext systems are springing up in Kansas City and elsewhere. Videotext systems are making a comeback in places like Albuquerque and Fort Worth, where Scripps Howard's *Albuquerque Tribune* and Capital Cities' *Fort Worth Star-Telegram* are making a go of modest, low investment videotext systems that give readers with computers access to electronically archived material that can't be fit into the daily newshole. However, the uncertainty of these new ventures is illustrated by the fact that the *Rocky Mountain News* and the

Omaha World-Herald recently shut down more ambitious and expensive videotext efforts, saying the demand for electronic newspapering in their markets isn't there yet.[4]

In fact, newspaper companies have jumped into new product development only as fast as the recession (and their bottom-line orientation) will allow. Gannett's new product development people are involved with marketing everything from a clothing line with *USA Today* logos to joining forces with Apple and the Associated Press in developing a multimedia news system delivered via the personal computer.[5] The "Edge of Knight-Ridder," an internal venture capital program, is developing a number of new newspaper-related products built around the company's electronic database services[6] while also planning for the day when the newspaper will be transmitted electronically through a portable, flat panel device that can be carried around like a magazine.[7] Meanwhile, newspaper executives are watching (nervously, in many cases) as new computer developments point toward the time when today's newspapers, television, computers, and the telephone will be blended together into one multimedia instrument.

Futurists say that all this is just the Information Age finally beginning to catch up with newspapers. Although the shape of tomorrow's media is still hazy, newspapers in print, they say, may become an obsolete form of information delivery. Paul Saffo, a research fellow at the Institute for the Future in Menlo Park, California, argues that paper is becoming outmoded as computers become society's principal way to store data. Despite the slowness of society to abandon paper, he notes that it usually takes about thirty years for a new technology to transform a society's main method of communication. "We'll become paperless like we became horseless," he says. "There are still horses. But little girls ride them."[8]

People shape the future, of course, by trying to anticipate it, and the future of newspapers will be influenced to a great degree by how today's newspaper executives size up the future and what they try to do about it. Amid all the flailing about as newspapers prepare for an uncertain tomorrow, three general strategies can be discerned: efforts to save the newspaper as it is, efforts to augment the newspaper electronically, and efforts to look beyond the newspaper in print.

The Future of the Newspaper As It Is

In recent years, front pages with more "points of entry" and "scannable" news, marketing programs developed in tandem with news departments, and "news-you-can-use" and reader-written features have proliferated. Sadly, newspaper executives cling to their belief in reader-oriented journalism with a near religious fervor even though there is little evidence that the focus on readers and the fixation on marketing, packaging, and redesigns associated with it has done much to improve newspapers' prospects.[9] Indeed, even the newspaper industry's own consultants now caution newspaper managers not to expect circulation growth from the adoption of reader-driven marketing formulas.[10]

As part of Knight-Ridder chairman James Batten's "customer obsession" campaign, the company's newspapers now perform two reader surveys a year and develop a "customer" plan to keep abreast of reader interests.[11] Ironically, the Boca Raton *News,* a key element of the campaign, has not prospered to the degree expected by its marketing-oriented editors. In 1991 the *News* dismissed two circulation managers after their departments allegedly overstated the newspaper's paid circulation—a sign of the pressure the newspaper is feeling to show results for Knight-Ridder.[12]

Journalists at Gannett newspapers have been told that their future depends on how well they adjust to the reader-driven changes coming from Gannett's "News 2000" program. However, the "News 2000" plan at the *Olympian* of Olympia, Washington—like at most other Gannett newspapers—was adopted without any new scientific research on what local readers really do want in their newspaper. The newspaper convened a few focus groups and asked readers to send in questionnaires. But the newspaper's plan, which called for a revamped format based upon brief, heavily packaged news items, extensive reader-service columns as well as redesigned coverage of community issues and themes and "news-you-can-use" data, looks suspiciously like a blueprint for the reader-friendly newspaper that has been promoted in such quarters as New Directions for News, the Poynter Institute, and Gannett headquarters.[13]

Despite the lack of in-depth research, Gannett executives defend "News 2000" as a way to respond to reader interests and the changing demographics of society. They say the program—promoted with a "news pyramid" designed at corporate headquarters to emphasize interaction with readers and information people need—has been tailored by local editors for their market and is not an attempt to impose a corporate vision on Gannett's local newspapers. Phil Currie, Gannett's vice-president/news, says "News 2000" is an acknowledgment by both the company and its editors that Gannett's newspapers must change to survive. Gannett hasn't abandoned the "idea that newspapers can work," as Currie puts it, but recognizes that "they have to work in different ways than they have" in the past.[14]

However, many Gannett employees object to the program as simply a company effort to apply the formulas used at *USA Today* at the local level. They say the program is the final jettisoning of any pretense of Gannett's once-vaunted policy of autonomy for its local newspapers. "News 2000," they complain, amounts to little more than a tightly engineered program of formula journalism. "We've always found a way around this corporate stuff, but this time I feel they've whipped us," says one veteran Gannett reporter. "They've whipped us into submission."

This same reporter also says its remarkable how smoothly the new format with its emphasis on short bursts of data and graphically oriented layouts can be transferred onto the computer screen. He sees the long-term impact of the program as ultimately phasing into Gannett's efforts at multimedia and electronic data delivery. "They're going to take all this—the glitz graphics and the three inch stories—and put it into a modem and send it into every home in town," he says. "I see this as the transition to telephonic newspapers."

The story of the 1980s was the way a new breed of market-oriented newsroom managers captured newsroom organization and—without doing much to alter the traditional hierarchical structure—added new layers of editors, graphic designers, market researchers, and human resources personnel. Now, these top-heavy and self-consciously managed systems are slowly being restructured to adapt to the new technologies making their way into newsrooms and to the new realities of a less profitable industry.

Susan Miller, Scripps Howard's vice-president/editorial, sees newspapers paying even more attention to marketing and readers—no matter where technology leads the industry. She predicts that the economics of the industry will lead to a thinning of midlevel management whose ranks were swollen as newspapers put more emphasis on the planning and packaging of the news product. She says the reader-driven and service-oriented newsroom of the future will contain fewer employees, and there will be more emphasis on teamwork and collaboration in the selection and presentation of the news. At the same time, Miller thinks that the leaner newsroom of the future will mean less bureaucracy and more power in the hands of frontline troops.[15]

Bill Baker, Knight-Ridder's vice-president/news, says many of the stresses on today's newsroom employees are the result of the industry's groping for answers in the 1980s—many of which didn't work out. He says newspaper companies' growing stress on innovation is also going to make entrepreneurial thinking in the newsroom more valued. He says a number of new information products being developed by "The

Edge of Knight-Ridder" program, for example, are the creations of long-time reporters who have "the appetite to follow through on them," as he puts it.[16]

Despite these optimistic prognostications, the pressures to plan and package the news product combined with the growing push for organizational control in corporate America leaves scant hope that newspaper managers will abandon the traditional hierarchy, give up power, or change their systems-oriented approach to management in any meaningful way. Even with today's emphasis on employee resource programs, the newspaper industry is not a good candidate to adopt the more flexible, employee-centered, bottom-up management approach that has spurred innovation in many high tech industries. Newspaper managers who have made their way up in a safe, monopolistic environment simply don't take easily to creative risk taking. The temptation to hire another consultant or do another readership survey or let an industry organization do the thinking for them will, in most cases, win out over cultivating their company's own ideas and then investing in them.

Ironically, improving the quality of the newspaper is the one strategy that too many newspapers have forgotten amid the news nuggets, readership surveys, and predictable, formula thinking that has come to dominate the industry. At the 1991 ANPA convention, for example, Tina Brown, the recently departed editor of *Vanity Fair* magazine, took the delegates to task for producing newspapers that are too bland and noncontroversial, copy television's ways, and are edited for people who don't read. She said the key to her magazine's success is the willingness to provide "extradimensional" news—the story behind the story, the repercussions of the story—that are presented in a human and dramatic fashion to lure the reader into long, in-depth stories. If there is no passion and vision in the news pages, she said, no amount of marketing or prettifying the news product is going to preserve a future for newspapers.[17]

Efforts to Augment the Newspaper with the Computer

Newspapers are making a marginal profit at best in their efforts to find an audience that wants access to an electronic menu of items, such as restaurant and movie reviews, expanded news stories, sports scores, advance classified ads, financial information, and public records. The most popular form of electronic access has been the telephone info-line, and newspapers like the *Kansas City Star* are integrating them into the full operation of the newspaper.[18] Videotext systems are still considered risky, but editors at the newspapers that have abandoned videotext as well as those that are pushing ahead agree that the market for electronic newspapering is growing. "The generation coming out of school who are very computer-oriented—these are the readers of tomorrow," says Gerry Barker, marketing director for the *Fort Worth Star-Telegram*'s "Startext" electronic newspaper, which has been in operation since 1984. "People have misjudged it. It's a social revolution that's happening out there. You can't throw dollars and technology at this and expect it to hatch. It's evolutionary. Just because we built a few Edsels doesn't mean the car is wrong."[19]

The editors of electronic newspapers, at least in these early stages, say they see their product as an enhancement, not a cannibalization, of the traditional newspaper in print. The editors at the *Albuquerque Tribune*'s "Electronic Trib," for example, say they offer products that don't duplicate what's in the news pages of the printed newspaper. They print the computer access number in the newspaper, and change it each day, so the electronic system is linked to the purchase of the printed newspaper.

David Carlsen, editor of the "Electronic Trib," doesn't believe an electronic newspaper means print journalists must make big adjustments in their approach to the job. The electronic version of the newspaper uses material from the newspaper's archives and wire services, and editors don't ask the staff to write anything special for the "Electronic Trib," Carlsen says. "I don't see the life of a reporter at the *Tribune* changing that much," he says.[20]

However, it is unlikely that electronic journalism won't ultimately change the environment for most newspaper journalists. Ideally, the advent of electronic newspapering could be a boon to in-depth reporting since the computer is capable of carrying details and expanded material that can't fit into the news columns. The newshole, shrunk at many newspapers by economic retrenchments, is suddenly unlimited in an electronic system, as Carlsen puts it. And this could encourage newspapers to expand their interest in specialized and enterprise reporting, which could be marketed to readers willing to pay for it.

And yet as electronic news becomes more important to a newspaper, the work of newspaper reporters will almost certainly become more update-oriented as electronic systems give newspaper customers access to news and information at any minute of the day. At the *Kansas City Star*, for example, reporters are asked to find or record sound bites and to look for supplemental data for the newspaper's audio- and videotext systems.[21] And new technologies in the newsgathering and newspaper printing business—along with the growing premium on quick-hit, easy-to-summarize information offered by electronic information services—could make newspaper reporting jobs more like those of their broadcasting counterparts. The work of newspaper reporters "will become much more real time than it is today," predicts Terry Maguire, senior vice-president of the American Newspaper Publishers Association. "Rather than once a 24-hour snapshot, we'll see the journalists participating in the continuing unfolding of the news for the reader."[22]

Many analysts blame the failure of early efforts at videotext on newspapers' attempts to transfer the newspaper in print too literally onto the computer. Knight-Ridder and other companies backed off from the marketing of their videotext operations when pilot programs showed customers resisting the high cost of the system and the awkwardness of having to scroll electronically through material. The success of the companies that have plunged ahead into electronic information systems has largely been due to the creation of interactive networks and their creativity in the treatment of the computer as a unique communications device. The experience of the pioneers in electronic data delivery indicates that many people prefer to use computers to communicate with each other rather than to sort through prepared information. In fact, early signs indicate that electronic newspapering is only likely to accelerate the trend toward reader-driven news.

Richard Baker, the director of corporate communication for CompuServe, a twenty-two-year-old computer communications company with more than nine hundred thousand customers, says the key to CompuServe's success has been the development of customized information and interactive bulletin boards for users who want to communicate with each other. "The newspaper's approach to news has to change in order to be successful in transmitting information electronically," Baker says. "Newspapers and magazines have to embrace the concept of sharing the creation of the news. There needs to be a willingness and openness to let the readers have a much greater hand in determining what's the news."[23]

In the near future, computer advances may actually stave off some of the more drastic prognostications for the newspaper in print. Already computers and new developments in satellite communications have allowed newspapers like the *New York Times* and *USA Today* to become national newspapers. Small and weekly newspapers, newsletters, and target-marketed publications, helped by the new computer desktop technology, have continued to flourish, and entrepreneurs seem to spring up almost daily as they try to exploit market niches that aren't covered in-depth by daily newspapers.

As with so many other businesses in an era of conglomerates and rapidly developing technology, the trend seems to be that the big get bigger, smaller operations bloom, and midsized companies are caught in the squeeze. That means midsize newspapers in medium-size markets will continue to feel the squeeze both from the national newspapers and the smaller publications that exist under their circulation umbrella. That explains in part why so many daily newspapers are putting such a big emphasis on local news and suburban coverage, including the proliferation of zoned suburban editions and the rebirth of "chicken dinner" local coverage that dropped out of newspapers for a time during the 1960s and 1970s. It also explains why daily newspapers, many of which have long published their own free shoppers and direct mail publications, are continuing to try to branch out by launching new publications of various kinds.[24]

In fact, as daily newspaper readership rates keep falling, there are those who believe that the best market in the future may be for the "tailored" newspaper aimed at better-educated, affluent segments of the market sought by advertisers. Computer automation may soon lead to the advent of newspapers that are distributed by "psychographical" rather than geographical zoning, as one ASNE report puts it.[25] This could mean newspapers that provide each subscriber with a package that contains the basic newspaper, the locally zoned edition, and whatever special interest sections a customer wants to buy. The "tailored" newspaper is expected to be made possible by such new technologies as full-page pagination, storage of pages on erasable laser disks, the use of lasers to burn page images on reusable press cylinders, sophisticated new mailroom systems, and satellite delivery of full-page images.

And yet the advances in computer technology have been viewed as a threat, as much as a boon, by many executives of the newspaper industry. Newspapers, for the most part, have resisted becoming all-service information companies while furiously fighting the efforts by telephone companies to enter the electronic data transmission business. Newspaper executives see the experience of the French Minitel organization, which gives telephone users in France access to telephone directories and a variety of interactive and communications services via minicomputers, as the model for how the telephone companies may use their monopoly powers to move in on newspapers' most lucrative business. However, while newspapers have lost court battle after court battle to the Baby Bells, a company like Prodigy, the IBM-

Sears consortium, has stepped into the market void left by daily newspapers, which have shown little interest in marketing electronic access to their news and information, data bases, or libraries.

Futurists chide the newspaper industry for expending so much effort fighting the Bell companies instead of jumping into the electronic information business themselves.[26] But newspaper traditionalists, who cringe at the idea of newspapers delivered via computer, shouldn't take great comfort in the newspaper industry's slow entry into the electronic data business. Communications historians note that older forms of communication technologies have always tried to forestall new communications advances. When those efforts have failed, as they invariably do, the traditional media are quick to link up with their former adversaries.

As newspaper companies lose faith in other efforts to revive the business, even the deepest sentimentality for ink on paper is unlikely to stop them from evolving away from the concept of the daily newspaper as it has traditionally been known. In fact, everything ultimately argues for a partnership between newspapers and the telephone companies—something that may already be happening. For example, the *Seattle Times,* whose publisher, Frank Blethen, has been one of the loudest critics of the Baby Bells, recently announced that the *Times* was negotiating to team up with USWest to be a data provider on the telephone company's information network.[27]

The Paperless Newspaper

With the coming developments in electronic data delivery, many newspaper futurists believe the newspaper in print faces a perilous future. They say videotext operations and the new computer pagination systems—where newspaper pages are fully designed and laid out on the computer screen—are simply crude, first steps toward the multimedia systems that will come to dominate the information industry. In software systems that are already on the market, computer users can pull from the computer's memory a variety of audio-visual material—including printed text, mobile graphics, video images, music, special effects—that let users create their own multimedia productions.[28]

These developments combined with the advances in computer-transmitted television present enormous implications for both newspapers and broadcasters. Digital broadcasting—where images are transmitted in a code used by computers rather than in analog waves now transmitted to television sets—promises to provide a truly multimedia system where text, graphics, and video images can all be transmitted to the computer screen. It doesn't take a rocket scientist to see that this development will increase the pressures to blend the now separate media forms, and companies in the U.S. and Japan have been hurrying digital technology to the marketplace much faster than many predicted.

Knight-Ridder officials are planning for the day—which they see arriving in this decade—when these blended media products will be available on a pocket-sized, mobile, flat display panel, and the newspaper can be dialed up on a miniature screen where stories are magnified at a touch.[29] With this technology, newspaper companies could find themselves in a ratings war of sorts for viewer attention against broadcast companies and other electronic competitors on other channels. In this environment, will newspapers become more like broadcast stations? Or will television become more like newspapers? Or will some kind of hybrid product emerge triumphant?

Roger Fidler, the director of new media development for Knight-Ridder, predicts a "bright future" for the "essence" of the newspaper and says he doesn't believe that the electronic tomorrow will fundamentally alter the job of newspaper journalists. But he acknowledges that the multimedia environment is likely to mean a reduced role for newspapers in print. "I don't see print disappearing," he says. "But I see it taking a different form. The question is not whether there will be newspapers in the next century, but who will publish them. I'm not convinced the majority of the newspaper companies today will be in business in the next century."[30]

In fact, many communications conglomerates, now integrated across newspaper and broadcast divisions, are well structured to take advantage of the multimedia developments. The much talked about 1989 merger of Time, Inc., and Warner Communications could signal the beginning of a trend where nonmedia conglomerates move into the news publication field, as General Electric with its takeover of NBC has done in television. Time executives justified the merger on the ground that by the mid-1990s, the media and entertainment industry will be composed of a limited number of global companies, and they wanted to be one.[31] But others saw the merger as a symbol on the business level of the merger of news and entertainment that has already occurred with much media content. Even the critics of the deal gloomily acknowledge that the future of the media business probably lies in the direction of the vertically integrated media-and-entertainment companies. These companies already have the capacity to do it all—develop the product, market the product, and write about the product in the news pages—as the entertainment, promotion, and news business blend into one. Madonna's enormous contract with Time-Warner is a good example of the mega-hype transforming the traditions that once kept news organizations separate from the celebrities they cover.[32]

Still, as they peer into a tomorrow of global media conglomerates and vast interlocking electronic information networks, newspaper traditionalists should be reassured by how stubbornly newspaper companies are clinging to the traditional concept of the newspaper in print. No matter what the new product—whether it is videotext or multimedia systems or new data base products—newspaper executives say their plan is to find ways to "leverage" the traditional newspaper, as Knight-Ridder's Baker puts it, into a stronger position and to produce a richer blend of information products to insure that the newspaper in print doesn't have to go it alone in the new information environment.[33]

At the same time, newspaper companies are chided by critics who claim that newspapers' loyalty to ink on paper is too strong. New technologies offer both dangers and challenges, they say, and newspapers often seem blind to both. Even if they want to change, many people, including industry insiders, are skeptical that newspapers will be able to adapt quickly enough to stave off economic peril. "We keep saying 'be entrepreneurial,' " says newspaper consultant Christine Urban. "But there are fundamental neurological synapses that entrepreneurs use that may be absent in some newspaper people."[34]

So what will it be like to be a journalist in the brave, new world of electronic information? The minimalistic journalism brought about by reader-friendly newspapering and other forms of marketplace journalism have done much to undermine journalism's higher purpose and to turn news into just another commodity in the marketplace. And as newspapers join the electronic competition, newspaper journalists are likely to find themselves ever more subject to the forces of constant technological change, the demands of perpetually updating the news for electronic services, and the pressures to think of their work more and more in marketing terms.

Unfortunately, the information anxiety that is causing much dejection in the newsroom isn't likely to abate. As with many other professions in the go-go 1980s, marketing and the bottom line have become the bywords of newspapering, and new information technologies offer much to encourage that trend. Fear and uncertainty are compelling factors in a field where editors are seeing robots in the backshop, interactive television, voice-activated computers, and a flood of new electronic data delivery technologies inundating the market. A world that has always changed under their feet now seems to be in permanent upheaval. In the years ahead, newspaper companies and newspaper professionals can probably expect to bump up and down on a rocky ride of diminished profit margins, failed efforts at experimentation, and intrusions into their markets.

That's the potential dark side. But there are also reasons to be optimistic. The endless newshole promised by computers does offer an answer to the ever shrinking news columns and could hold hope for journalists who have grown frustrated by the economic retrenchments and design gimmicks that have increasingly circumscribed the life of those who produce the text. Newspapers have always been at the base of the information pyramid, providing much of the in-depth information that is then compressed and marketed by the electronic information purveyors. As the explosion of information continues, there will be even more need for highly skilled journalists to dig through it, filter out what's important, and help put it into perspective. The demand for more specialty reporting skills, the opportunities for more creative and analytical writing, and the chance to use data bases to do more sophisticated investigative reporting are all potential upsides of electronic newspapering.

Newspaper journalists should also take heart in the fact that virtually none of those who gaze into newspapering's future are predicting the near-term demise of the newspaper in print. Technology so far has been unable to match the efficient way the eye can scan the newspaper page or the way newspapers can be folded up and carried around—or the way a newspaper can be read over coffee and bagels on a Sunday morning.

Journalists should be encouraged by the way newspaper companies' top executives are talking about how they must capitalize on the newspaper's strengths if they are going to survive in the new Information Age. And the newspapers' strengths are many, and most of them promise to give newspapers a big edge in a multimedia environment. Newspapers, in most instances, have bigger and better newsgathering staffs than their broadcast counterparts—or any of the other potential electronic competitors for that matter. Newspapers understand their local or their speciality markets. And newspapers can offer an intelligent voice in a world where the cacophony of other media seems to be drowning the public in noise it doesn't want to hear. "There are things about a newspaper that are attuned to the human spirit, and it'll be there forever," predicts Knight-Ridder's Baker.[35]

CHAPTER THIRTEEN

Fighting the Good Fight Within

Speak truth to power.   —Old Quaker saying

It's tougher to admit openly that you're frustrated about your ambitions to change the world.. . . . When you become alienated from your calling, that's a really severe problem.
—David Hawpe, editor of the *Courier-Journal* in Louisville, about journalists leaving the business

You can find out more in one night of drinking with the capital press corps than you do in six months of reading daily papers. Straight journalists know but don't tell. The establishment structure keeps them from it.
—Molly Ivins, columnist, the *Fort Worth Star-Telegram*

The newsroom is not nirvana. . . . But the organizations for which journalists work need not make them intellectual or ethical eunuchs, at least not without individual consent.
—Ed Lambeth, *Committed Journalism*

PAUL HENDERSON is just the kind of reporter—intense, streetwise, a righter-of-wrongs knowledgeable about everything from the police beat to the complex workings of government—that the newspaper business, or at least the newspaper business of myth and lore, wants in the newsroom.

And when Henderson won the Pulitzer Prize in 1982 for a series in the *Seattle Times* that exonerated a man unjustly convicted of rape, a series that, through dogged digging into court records and determined probing into questionable police tactics, raised the traditional craft of police reporting to an investigative art, he was hailed by those who believed in the time-honored tradition of the journalist-as-pursuer-of-justice.

However, three years later, Henderson was out of the newspaper business and running his own private detective agency. Within weeks of winning the Pulitzer Prize, he had clashed with the new breed of managers at the *Times* who wouldn't tolerate his crusader's temperament, his maverick lifestyle, and his independent work habits. "It wasn't the best time for someone like me to win a Pulitzer Prize," Henderson says. "The *Times* was in transition and management wasn't going to tolerate reporters who did things their own way. The working environment was becoming oppressive—regimented, almost militarized. . . . From my perspective, management was hell-bent to take the fun away. It was starting to seem like a corporate sweatshop."

Henderson, whose twenty-three-year reporting career was modelled on the *Front Page* tradition of the hard-driving, hard-drinking reporter, admits he wasn't the best candidate to survive the new MBA-style journalism. "I think they really would have liked to reform me," he says. "But I didn't reform too well."[1]

Henderson discovered—as many have before him—that the career of a newspaper reporter isn't necessarily a smooth or comfortable one. Even long before the advent of modern, market-driven journalism, newspaper reporting, with its stresses, deadlines, and the constant risk of burnout, wasn't a profession where it was easy to grow old gracefully. While people in professions such as law or medicine can expect to be treated with greater respect as they gain seniority and experience, newspaper reporters often work for employers who believe that the reporting business—with its ever ready supply of young journalists eager to work for low wages—is a young person's profession. The professionalization of newspapering has improved the situation at a few, top-quality newspapers and for correspondents in Washington, D.C., and overseas bureaus. But at most newspapers, newsworkers who don't move up into management or leave to take jobs outside the business face the prospect of ending up "hunched and broken" over the copy desk, to borrow a phrase from the movie *Front Page*.

Even before MBAs arrived to restructure newsroom management, reporters had to live with the tensions of a business that tended to attract strong-willed and ego-driven people and then organized them into a bureaucracy to do their work. Back in 1973, Leon Sigal captured that frustration when he quoted *New York Times* veteran reporter Homer Bigart's timeless observation, "I never read my stories in the paper any more. It's a safe way to avoid ulcers. You can't win. You finally come to the point where you either have to take it or quit. People have tried to fight back, but they get nowhere. You can't beat newspaper bureaucracy any more than you can beat any other kind of bureaucracy."[2]

The new corporate managers have put their own imprint on this formula, but it is still a tough business to be a newspaper reporter today, and in many ways it is tougher than before. The "creative tension" in today's MBA newsroom can make for an eat-or-be-eaten atmosphere, says William Davis, a Guild officer at the Knight-Ridder owned *San Jose Mercury News.* "They want people climbing all over each other," he says of Knight-Ridder's management philosophy. "They say, 'you know, the cream rises to the top. One out of ten of you will make it.' The other nine, if they are ragged and bloody, well 'we'll just kick them out the door and replace them.' They're turning newspapers into a Wall Street operation. . . . It's become a cutthroat business."[3]

Of course, the frustrated, bitching, disillusioned reporter is a stereotype of the business—and editors will say that no one can outdo reporters in their collective belief that the world is in conspiracy against them. Still, there is substance to the laments of journalists that today's MBA-type managers aren't just bringing marketing principles to the business but are eroding the idealism and undermining the traditional values of the profession.

In this era of corporate journalism, the stories are "very safe, very predictable, homogenized journalism for the most part," says Michael Wagner, an investigative reporter now with the *Sacramento Bee.* "You're talking about a finite universe of people who are proud of what they're doing, who feel like they're following the American journalistic dream. And it's a shrinking universe."[4]

Many journalists are finding it tougher to question authority out in the world when they are being pressured to become loyal corporate soldiers inside their organizations. To fit into the newspaper's design and packaging needs, preplanning is essential and reporters are expected to fulfill their role within the system dutifully and without complaint. Editors who need to allot space in the news pages well in advance prefer stories that are predictable, come in with plenty of lead time, and fit the preconceptions that have already been discussed in editorial meetings. Packaging takes coordination among graphic artists, photographers, page designers—and a reporter's work often proves to be little more than grist for the design team's mill. In this system, it's easy to find the reporter reduced to a researcher, a gatherer of information, a functionary in the plan-package-and-market-the-newspaper bureaucracy. No matter how fervent their protests, the lives of newsworkers have become increasingly circumscribed by performance standards and management systems designed to insure greater productivity, by bosses trained in the new techniques of scientific management, by readership research and surveys, and by editors who have joined the marketing team. "This system has nothing to do with journalism," says Ivan Weiss, a veteran wire editor at the *Seattle Times*. "It has everything to do with bureaucratic control, and bureaucratic control is the enemy of all journalists."[5]

The pain felt by newsworkers in these circumstances has been magnified by the swift transition from the 1970s, when journalists—drawing their sustenance from the protest and the antiestablishment feelings of the time—actually promoted "reporter power" movements, pushed for more democracy in the newsroom, and identified with the dissenters in the streets.[6] Investigative reporting blossomed in newspapers both large and small in the aftermath of the Watergate scandal—almost to the point that, as press critic Irving Kristol charged, the press had become "pathological" in its negative attitude toward government and large institutions.[7]

In fact, the phrase "adversary journalism"—used proudly by reporters to describe their activities during the years before and after Watergate—has become almost a dirty term to newspaper executives in the conservative atmosphere of the Reagan-Bush years. The movement away from adversary journalism was well illustrated at a 1983 gathering of the Investigative Reporters and Editors organization, of all places. There a number of editors complained that investigative reporting had lost much of its public support by going after minor targets, abusing the use of unidentified sources, and indulging in an "awesome and asinine assortment of sins," as Frank McCulloch, then McClatchy executive editor, put it. "We have become too full of ourselves," McCulloch told the group. "We have been arrogant. We have been rude. We have been elitist. We have been inaccurate. We have been insensitive. We have been unfair. . . . We sometimes get so caught up in the pursuit of a quarry that we lose all sense of scale and proportion."[8]

With that kind of self-flagellation from an advocate of investigative reporting, it's easy to see why investigative reporting waned during the Reagan years. In a 1981 speech, Bob Porterfield, a Pulitzer Prize winning investigative reporter at both the *Anchorage Daily News* and the *Boston Globe*, complained that newspapers, and particularly chain-owned newspapers, were keeping reporters busy with routine coverage and were unwilling to give them the time to do serious probing. "The volume of hard investigative journalism has dropped off considerably," Porterfield said. "There was a real increase in investigative reporting after the Watergate stories, but now a lot of newspapers are not really making the commitment."[9]

The backlash against the aggressive and freewheeling journalism of the 1970s, while not directly attributable to the move toward MBA-style management of the newsroom in the 1980s, has certainly been reinforced by it. Newspaper executives who are fixated on the market-place are going to be more reluctant to offend. In fact, it is easy for newspaper executives schooled in the art of pleasing readers—and advertising managers and marketing directors and money-managers from corporate headquarters—to simply lose the habit of upsetting anyone. Clearly, the goals of the corporate journalism of the 1980s and 1990s have proved to be incompatible with a style of journalism that has the avowed purpose of shaking up the establishment.

In his book, *Last Stand,* former *Missoulian* reporter Richard Manning describes how a team of Lee executives arrived in the Montana town one night to quite literally redesign the newspaper into a mini-version of *USA Today.* [10] In short order, Manning says, a "subversive" reporter like himself, whose hard-hitting coverage of abusive logging practices by the timber industry had raised hackles, found himself pulled off his beat by his Lee editors—and he quit. As he put it,

> My bosses and the newspaper business in general had banished the sense of purpose that had initially attracted me. Instead, the spirit of journalism had become identical to that of cutting trees, selling shoes, and running the nation's savings and loans. . . . Corporate journalism had no room for troublemakers, especially if that trouble accrues on the desks of fellow MBAs. . . . One cannot ask questions, as reporters are trained and bound to do, without causing trouble. And one cannot ask questions without sooner or later tasting hemlock. [11]

As long ago as 1970, Carey McWilliams, the long-time muckraking editor of the magazine the *Nation,* identified the modern marketing movement among publications as a major threat to investigative reporting. [12] And editors, like much of the rest of society, may have simply grown exhausted from the social tensions of the 1960s and 1970s. In a time of laissez-faire politics and social and moral retrenchment, intrepid journalism simply hasn't been in fashion. "You don't see a lot of Watergate-inspired stories in papers in the U.S. anymore," says John Kolesar, now retired from his last job as managing editor of Gannett's *Courier-Post* in Cherry Hill, New Jersey. "I guess the editors are like the readers: they've apparently changed the kinds of stories they like. They'd rather read about sugarless desserts than about the Democrats who have padded the payroll in the courthouse." [13]

The market-minded editors of today wouldn't put it so bluntly, but they may have unconsciously decided, as Curtis MacDougall quotes one New Jersey editor of many years ago, that reform simply isn't worth the price:

> Crusading is a rich man's game. . . . You lose advertising, you lose circulation, you even lose prestige. . . . No one gives a damn! The friends appreciate the service you have done for a few minutes, and then forget it immediately and completely. But the enemies you have made never forget. . . . I have discovered that the people hate a crusader and love a pussyfooter. Since I adopted my new policy of barring crusading, everything is running along smoothly and without any fuss or bother. . . . Everybody slaps you on the back and says you're a good fellow. We just shut our eyes to everything, and then everybody's happy.[14]

And yet the reform spirit—largely dormant as it may be today—continues to lie at the root of the journalistic tradition. In his now classic study of *Time, Newsweek,* CBS-TV and NBC-TV, Herbert Gans found "reformist" views to be at the core of journalists' "enduring values," which he associates with the Progressive movement of the early twentieth century. Gans maintains that journalists as a group aren't strongly liberal or conservative, in a traditionally partisan sense, but they do hold many of the values of the Progressives: an advocacy of honest, meritocratic, and antibureaucratic government, an antipathy to political machines and demagogues, a dislike of bigness, and a belief in responsible capitalism. "When journalists are unwilling to describe themselves as liberal or conservative, and prefer to see themselves as independents, they may be sensing, if not with complete awareness, that they are, as a profession, Progressive reformers," Gans says.[15]

Conservatives have been effective in portraying these reform instincts as something dangerously liberal and a threat to the social order. Conservative scholars—like Robert and Linda Lichter and Stanley Rothman—have found a ready audience for their view that journalists' liberalism, elitism, and antiauthoritarian attitudes alienate them from the rest of the country. In their study, *The Media Elite,* the Lichters and Rothman argue that social control inside the newsroom isn't what it once was and that the reins of power are no longer in the hands of publishers. As a result, they say, the upper class liberalism of journalists and their hostility toward government now permeate journalism.[16]

The top executives of newspapers—not exactly leftist radicals themselves—were easy to convince. After all, if market forces rule the day—and readers voted for Ronald Reagan and George Bush's free market philosophy in large numbers in the 1980s—it was a logical next step for newspaper executives to become ever more deferential in their coverage of the capitalist institutions that conservatives so revere.

Still, despite periods of exhaustion and cynicism, progressive values and the reform instinct do flicker (if sometimes faintly) in the hearts of journalists. Those who accuse journalists of harboring a point of view because they don't believe in pure objectivity, in moral neutrality, in total disengagement from social issues are in many cases right. The most aggressive journalists usually believe in being fair-minded and evenhanded and impartial—but only up to the point where crusading is called for. After all, Finley Peter Dunne's proper definition of the journalist as someone who comforts the afflicted and afflicts the comfortable is hardly a politically neutral one. Whether it's labeled investigative journalism or advocacy journalism or adversary journalism, many journalists do view themselves—self-appointed as they may be—as the conscience of the community. As Mitchell Stephens points out, the oldest traditions of American journalism are those of rabble-rousing, dissent, and caustic commentary. " 'Minds and hearts' were not turned to revolution in America by newspapers that struggled to find a balancing quote from George III," Stephens says.[17]

Yet newspapers weren't owned by large conglomerates and run by their marketing-minded editors in the days of the American Revolution. Editors who advocated rebellion from England were giving readers what they wanted to read, but they were also willing to risk all for a principle. The issue of conscience for today's corporate editor seems to be, as the *Seattle Times*'s executive editor Michael Fancher puts it, whether "journalistic quality" and a "marketplace orientation" are compatible. He concludes that they are, of course. And Fancher's other worry? What to do about those journalists who don't embrace this concept—who feel that newspapers must have "a special social commitment" and "be more than a banner waving in the marketplace wind?" Fancher leaves this question unanswered.[18]

One suspects that the embers of reform will continue to glow in the soul of today's journalists, and those reformers will continue to be irksome to their own news organizations, as they have been in the past. Long before the advent of MBA journalism, newspaper organizations had ways—some formal but most informal—of keeping would-be activists in check inside the newsroom. A long line of academic scholarship confirms that reporters do operate under constraints, many of them subtly but intentionally imposed within the newspaper organization in order to keep reporters in line.[19] The work of many scholars who have examined newsroom behavior can be summed up in the saltier language of Hillier Krieghbaum:

> Most media executives do not have to compile a so-called "shit list";
> the always-present desire to please the boss exists among a vast

majority of those on any payroll. It all may be rather subtle but it doesn't have to be outlined in office memoranda. And the concept that one can always quit if too much professional misconduct is asked in return for salary, may be better in theory than in practice, especially if one has a wife, two children in college, and a large mortgage.[20]

Scholars of journalism never cease to take pleasure in pointing out that companies in the business of making a profit—as newspapers most definitely are—aren't likely to attack the basic premises of the economic system. Media scholars like Herbert Gans, Gaye Tuchman, Michael Schudson, and James Carey have been particularly fascinated with how the principle of "objectivity" has allowed newspapers to hide their biases, their economic motives, and the myth of a benign capitalism behind a "scientific" presentation of the news.[21] Ever since Walter Lippmann wrote that news is "precise in proportion to the precision with which the event is recorded,"[22] communications theorists have been picking apart the view that anyone, but particularly journalists, can "bring to light the hidden facts" and pinpoint the true nature of things in an objective, unbiased manner, a power Lippman himself reserved only for "experts" working in independent government agencies.

David Paletz and Robert Entman portray the media as a key pillar in the maintenance of the status quo. The media's routines are deeply imbued with "consensus values and elite perceptions," they say, and the media "bend into conformity" any threats to the social order by the way they cover conflict and dissent. "Journalists work in bureaucratic organizations characterized by hierarchy, division of labor, and routinization of working operations through relatively standardized rules and procedures," they say. "The purpose is efficiency in the gathering, describing, and transmitting of news. . . . The result: packs and reliance on official sources."[23]

Douglas Birkhead goes so far as to say that journalists aren't true professionals because they've never developed a professional ethic that is distinct from the business needs of their employers. Birkhead argues that what journalists consider their professional values—objectivity, detachment, performance on deadline—are really little more than tools management uses to control reporters in the newsroom. By avoiding value judgments and maintaining a "disinterested" view of the world, reporters retain their integrity in only the narrowest, technical sense, he says. As a result, corporate objectives become sanctified as the profession's ends and values.[24] Even the idealism that underlies the profession and its tradition of social reform are dismissed by media critics who say this is little more than a way the system lets journalists vent steam. As J. Herbert Altschull describes it,

> Nothing gratifies the individual journalist more than a successful challenge to power, even as Don Quixote rejoiced in tilting at windmills. There is built into journalism the *possibility* of inducing change and of helping to create a world that is more just and more peaceful; it is this possibility that has fired and continues to fire the imagination of journalists everywhere on earth. Political and especially economic reality, however, severely circumscribes these possibilities.[25]

Scholarly studies of the newspaper business can leave a hollow feeling inside the working journalist (or the ex-journalist, for that matter). For one thing, scholars always seem to get such satisfaction in exploding myths, such as the belief in objectivity, that most journalists long ago discarded in favor of more realistic standards like "fairness" and "impartiality." Secondly, the cynical view of reporters as manipulated and self-deluded puppets of their bosses—or "agents for others," in the scholarly language of Edward Jay Epstein[26]—is not only unflattering but, for many of the best journalists, untrue. Journalists, more than anyone, are aware of the constraints under which they work. But the realities of work life mean that many reporters find a way to do good work at the newspaper where they are employed whether or not that newspaper concurs with their idea of what good journalism is. Few journalists are so fortunate to report, as does *Washington Post* political writer David Broder, that never in his career has he had a story censored or bent to commercial dictates within the newspaper. "As a hired hand, I am not sure I can explain this remarkable forbearance," he says. All of his editors, he adds, "seemed to accept that with great influence went great responsibility."[27]

Of course, Broder stretches modesty by calling himself a hired hand. Not only is he a Pulitzer Prize winner and a nationally recognized political columnist, but he works for one of the wealthiest newspapers in the country, which (quite literally) can afford its high principles. Broder should hardly find it a surprise that as one of America's most distinguished journalists he has always been treated well by his employer. He also seems conveniently to forget a publicized and somewhat nasty dispute with his editors over political coverage when he resigned from the *New York Times* many years ago.[28]

So how do reporters survive in a business that, unless they are lucky enough to become David Broders, may promise them a short and tension-filled career, a workplace where market principles take precedence over journalistic ones, and an environment where their values are increasingly being circumscribed by the profit margins? There is no simple answer, of course. The simplest ethic, and one subscribed to in principle by many reporters, is outlined by John Merrill, whose ideal journalist "resists all controls; he observes the law, rendering unto Caesar what is Caesar's, but morally he is his own man. Even his boss can't touch him. . . . Freedom can be preserved only if that lonely journalist is unfettered, acting on the basis of his own 'reason, sensitivity, and commitment.' "[29]

Merrill's vision of the reporter's role is an attractive one—and it is one many of us have held as an ideal. However, as Paul Henderson and others of us have learned, the "lonely" journalist often isn't left alone with his or her conscience in this world of aggressive management, planned-and-packaged news, and the closely monitored workplace. Reporters increasingly find themselves facing editors, like the *Seattle Times*'s Fancher, whose motto, as he opened his article in the *Gannett Center Journal,* is "change or be changed."[30]

Basically, I suppose, conscientious journalists may simply have to renew what has always been an age-old adage for the good journalist: fight on, both inside and outside the organization. In an era when the bottom line limits the vision of so many newsroom managers, it's more important than ever for reporters to remember that they shouldn't define their job only the way their bosses define it for them. This means that reporters may find themselves not only doing battle with the bureaucrats, the politicians, and the public relations wizards on the outside, but they may need to struggle mightily against the management systems within their own newsroom. Determined reporters have always worked at two levels: one level to keep the company off their backs, the other to pursue the stories that they know are valuable and important to the public. This may mean that a reporter won't be deemed a "team-player"—but that, in the end, may be the price of committed journalism. As witnessed by much of the guilty, uncomfortable talk at gatherings of news executives, many editors are not *proud* of their new-found market orientation. And they are likely to accept, even if at times grudgingly, the reporter who is motivated to go beyond the packaged version of events, to dig deeper, and to come up with the real story.

Kent MacDougall explains how even a radical journalist can work within the establishment structure to get stories that challenge the status quo into the newspaper. The traditions of the news business, he says, make it possible, even at editorially conservative newspapers like the *Wall Street Journal* and the *Los Angeles Times,* where he worked, to cover topics that run counter to mainstream thinking as long as those stories stay within the standards of fairness and acceptable reporting methodology.[31] Few reporters are avowed socialists like MacDougall, but many do share his interest in covering the plight of the underprivileged, the views of dissenters, and the generally unexamined assumptions about the way the economic system works. At most newspapers, reporters usually still have some latitude about what stories they cover. Wiliness in how to cover a controversial topic, a tactful choice of words and phrasing in writing the article, and a portion of outright determination to make the internal newsroom bureaucracy work to their advantage can get reporters a long way. Editors—even the most market-minded editors—are seldom going to spurn an excellent piece of journalism, no matter what the topic. As Michael Schudson says, "Enterprise journalism, like interpretive reporting, may have its traditions and may have its rewards, but it will not have its handbooks. It requires mature subjectivity; subjectivity tempered by encounters with, and regard for, the views of significant others in the profession; and subjectivity aged by encounters with, and regard for, the facts of the world. There is no text for this."[32]

Frustrated reporters, of course, can always quit—and many do. But an honest examination of one's conscience (an examination that the conscientious reporter does regularly throughout a career, if not everyday) will probably convince most reporters that if they still have the fire and the drive and the love of the business left within them, there is no better place, despite the compromises, to make a difference than in the mainstream press. The purity of purpose in point of view journals and the alternative press—and there are fewer of these "pure" publications around, too, as market pressures seep in everywhere—is always an attractive option. So is the angry journalist's fantasy of founding his or her own publication, which desktop technology is making an increasingly realistic possibility, or the tired journalist's dream of going off to some idyllic location and editing a small weekly. In a fundamentally romantic profession, there is always a fantasy to pursue. But carrying on within the mainstream press is not necessarily the futile task that critics and scholars of the press would have us believe. As Carey McWilliams puts it, "reform journalists may not be 'movers and shakers,' but they do edge the world along a bit, they do get an innocent man out of jail occasionally, and they do win a round now and then—sometimes a significant round."[33]

The movement toward marketplace journalism has made the job of the reform-minded reporter, which has always been difficult, more difficult. But the journalism of the last twenty years has also brought plusses for reporters—better salaries (in some places), a stronger professional ethic, higher social status, better training and education, and enhanced respect (even from some editors) for expertise and specialty skills.[34] Editors, too, are a more sophisticated breed—even if their sophistication includes knowledge of the "realities" of the marketplace that many reporters wish wouldn't quite so absorb them. But editors aren't a monolithic bunch. And much of the marketing propaganda of the industry is viewed as skeptically by some editors as it is by their newsroom employees. Whether it's in service to readers, or advertisers, or survey researchers, or the marketing department, serious journalism will collapse if journalists give up and declare themselves simply Epstein's "agents for others." "Any given year's crop of investigative journalism will refute such an assertion," says Ed Lambeth. "The point, in fact, is that journalists, as a group, have enough professional competence and enough moral freedom to fully face and accept the responsibilities implied by the constitutional protection granted them."[35]

CHAPTER FOURTEEN

The Future
of the Word

Newspaper work is valuable up until the point
that it forcibly begins to destroy your memory.
A writer must leave it before that point.
—Ernest Hemingway, discussing his experience on the *Kansas City Star*

Sometime in the early 1970s, newspaper reporters started thinking of themselves as writers. But their job is to dig out information that
somebody has asked for. We're in the reporting
business. If you want to write, go work for a
book! —Philip McLeod, editor of the *London
(Ontario) Free Press*

Words were imbued with power. The names of
gods were part of the essence of being, and the
influence of the scribe was reflected in the
deities.
—Harold Innis, describing Egyptian culture in
Empire and Communications

With this young generation, everything is image and impression. The written word is no
longer very important to them. . . . We're going
to have to adjust.
—Joseph McGuff, recently retired editor of the
Kansas City Star

NEWSPAPERS aren't the only place where the printed word is under
assault. With the publishing industry increasingly a bottom-line, mass-
marketing venture, writers—particularly good, serious fiction and non-
fiction writers—have fewer outlets for their efforts. The best of our arts
and opinion magazines, where fine prose and deft argument are still
prized, struggle on in an ever more crowded marketplace of trade
journals, specialty magazines, and slick target-marketed publications.
Small literary magazines try to carry on the tradition of poetry and
short stories, but for the most part few people read them. Book publishing, once a cultured, family-owned business, has come under the
control of the conglomerates, and independent book stores have been
pushed out of business by chains that market books like so much other

shopping mall ware. Profiteering is cheapening the printed word, with romance novels, action thrillers, and fad and self-help books increasingly the literary heritage we are passing on to the future. "The conglomerateer has bred an atmosphere of fear, cynicism, rapaciousness, and ignorance that has been ... destructive to serious publishing," says Ted Solotaroff, a former senior editor at Harper and Row. The cost, he adds, can be reckoned by the number of dedicated publishers and editors who have been "driven out or demoralized or corrupted." [1]

A love of the daily newspaper and a nostalgia for ink on the printed page may seem like strange passions to hold for a business that grew up amid news hucksters like James Gordon Bennett and "yellow" journalists like William Randolph Hearst and Arthur Brisbane. Yet we have reached the day where the daily circulation newspaper, once seen at the forefront of mass culture, has become a haven for historians, a residue of intelligence and perspective, a place for leisurely browsing and the savoring of the printed page in a world where the modes of electronic communication are proliferating at a dizzying pace. Much of this is possible because newspapers—at least, the better ones—have improved so much over the last century. However, as print literacy has grown less prized in our culture, the places where words are valued seem to be growing fewer and fewer, too.

The future of the printed word does not look promising in this age of electronically transmitted information, multimedia technology advances, and media moguls mesmerized by expansion and the bottom line. If it isn't marketplace forces and a fickle and distracted public working to reduce the outlets for serious writing, it's the progress of the electronic age with its promise of a world where everyone is staring, hypnotized, into banks of video screens. Marshall McLuhan and the other media theorists offer the supposedly reassuring thought that the word won't disappear; it will simply be reshaped by the demands of the new electronic forms of communication. This, however, is hardly comforting to those who worry that the wired world may be losing the discipline of mind, the depth of imagination, and the creativity of spirit that an intimate involvement with the printed word has produced for the culture. As television critic Michael Arlen puts it:

> Just because an electronic circuit looks circular, or sounds circular, and just because the hippy teen-agers that McLuhan admires so much ... go floating about absorbing sense impressions and otherwise having a fine old time, doesn't seem to me much of a reason for supposing that we're going to start wanting to do without logic—

intuitive, deductive, analytical, linear, call it what you will. After all, logic, brains, intellect, sustained formal thought are how we splendid, wonderful people got to be so splendid and wonderful in the first place.[2]

Critics of electronic culture, beginning with Henry David Thoreau, have long lamented the fact that the forms of communication may advance, without the forms of thinking that are communicated necessarily keeping pace. From Thoreau's comment about the telegraph ("But Maine and Texas, it may be, have nothing important to communicate")[3] to Roszak's worries about the computer data base explosion ("An excess of information may actually crowd out ideas, leaving the mind . . . distracted by sterile, disconnected facts, lost among shapeless heaps of data"),[4] scholars and thinkers have complained that our fascination with the modes of communication outweighs our worries about the emptiness of what is communicated. Critics point to the underlying danger of a communications technology that is driven not by the importance of the message, but by the demands of profit. On this level, even McLuhan, enthusiastic as he may have been about television, understood the dangers inherent in the centralizing powers of electronic technology. "Leasing our eyes and ears and nerves to commercial interests is like handing over the common speech to a private corporation, or like giving the earth's atmosphere to a company as a monopoly," McLuhan wrote.[5]

This book has been mostly about newspapers. But as we've seen, newspapers are fast being swept up in a communications revolution that—despite all the talk about video technologies, fiber optics, digital television, and interactive data bases—is really about marketing. In the same way that the merchandisers and advertising agents have always worked, the electronic hucksters are everywhere, trying to entice us with the promise of ever more relevant news and up-to-date information, to lull us with fantasy and excite us with titillating entertainment, and to insinuate themselves ever deeper into our senses. Whatever shape the word takes in the future—whether it is in the form of electronic imagery or computer pulsations or the word on newsprint—its meaning will be dictated by the powers that are right now blending all our modes of communication into a marketing, entertainment, and economic juggernaut they believe to be irresistible. The technology may be the driving force, but the motivations are very human—the desire for power, for control, for bureaucratic gain, and, most important, for unceasingly mounting profits.

Newspapers have been a comfortable refuge in this multimedia vortex: a real, hands-on product, with texture, the feel of real print that requires the old-fashioned skills of discernment and literacy. For a relatively small amount of change, you get a pretty good service: reporters who go out and track down the issues and events of the day, editors selecting from the universe of information what seems most interesting and relevant, analysts and columnists who try to put the crazy world into perspective, pages that can be scanned quickly and comfortably with the human eye. Anyone who hasn't been able to soothe his or her nerves by picking up the *New York Times* (ah, yes, nothing is so earthshaking that it can't fit into the staid, old format) hasn't discovered one of life's finest nonchemical tranquilizers.

However, the newspaper is fast being transformed by the same marketers who are peddling the electronic tomorrow—and who, if the time is right, will happily merge it into the all-service, all-purpose electronic information conglomerate. Corporate journalism—like corporate hamburgers and corporate mini-marts and corporate gas stations—is already at hand in many one-newspaper towns where that newspaper is chain-owned. The homogeneity of thinking that produces the "Big Mac" is now at work in the packaging and marketing of everything from *USA Today* to many local newspapers. The personality of newspapers is fast disappearing beneath a cascade of computer graphics, eye-catching packaging, and marketing slogans. Stories are being written to "convey information"—not to unearth hidden facts, develop important themes, or delight with an intelligent turn of phrase. Readers are being told lots about themselves—how they can cope, how they can evaluate their financial options, how their lives compare with those of the rich and famous—and the result is newspapers with less and less content. "The world of our making becomes ever more mirrorlike," Daniel Boorstin writes.[6]

The new corporate-minded editors say they are just giving readers what they want. Yet they do not really know what readers want. Surveys can be read in any number of different ways, and that is why they have done the newspaper business so little good. The surveys consistently show that people support investigative reporting, that they want more serious foreign and national news in the newspaper. Yet readers call in most frequently when they are insulted by a columnist or when their favorite comic strip is canceled. The readers of newspapers want their newspapers to be good—to be solid and informative and interesting—whatever that may be. They look to journalists to define for them what is interesting and important. Readers can't find it a pretty picture to see journalists looking out at them, asking plaintively, "What in the world can we do to please you?"

Oddly, we live in an age where public opinion—what is, ostensibly, supposed to be a measurement of our opinions—has terribly complicated our lives as well as the job of the media. It's an exaggeration to say that the media shape our values, just as it would be overstating matters to say that we as individuals can change the shape and the nature of the media. Rather, it's a reciprocal feedback process that creates our communications environment—echoes of public opinion echoing out into the land, trend seekers shaping trends, events becoming media events before we can begin to understand what they truly signify. But more than anything, the gauging of public opinion has become big business. Mass production and mass marketing have made it necessary for manufacturers, advertisers, retailers—and now the media, every bit as much as anyone else—to know the preferences of everybody about everything.

Boorstin notes that until the rise of liberalism in Europe "opinion" was closely identified with error and to say something was "mere opinion" was a way of saying that the notion was hardly worth consideration. But these days, opinion is qualified by such words as common, general, or public, and the emphasis has "shifted from its uncertainty" to something else—"to its power." Opinion—something that was at first personal—has grown into a vast and dominant public institution, a monolithic force.[7] And it is the needs of mass marketing and mass advertising—not the commitment to the struggle for truth in a democratic society—that motivate the temperature takers of mass opinion.

In this world of relative truth, the act of communication has lost much of its power. Boorstin points out that one of the earliest definitions of the word "communicate" was, in sixteenth-century England, part of the definition of God.[8] Originally, Boorstin says, the word "communicate" implied "community," and it meant somehow to make common, to share. In our world of "overcommunication," however, we have reduced the concept to the task of imparting information, to conveying something, anything, to a market that has been gauged to be receptive. "We witness the cheapening of the word," Boorstin says. "Wherever we go and wherever we look, we see and hear words—mostly messages we would rather not receive. Once, the word was sacred, a synonym for the Word of God, that which has a special sanctity. But now, words are everywhere and inescapable."[9]

The cheapening of the word in our culture of overcommmunication is a near universal lament among media philosophers. Innis emphasizes the sacred character of writing and the power of the word in early Egyptian and Hebrew culture. "Word, wisdom, and God were almost identical theological concepts," he says.[10] Postman notes that the "God of the Jews was to exist in the Word and through the Word, an unprecedented conception requiring the highest order of abstract thinking."[11] Ong carries this idea forward by his reverence for the holiness of the word as "a primary point of entry for the divine."[12]

Boorstin, Ong, Postman, McLuhan, and Innis would argue among themselves about what mode of communication offers the most promise to retain—or the greatest threat to destroy—the tradition of the word as sacred. In that debate, I side with those who put their faith in the strength of the written word as the underpinning of society. It is the written word—or the spoken word trapped, as they say, in its written form—that has the greatest chance to preserve the sacred nature of communication from the onslaught of technology, mass marketing, and public opinion pulse taking. As any child who has discovered the joy of writing can tell you, there is nothing that can compare with the possibilities of the written word. The written word gives meaning—lasting meaning, resonating meaning, a meaning that touches the depths of the spirit. Communication by written word requires hard work, discipline, deep concentration—but it lets us learn things about ourselves that we can learn no other way. The written word, to use modern psycho-lingo, is self-empowering. It also points to the higher power that is within us all—the divine power of the word, as the Hebrews understood it, or as the writer of the Book of John expressed it in the Christian context, "And the Word became flesh and dwelt among us, full of grace and truth."[13]

In their prohibition against the building of graven images, the Hebrews recognized a spiritual principle that is transferable to our electronic culture—namely, that when we are mesmerized by the image, it is harder to see through to the sacred truth of things. Worship, our religious traditions tell us, is about words and silence and communication with a higher power—and not about holding up ourselves and our images of ourselves as the mirror of reality. But that, sadly, is what television and video technology and the ever present measurement of public opinion are all about.

As the economic facts stand, the future of the word is to a troubling degree in the hands of the marketers of words, makers of images, and maximizers of profit who are running our communications corporations. Of course, the power of the word has always been the greatest tool of resistance against those who would have money run the world. However, it is becoming more difficult to get this message through the gates of the media conglomerates. It is in the nature of the conglomerateers that they will define the market, poll the market, produce the product, market the product, and then measure the satisfaction of the customers. If they want to treat the word as just another ingredient in the blending of the marketing mix, they will.

Against this discouraging backdrop, there are some hopeful signs. The rise of the new journalism and the success of expansive, narrative journalism practiced by writers like David Halberstam, Gay Talese, Tom Wolfe, and John McPhee have invigorated our business and raised the standards of good journalism, even in newspapers. The "literary" journalists like Truman Capote and Norman Mailer and Joan Didion have carried much of what is left of our literary tradition in this era of blockbuster best-sellers and chain-owned bookstores. The stylists, the satirists and the cleverest of columnists—the George Wills and the Dave Barrys and the Mike Roykos and the Ellen Goodmans and the Tom Boswells—have achieved a level of prose once seldom seen in the world of newspapers. The U.S. with its democratic roots and its birth in the era of cheap printing has always fostered a remarkable kinship between journalism and literature. The Twains and the Dreisers and the Cathers and the Hemingways might never have gotten their start if they hadn't had jobs on newspapers where they could develop their craft and then transcend it.

Right now, journalism seems to offer the best and the worst of possibilities for our literary future. On one side of the scale, we have the marketers and the word packagers and the information brokers. On the other side, we live in an "age of journalism," as some have dubbed it, with booklength, high-quality journalism finding a solid market among the public and helping to elevate the level of prose in newspapers and periodicals. On the tilt of this scale, the future of journalism—and, perhaps, much of what remains of our literary tradition—depends.

Just as I'm confident that good reporters will keep up the good fight, so I believe that readers aren't about to give up on good journalism or the daily newspapers that practice it—as long as newspapers don't give up on them. The newspapers that devote themselves to filling their pages with real news, enterprise reporting, good writing, and intelligent analysis will survive and prosper, I am convinced, despite the pressures from the marketplace, the beguilements of video culture, and the abandonment of reading by some segments of the public.

Newspapers that take their cue from television may be trying to swim with a current that has already shifted in the other direction in this country. Everywhere—from Congress to the legislatures to the schools and universities—there is a push to boost reading and literacy skills. Americans have figured out that the Age of Information is upon them. While their motives may be mostly economic, the pendulum seems to be swinging back to the cause of something other than video literacy. Newspaper editors risk the loss of the advantages they have over television if they don't give readers something more than what their television screens offer.

As much as we salute television's sway over us, we also recognize its ephemerality. Television libraries are rare. Few people seem interested in using their video equipment to record television shows for posterity. The rare scoops on television news are usually forgotten—evaporating quickly into the video void. Words that come over the airways don't have the staying power of words on the written page. We may become a society without a collective memory, but I doubt it. Television is now paying the price for its own evanescence. Video images have great potency, but, like dreams, they disappear—insubstantial, and soon forgotten.

Daily newspapers have never had a better opportunity to offer a true alternative to the video culture and the pied pipers of marketplace journalism. People know they live in a complex and confusing world. And those readers who know the value of staying informed will be the first to know if their newspaper isn't giving them "good" information. They have too many alternatives if newspapers offer only a quick and shallow interpretation of events.

Daily newspapers, it seems to me, face a clear choice. They can continue to go down the path of trying to match television as an entertainment and visual medium—where they will finish far behind. Or they can provide the depth and context and perspective that society can't find in other media. If marketing and pleasing the public become the primary reason for their existence, newspapers risk the loss of their identity and the abandonment of any claim to the public conscience.

This is not Luddite talk. In this electronic era, newspapers may have to expand their format; they may have to update their methods of delivering the news; they may have to expand their pact with the world of computers by broadening their functions and providing more in-depth data delivery services. But even as the computer comes more to dominate our lives, writing, I'm confident, will continue to be at the base of the unfolding Information Age. By that, I mean writing that is more than just conveying information. The written word has always provided the weave and fabric of our culture. When words rest in software, they don't necessarily lose their allure. In fact—given the flexibility of the word processor—writing becomes even easier. The medium changes the outcome somewhat, to be sure. But as long as there are real writers and real thinkers at the keyboard, I'm not worried.

I heartily disagree with Walter Lippmann who gave up on newspapers as inherently biased and limited in their ability to penetrate to the truth of things. This shortchanges a business that has matured since Lippmann's time, expanded its definition of news, and deepened its perspective on events. The best newspapers have managed to enrich their prose, incorporate the tools of investigative reporting, free reporters from the constraints of "objective" journalism, and borrow from the techniques of narrative historians without becoming elitist instruments of communication. If newspaper owners can adjust to profit levels that don't necessarily put them at the top of the list for U.S. industry, they can put out a product that will continue to merit the protections that our forefathers believed were indispensable to the proper functioning of the republic.

In this era of conglomerates and concentrated ownership, the tentacles of the big media companies are reaching everywhere, connecting with their electronic competitors and entertainment combines, plugging up the remaining independent media outlets, and extending their hold even into our smallest communities. Like chain-owned day care centers, chain-owned medical facilities, and chain-owned nursing homes, big media chains are increasingly insinuating their economic aspirations into the rhythms of our births, our experience of our lives, and our departures. The "captains of consciousness," to use Stuart Ewen's phrase, are extending their influence into places where no one invited them—and where we may not fully recognize them for what they are when they have taken over.

Still, it would be a mistake for newspaper traditionalists—whether readers of newspapers or journalists who work for them—to believe that the trend toward market-oriented journalism is an irresistible one. At all levels of every media corporation are media people who believe in—or, at least, believe that they believe in—the traditional values of public service and the principles of public trust that are the bedrock of the profession. Most believe in the myths of the intrepid, truth-seeking newspaper and the independent, free-thinking journalist, and they don't, for the most part, want to stamp them out. Despite what the media scholars say, the myths of this business—and the idealism that underlies them—are important. They are the leverage for those who believe that newspapers aren't just another commodity in the marketplace. They stand between the newspaper business and newspapers degenerating into just another product.

Maybe someday we'll wake up and realize that the antitrust statutes couldn't be used for a better purpose than to check the growing concentration in our communications industry. Maybe someday we'll change the tax laws so they don't favor the conglomerates—both in the media and the rest of American industry. Maybe someday we'll tire of mergers and profiteering and living in the shadows of the expanding corporate giants. Until then, journalists who are committed to the cause of good journalism must wage the good fight on the inside against the forces of marketplace journalism. And we on the outside who treasure that cause will continue to read daily newspapers—and to keep the faith.

AFTERWORD

I had the privilege—both wonderful and painful as it proved to be—to work in what may turn out to be remembered as the golden age of newspaper journalism. For many in my generation, life has been about the fading of the 1960s and 1970s, and that's true in newspaper work, too. The idealism kindled by the Civil Rights movement, the moral agony of the Vietnam War, the turmoil of protests, Watergate, and the rise of the counterculture—the experiences of that era reshaped our profession as profoundly as they did the country as a whole. It was a heady time, and those of us who shared in it—even if in newsrooms far from the centers of power—imbibed the atmosphere deeply.

In my own career, I have had experiences that, for the most part, allowed me to keep alive the passion of those idealistic times. I can remember how deeply impressed I was as a graduate student in the Kiplinger reporting program at Ohio State University during a visit to Washington, D.C., when the city was in the grip of Watergate. On a trip organized by our Kiplinger "professor," Stuart Loory (a former White House correspondent for the *Los Angeles Times* among other interesting career stops), we visited with a top White House aide to Richard Nixon who was planning the president's impeachment defense; we met with a member of the House Judiciary Committee preparing impeachment charges against Nixon; we had get-togethers with Harry Rosenfeld, the *Washington Post* metropolitan editor who oversaw the newspaper's Watergate coverage, and Sy Hersh, whose reporting on the My Lai massacre had made him a hero to young journalists; and we watched an acid-tongued Jerry Warren handling a press briefing with the angry, unruly White House press corps of that era. Loory had earlier helped me obtain a grant to travel throughout the South investigating the Nixon administration's strategy of blunting the activism of VISTA (where I had served as a volunteer) and other War on Poverty programs. But most of all I owe to Loory the special opportunity to learn my craft from such a principled professional, from someone who instilled in us the values of enterprise journalism, the necessity of taking a stand in our stories, and the importance of never losing our sense of outrage at injustice.

In my first reporting job at the *Lansing State Journal*, I was given the unusual chance to pursue stories—about redlining in poor communities, conflict of interest on the city council, and skulduggery in the awarding of city favors—that were in amazing congruence with my activist background. I was entrusted with a number of investigative tasks, including the probing of football recruiting irregularities at Michigan State University, which rankled local boosters but was pursued by my managing editor, Ben Burns, with an enthusiasm that would be unheard of in today's atmosphere of "reader-driven" newspapering. I remember one day in particular, after a prisoner had made a helicopter escape from a nearby prison, when Burns and Hal Fildey, the newspaper's two top editors, sat along the copy rim, watching me working the telephone and joking that if I kept at it, I might become a real reporter someday. It was a rare experience to work for editors who were interested in the substance of a reporter's work and believed in their reporters, and as I became enmeshed in the "plan-and-package" atmosphere of the MBA-run newsroom, I came to appreciate the memory of it all the more.

During my years in Washington, D.C., I worked alongside other young reporters, like those at Ralph Nader's now defunct Capitol Hill News Service, who were inspired by Watergate and caught up in the reform mood that had vitalized the Washington press corps. We pursued our own versions of official malfeasance and did the local angle versions of stories—Abscam, Koreagate, and various semiscandals in Congress—that flowed from Watergate and the subsequent reforms. At the Gannett bureau, we labored in relative obscurity (in those pre-*USA Today* days, we often had to spell Gannett to a source), but we were a hard-working, ambitious bunch, and we did solid work for our appreciative, small-city newspapers. Before his ascendancy to the top of Gannett, John Curley, who was then our bureau chief, took pride in the development of new talent and the servicing of Gannett's far-flung newspapers with first-class journalism. To this day, I look back with fondness to that brief heyday at Gannett, before the shadow of *USA Today* fell across the news service, when the company still believed it could build a name by the quality of its journalism and when it spent real money on positioning the news service as the centerpiece of its push for recognition.

Even when I came to work for the *Seattle Times* in Olympia, I was able to get stories with a hard edge into a newspaper that, despite its embrace of marketplace journalism, didn't shy away from an occasional foray into rough-and-tumble newspapering. The *Times* never became the *Los Angeles Times* of the Northwest, as one top editor described the newspaper's ambition when I joined the staff, or even one of the top ten newspapers in the country, as was the openly expressed goal for many years. But during my time there—and since I have left—the newspaper has had its triumphs. The *Times*'s tendency toward complacency and its lack of consistently aggressive newspapering is more the result of bureaucracy and a newsroom managed for the marketplace than it is a lack of talent among the many good journalists who work there.

I can remember often thinking to myself during my years in the business, "They pay you for this?" I never ceased to marvel at how much rabble-rousing could be done within the bowels of the mainstream press. Of course, as time went on, the frustrations and the petty humiliations of newsroom life began to bite more deeply, and I, like many before me, decided it was time to get out with my self-respect intact. But for the most part I never lost my love for the work—and I never lost that thrill of pinning down an important story with a raising of my fist and a "gotcha."

I suppose I expected that it would all come to an end in ways that would be dramatic and apparent. I never imagined that the cause of change-the-world journalism would be taken away from us in a fashion that, at first, seemed so nebulous and so difficult to identify. I can still remember reading Mike Fancher's call for marketplace journalism in the *Gannett Center Journal* and saying to myself, "So this is what is happening?" Like many of my colleagues, I sensed the business was changing around me in important ways, but it took my exiting the *Times* and the research that went into this book to fully comprehend it.

An old Gannett colleague who worked with me in both Lansing and Washington, D.C., once asked soon after I'd left the newspaper business for academia what I told my students about the transformation we had seen take place in the newspaper business. Are you honest with them, he asked me, about what they are getting into? I don't remember exactly what I told him. But I know that I have always believed that good journalism comes from the heart of good journalists, and it is in the heart of the profession that I take inspiration—and that I don't believe will ever be squelched, not even by legions of MBA editors.

APPENDIX OF TABLES

TABLE 1

Distribution (%) of Perceived Changes in Newsroom Policy by Type of Newspaper[1]

			Type of Newspaper		
Change Reported[2]	(106) Small Family	(76) Small Chain	(125) Large Family	(118) Large Chain	Average
Management	25.3	22.7	27.6	21.8	24.3
Coverage	13.6	12.2	21.8	11.4	15.0
Design/Appearance	9.1	21.0	14.6	14.3	14.6
Marketing	8.6	6.6	8.4	13.2	9.6
Content	2.5	8.8	3.4	15.7	8.0
Profits	4.0	4.4	3.8	13.2	6.8
Staff	15.1	4.4	2.7	4.6	6.3
Ethics	1.5	1.1	6.9	0.7	2.7
Other	20.2	18.8	10.7	5.0	12.6
	100[3]	100	100	100	100

Chisquare = 71.3, 24 df, p<.001.

1. Percents are based on the number of changes reported by 429 respondents (861). Each respondent could identify up to four changes.

2. Question: "First, we're interested in identifying any changes in business and/or journalistic policies that may have taken place at your newspaper. Please describe briefly any changes that have been made in the past few years."

3. In this and following tables, numbers don't always add up to exactly 100 due to small rounding differences.

TABLE 2

Distribution (%) of Recent Journalistic and Business Changes in Management Policy at Four Types of Dailies[1]

	Type of Newspaper				
Policy Change[2]	Small Family	Small Chain	Large Family	Large Chain	Total
Business sector	51.5	61.5	48.8	77.1	63.2
Journalism sector	25.0	16.1	34.9	11.5	22.6
Other change	23.5	22.4	16.9	11.5	14.2
	100	100	100	100	100

1. Percent is based on the total number of policy changes (861) identified by 429 respondents.
2. Question: see table 1.

TABLE 3

Distribution (%) of Perceived Changes in Newsroom Policy by Type of Change and Newspaper Type

	Type of Newspaper				
Change Reported[1]	Small Family	Small Chain	Large Family	Large Chain	Average
Management:					
journalistic	50	34	32	16	32
business	50	66	68	84	68
N =	50	41	72	61	224
Coverage:					
journalistic	41	64	75	31	57
business	59	36	25	69	43
N =	27	22	57	32	138
Design/Appearance:					
journalistic	69	37	39	55	46
business	31	63	61	45	54
N =	18	38	38	40	134
Marketing:					
journalistic	0	0	0	0	0
business	100	100	100	100	100
N =	17	12	22	37	88
Content:					
journalistic	40	12	11	2	8
business	60	88	89	98	92
N =	5	16	9	44	74
Profits:					
journalistic	0	0	0	0	0
business	100	100	100	100	100
N =	8	8	10	37	63

TABLE 3 (*Continued*)

Change Reported[1]	Small Family	Small Chain	Large Family	Large Chain	Average
Staff:					
journalistic	13	0	71	62	29
business	87	100	29	38	71
N =	30	8	7	13	58
Ethics:					
journalistic	100	50	22	0	32
business	0	50	78	100	68
N =	3	2	18	2	25
Unclassified[2]	20	19	11	5	13

1. Question: see table 1.
2. Includes all changes that could not be coded as reflecting a business or journalistic policy.

TABLE 4

Distribution (%) of Reasons Why Quality of Newspaper Got Better at Four Types of Dailies[1]

Reason[2]	Small Family	Small Chain	Large Family	Large Chain	Total
Staff improvement	30.5	17.1	32.9	39.8	31.3
Design/appearance	17.1	35.7	23.1	10.2	20.9
Improved mgmt.	22.0	24.3	16.1	20.4	19.8
More competition	8.5	11.4	18.2	13.3	13.7
Research & Techn.	20.7	8.6	2.1	6.1	8.1
More money/support	0.0	0.0	5.6	8.2	4.1
Miscellaneous	1.2	2.9	2.1	2.0	2.0
No. of staffers	100	100	100	100	100
who say quality got better (%) =	51.9	57.9	72.4	51.7	60.0

1. Percentages in table are based on the total number of reasons given by staffers (393) for quality improving.

Chisquare = 59.9, 21 df, p < .001

2. Question: "If the quality of the newspaper has improved, what do you think is responsible?" (Asked of all respondents who answered to a previous question that quality had improved.)

TABLE 5

Distribution (%) of Reasons Why Quality of Newspaper Got Worse at Four Types of Dailies [1]

| Reasons [2] | Type of Newspaper | | | | |
	Small Family	Small Chain	Large Family	Large Chain	Total
Management	18.6	46.2	31.6	32.1	30.8
Cutbacks	39.5	19.2	15.8	21.0	24.9
Content	23.3	19.2	15.8	21.0	20.7
Coverage	4.7	7.7	10.5	16.0	11.2
Appearance	9.3	7.7	15.8	9.9	10.1
Technology	4.7	—	10.5	—	2.4
No. of staffers who say quality	100	100	100	100	100
got worse (%) =	48.1	42.1	27.6	48.3	40.0

1. Percentages in table are based on the total number of reasons given by staffers (169) for quality getting worse.

Chisquare = 44.1, 12 df, p < .001

2. Question: "If the quality has gotten worse, what do you think is responsible?" (Asked of all respondents who answered to a previous question that quality had gotten worse.)

Table 6
Distribution (%) of Effect of Policy Change by Type[1]

Effect of Change[2]	Type of Change								
	Profit	Mktg	Ethics	Content	Staff	Coverage	Mgmt	Design	Misc
Balance worse	90.3	57.1	54.2	50.6	49.4	36.0	34.1	30.2	32.6
Balance improved	3.2	29.5	33.3	25.8	30.4	54.4	45.3	55.2	32.6
No effect	6.5	13.2	12.5	23.6	20.3	8.8	20.6	14.7	34.8
N =	100	100	100	100	100	100	100	100	100
	62	105	24	89	79	136	223	116	46

Summary: 44.1 percent of the changes identified by staffers were seen as making the business/journalism balance worse; 38.9 percent of the changes were seen as making the balance better; 17 percent were seen as having no effect.

1. Chisquare = 21.9, 6 df, p < .001
2. Question: "How have these changes affected the balance between journalistic and business principles? Have they improved the balance, made it worse, or had no effect? Please answer for each change listed above."

TABLE 7
Correlations Between Policy Emphasis Indexes ($n=429$)

Policy Index	Profit	Customer	Integration	Policy Emphasis On Control	Community	Citizen	Autonomy
Profit emphasis		$.12^1$	$.23^2$	$.17^1$	$-.59^2$	$-.40^2$	$-.41^2$
Reader as customer			$.16^2$	$.30^2$	.05	$-.02$	.07
Mgmt. integration				$.14^1$	.07	.10	$-.05$
Mgmt. control					.08	.12	.06
Serve community						$.63^2$	$.61^2$
Reader as citizen							$.51^2$
Editorial autonomy							

1. p<.o1
2. p<.oo1

TABLE 8

*Mean Newsroom Policy Emphases by Business and
Journalistic Orientations*

Business Sector	Mean	Journalistic Sector	Mean
Reader as customer	3.45	Editorial autonomy	3.36
Profit	2.82	Reader as citizen	3.19
Management control	2.80	Serve community	3.13
Management integration	2.80		

TABLE 9
Mean Value of Newsroom Policy Scales by Newspaper Size and Ownership

Policy Index	Type of Newspaper				Grand Mean	S. Dev.
	Small Family	Small Chain	Large Family	Large Chain		
Reader as customer	3.43	3.34	3.28	3.73	3.45	.53
Editorial autonomy	3.58	3.19	3.44	3.17	3.36	.67
Reader as citizen	3.27	3.01	3.23	3.18	3.19	.68
Serve community	3.41	2.97	3.18	2.93	3.13	.65
Profit emphasis	2.64	3.08	2.66	2.97	2.82	.71
Mgmt. integration	2.85	2.91	2.74	2.74	2.80	.66
Management control	2.65	2.75	2.81	2.98	2.80	.56

NOTE: Underlined means are significantly different from nonunderlined means at the .05 level, Sheffes' test.

TABLE 10

Mean Value of Newsroom Policy Scales by Newspapers in Competitive and Noncompetitive Markets
(NC = noncompetitive; C = competitive)

			Type of Newspaper			
Policy Index	NC Family	NC Chain	C Family	C Chain	Grand Mean	S. Dev.
Reader as customer	3.39	3.47	3.30	3.70	3.45	.52
Editorial autonomy	3.53	3.16	3.48	3.20	3.36	.65
Reader as citizen	3.30	3.34	3.19	2.86	3.19	.66
Serve community	3.24	2.97	3.38	2.92	3.13	.62
Profit emphasis	2.66	2.96	2.64	3.06	2.82	.69
Mgmt. integration	2.68	2.80	2.92	2.83	2.80	.66
Management control	2.61	2.82	2.89	2.97	2.80	.54

NOTE: Underlined means are significantly different from nonunderlined means at the .05 level, Sheffes' test.

TABLE 11

Varimax Factor Matrix for Dimensions of Job Satisfaction

Dimensions		
Internal	External	Internal Satisfaction (.<u>65</u>)[3]
.71	—[1]	Supervisor goes out of way to help
.70	—	How often you are in the dark
.57	.33	Management makes you feel important
.55	—	Chances of raise for good work
		External Satisfaction (.<u>61</u>)[3]
—	.81	Contribute something to community
—	.68	Newspaper work satisfying & rewarding
.34	.59	Feel pride in product
.32	.49	Your newspaper compared to others
2.79[2]	1.15[2]	
31.1%	12.8%	

1. Factor loadings <.30 not shown.
2. Denotes Eigenvalues for factor.
3. Chronbach reliability coefficient.

TABLE 12

Mean Job Satisfaction by Category of Recent Policy Change[1]

Policy Change	Job Satisfaction	
	Internal	External
News coverage	3.02	3.35
Management	2.79	3.14
Marketing emphasis	2.79	3.11
Ethics	2.66	3.29
Design/Appearance	2.64	3.08
Staff	2.54	3.09
Profit emphasis	2.52	3.12
News content	2.50	3.24
Other	2.52	3.06

1. $(F = 2.11, p < .03)$ $(F = 1.71, p < .10)$

TABLE 13

Correlations Between Job Satisfaction and Policy Emphasis

	Job Satisfaction	
Policy Emphasis	Internal	External
Profit emphasis	−.33[1]	−.30[1]
Reader as customer	−.02	.07
Management integration	.09	.02
Management control	.02	−.05
Serve community	.46[1]	.40[1]
Reader as citizen	.44[1]	.30[1]
Editorial autonomy	.44[1]	.33[1]

1. $p < .001$

TABLE 14

Mean Values of Change in Newspaper Quality, Comfort with Management Policy, Perceived Management Style, and Perceived Policy Balance by Type of Policy Change

Policy Change in	Change in Newsp. Quality	Comfort with Policy	Mgmt. Style	Policy Balance	
				Improved	Worse
News coverage	4.24	3.50	4.35	1.71	.88
Management	3.89	3.12	4.61	1.31	.99
Ethics	3.88	3.19	4.38	.38	1.75
Design/Appearance	3.70	2.87	4.76	1.28	1.19
News content	3.44	2.88	4.88	.84	1.48
Staff	3.38	2.73	3.88	.46	1.62
Profit emphasis	3.26	2.37	5.37	.42	1.95
Marketing emphasis	2.88	3.04	4.80	.72	1.68
Other	3.68	3.03	4.11	1.14	.73
NOTE:	$F = 2.79$ $p < .005$	$F = 1.51$ $p < .15$	$F = 1.74$ $p < .09$	$F = 4.60$ $p < .001$	$F = 3.57$ $p < .001$

TABLE 15

Correlations Between Job Satisfaction and Change in Newspaper Quality, Comfort with Policy, and Perceived Management Style

	Job Satisfaction	
Correlate	Internal	External
Comfort with policy	.56[1]	.41[1]
Management style	−.40[1]	−.28[1]
Change in newspaper quality	.29[1]	.27[1]

1. $p < .001$

TABLE 16
Mean Job Satisfaction by Impact of Changes in Policy Balance

| | Job Satisfaction | | | |
Impact on Balance	Internal	External	F[1]	p<[1]
1st change listed (n = 259)[2]				
Improved balance	2.94	3.26		
Worsened balance	2.47	3.05	15.7	.001
No effect	2.69	3.13	7.68	.001
2nd change listed (n = 219)				
Improved balance	2.98	3.28		
Worsened balance	2.42	3.07	20.4	.001
No effect	2.74	3.09	7.08	.001
3rd change listed (n = 159)				
Improved balance	2.98	3.25		
Worsened balance	2.48	3.08	10.2	.001
No effect	2.64	3.10	3.23	.04
4th change listed (n = 107)				
Improved balance	2.92	3.28		
Worsened balance	2.36	3.10	9.01	.001
No effect	2.82	3.01	3.59	.03

1. The first row includes F p< for internal job satisfaction; the second row for external.
2. N is based on those respondents who listed a recent policy change.

TABLE 17
Mean Job Satisfaction by Size and Ownership of Newspaper

| | Type of Newspaper | | | | | |
Job Satisfaction	Small Family	Small Chain	Large Family	Large Chain	F	p<
Internal	2.84	2.53	2.80	2.64	4.48	.004
External	3.23	3.03	3.13	3.13	3.02	.03

TABLE 18
Mean Job Satisfaction and Comfort with Management Policies by Newsroom Position

	Top Mgmt.	Clerical	Midlevel Editors	Copy Editors	Photo.	Reporters
Internal job satisfaction	<u>2.99</u>	2.79	2.75	2.73	2.67	2.66
External job satisfaction	<u>3.27</u>	2.82	<u>3.23</u>	3.01	3.03	<u>3.18</u>
Comfort with mgmt. policies	<u>3.50</u>	3.14	<u>3.23</u>	3.00	2.88	2.81

NOTE: Underlined means are significantly different from nonunderlined means at the .05 level, Sheffes' test.

NOTES

Introduction

1. Memo obtained during the author's employment with the *Seattle Times,* 1987.

2. Neil Nordby, "What a Decade!" *Editor and Publisher,* March 10, 1990, 7–9.

3. Thomas B. Rosenstiel, "Editors Debate Need to Redefine America's Newspapers," *Los Angeles Times,* April 13, 1991, p. A18; W. Dale Nelson, "Riding Out the Storm," *The Quill,* April 1991, 14–17.

4. Michael Fancher, "The Metamorphosis of the Newspaper Editor," *Gannett Center Journal* 1 (Spring 1987): 69, 80.

5. Gene Goltz, "Reviving a Romance with Readers Is the Biggest Challenge for Many Newspapers," *Presstime,* February 1988, 16–22.

6. "Gannett's News 2000 Project Builds on Community Ties," *Presstime,* July 1991, 50; Pam Janis, "News 2000 Lays Foundation for Success," *Gannetteer,* September 1991, 4–5; Nancy Green, "Featuring NEWS 2000," *Leadtime,* Summer 1991, 2.

7. John Sedgwick, "Putting the Customer First: How CEO Jim Batten Gets Knight-Ridder Employees to Think Like Marketers," *Business Month*, June 1989, 28–35; Sally Deneen, "Doing the Boca," *Columbia Journalism Review*, May/June 1991, 15; "Boca Watch," *NewsInc.*, February 1991, 19–23.

8. *Creative Marketing Strategies to Win Readers and Advertisers* (Washington, D.C.: American Newspaper Publishers Association, 1986), 16; Lisa Benenson, "All Shook Up," *NewsInc.*, September 1990, 20–23.

9. Joe Morgenstern, "*L.A. Times:* The Fat Paper in the Fast Lane," *Columbia Journalism Review*, July/August 1990, 33–37; Bruce Porter, "The 'Max' Factor at *The New York Times*," *Columbia Journalism Review*, November/December, 1988, 29–35.

10. Doug Underwood, "The Newspapers' Identity Crisis," *Columbia Journalism Review*, March/April 1992, 26.

11. Mary Alice Bagby, "Transforming Newspapers for Readers," *Presstime*, April 1991, 20, 24.

12. Underwood, "When MBAs Rule the Newsroom," *Columbia Journalism Review*, March/April 1988, 23–30.

13. Bill Walker, "Why I Quit," *San Francisco Bay Guardian*, July 18, 1990, 40.

14. Underwood, "Marriage of Convenience in Seattle: A Look at the Joint Operating Agreement Five Years Later, and Its Effect on the Dailies' Ability to Deliver the News," *Pacific Northwest*, May 1988, 43–45.

15. Philip Weiss, "Invasion of the Gannettoids," *The New Republic*, February 2, 1987, 18–20, 22.

16. Paul Henderson, who won a Pulitzer as a *Times* reporter in 1982, said, "I'd never fit the mold they had in mind for their employees. Individuality is one of the most important aspects a newspaper has. I don't know what is served by trying to make everybody act and think alike. That seems to be the goal there—the cloning of the *Seattle Times* newsroom." (Quoted in Underwood, "Marriage of Convenience," 44.)

17. Conrad C. Fink, *Strategic Newspaper Management* (New York: Random House, 1988); John M. Lavine and Daniel B. Wackman, *Managing Media Organizations: Effective Leadership of the Media* (New York: Longman, 1988); Robert H. Giles, *Newsroom Management: A Guide to Theory and Practice* (Indianapolis: R. J. Berg, 1987); Philip Meyer, *The Newspaper Survival Book: An Editor's Guide to Marketing Research* (Bloomington: Indiana University Press, 1985).

18. Underwood, "MBAs," 23–30.

19. Ibid.

20. Underwood and Keith Stamm, "Balancing Business with Journalism: Newsroom Policies at 12 West Coast Newspapers," *Journalism Quarterly* 69 (Summer 1992): 301–317; Stamm and Underwood, "The Relationship of Job Satisfaction to Newsroom Policy Changes," *Journalism Quarterly* 70 (Autumn 1993): 528–41.

1. The Party Is Over—Where Are the Readers?

1. *Keys to Success: Strategies for Newspaper Marketing in the '90s* (Washington, D.C.: American Newspaper Publishers Association, 1989), 18.

2. Goltz, "Reviving a Romance," 16, 18.

3. Steve Star, telephone interview with the author, December 1987.

4. Bagby, "Transforming Newspapers," 20.

5. *Keys to Success,* 4.

6. Nelson, "Riding Out the Storm," 14–17; "The State of the Industry," *NewsInc.,* May 1991, special supplement; Subrata N. Chakravarty with Carolyn Torcellini, "Citizen Kane Meets Adam Smith," *Forbes,* February 20, 1989, 82–85.

7. Rosenstiel, "Editors Debate," p. A18.

8. Bagby, "Transforming Newspapers," 18.

9. Carl Sessions Stepp, "When Readers Design the News," *Washington Journalism Review,* April 1991, 20–24. Stepp has identified some of the characteristics of reader-driven news as:

- Broader definitions of news to appeal to young people, minorities, women, and other groups targeted by advertisers and circulation managers. This means lots of home, family, and career stories that focus on topics like parenting, women's careers, real estate, environment, consumerism, health and fitness, medical advances, and technology.
- Cozier relations with readers via focus groups, fax machines, hotlines, and other quick action to satisfy their wishes.
- Continuing redesign around sleeker graphics, bolder colors, shorter stories, more indexes and quick read items, and lots of "points of entry" to make newspapers more scannable and accessible to busy readers.
- The blurring of soft news and hard news with lifestyle topics, once considered the domain of feature sections, moved to the front page.
- Less coverage of government and other traditional beats.

10. Bagby, "Transforming Newspapers," 18.

11. "Reinventing How Newspapers Go to Market," *Presstime,* June 1991, 28–38; Richard O'Mara, "The Flight from Newspapers," *The Quill,* March 1990, 34–37; Chakravarty and Torcellini, "Citizen Kane," 82–85; Goltz, "Reviving a Romance," 16–22.

12. Joe Logan, "2014: A Newspaper Odyssey," *Washington Journalism Review,* May 1989, 37–38, 40.

13. Chakravarty and Torcellini, "Citizen Kane," 82.

14. Underwood, "Retail Stores and Big-City Newspapers," *Columbia Journalism Review,* September/October 1990, 33–35.

15. Susan Miller, "The Total Newspaper," in *Newsroom Management Handbook* (Washington, D.C.: American Society of Newspaper Editors, 1985), Chapter 20, p. 1.

16. Miller, "American Dailies and the Drive to Capture Lost Readers," *Gannett Center Journal* 1 (Spring 1987): 56–68. For a booklength history of

the project, see Leo Bogart, *Preserving the Press: How Daily Newspapers Mobilized to Keep Readers* (New York: Columbia University Press, 1991).

17. Ruth Clark, *Changing Needs of Changing Readers* (Reston, Va.: American Newspaper Publishers Association, 1980).

18. Miller, "Lost Readers," 60.

19. Madelyn Jennings, "The Changing Workplace: As Workers' Jobs Evolve, So Do Their Attitudes," *Newspaper Controller*, September 1982, 2.

20. Goltz, "The Strong Demand for Newspaper Consultants," *Presstime*, August 1988, 28–35.

21. Larry D. Franklin, "Target Marketing: Opportunity for Publishers and Advertisers," *Newspaper Controller*, February 1980, 1–2.

22. Elise Burroughs, "Modern Marketing Makes Its Mark," *Presstime*, December 1981, 4–9.

23. Goltz, "Today's Researchers Will Tackle Anything," *Presstime*, July 1987, 6–9.

24. Burroughs, "Modern Marketing," 4.

25. *Creative Marketing Strategies*, 18.

26. Goltz, "Today's Researchers," 6–7.

27. Arnold Ismach, "The Economic Connection: Mass Media Profits, Ownership, and Performance," in Everette E. Dennis, Arnold H. Ismach, Donald M. Gillmor, eds., *Enduring Issues in Mass Communication* (St. Paul: West, 1978), 257–258.

28. Bogart, "How U.S. Newspaper Content is Changing," *Journal of Communication* 35 (Spring 1985): 82–90.

29. Ibid., 84–86. See also Bogart, "Newspapers in Transition," *The Wilson Quarterly*, special issue, 1982, 68–69; Bogart, *Press and Public: Who Reads What, When, Where, and Why in American Newspapers* (Hillsdale, N.J.: Erlbaum, 1981), 247–272.

30. Goltz, "Reviving a Romance," 16–17. Bogart noted that the decline in circulation penetration slowed slightly from 1977 to 1983 and even more so from 1983 to 1987. However, the decline has continued into the 1990s. See also Bagby, "Transforming Newspapers," 20.

31. Ray Laakaniemi, "Written by Pros, Read by Amateurs: Analysis of Trade Speeches on Improving Newspaper Content," *Newspaper Research Journal* 9 (Fall 1987): 31–40.

32. Clark, *Relating to Readers in the '80's* (Washington, D.C.: American Society of Newspaper Editors, 1984).

33. Clark, "The Return to Hard News," *Bulletin* of the American Society of Newspaper Editors, September 1983, 23–25.

34. Bogart, "Newspapers in Transition," 64–65; Bogart, *Press and Public.*

35. Bogart, "The Public's Use and Perception of Newspapers," *Public Opinion Quarterly* 48 (Winter 1984): 717.

36. Bogart, *Press and Public*, 245, 249–252.

37. Ibid., 254. Bogart notes that there were early voices decrying the move toward market journalism. In 1976, William Hornby, the former executive editor of the *Denver Post*, warned of the dangers of the " 'Market' Thinkers" and said, "The newsroom has always needed, and never more than today, a more farsighted management ethic than that based merely on moving to a

customer a product he wants. The newspaper is an institution that sets out to do more than just maximize its market." (Hornby, "Beware the 'Market' Thinkers," *The Quill,* January 1976, 16.)

38. Christine D. Urban, "10 Myths About Readers," *Bulletin* of ASNE, July/ August 1986, 19–21.

39. Underwood, "MBAs," 24.

40. Ibid.

41. Sara M. Brown, "The Selection and Development of First-Level Editors," *Presstime,* March 1988, 19.

42. Ellis Cose, *The Press* (New York: Morrow, 1989), 21.

2. *The Marketers and Managers Move In*

1. Memo with accompanying charts obtained from *Quad City Times* editor Dan Hayes, October 27, 1987; Stuart Schwartz, telephone interview with the author, December 1987.

2. Underwood, "MBAs," 28. Schwartz says, "What Gannett is doing with its national newspaper, Lee is doing with its local newspapers. I think Lee is leading the industry right now." For the views of a former reporter at the Lee-owned *Missoulian* in Montana who has lived through these changes, see Richard Manning, *Last Stand: Logging, Journalism, and the Case for Humility* (Salt Lake City: Peregrine Smith, 1991). See also Nathaniel Blumberg, "The *Missoulian* and Lee," *Treasure State Review of Journalism and Justice,* Winter 1991, 5–8. Blumberg, the former dean of the journalism school at the University of Montana, details a list of grievances with Lee's management of the *Missoulian,* including "goofy" headlines, top play to trivial stories, editing errors, a lack of political and government reporting, understaffing, and deferential coverage of the business community.

3. M. L. Stein, "A Futuristic Look at Newspapering," *Editor and Publisher,* January 2, 1982, 16.

4. Perhaps the best profile of the new breed of marketing-oriented newspaper executive is in Andrew Kreig, *Spiked: How Chain Management Corrupted America's Oldest Newspaper* (Old Saybrook, Conn.: Peregrine Press, 1987), 76–109, 124–129. Kreig's portrayal of former *Hartford Courant* publisher Michael Davies (who is now with the *Sun* in Baltimore) fits the profile of many of today's executives who have been brought in to improve newspapers' relationship with readers. Davies, Kreig says, surrounded himself with corporate loyalists, joined local business and civic groups, pushed public relations and image-improvement techniques for the newspaper, and promoted suburban coverage and special sections supportive of advertising interests. In a speech to the 1985 ANPA convention, Kreig quotes Davies as saying, "If there's one thing an editor-turned-publisher discovers very, very quickly, it is that 'profit' is not a four-letter word. Going from running a newsroom of about three hundred to worrying about the present and future welfare of about fifteen hundred employees is very, very sobering and gives one a very quick and deep appreciation for those who bring in the revenue—and bring it in reliably." Davies added, "The newsroom has to be included in strategic planning and

overall company goals. I don't believe that equates with selling out or lowering standards at all."

5. Paul S. Hirt, "The Total Newspaper—A Progress Report," in Donald B. Towles, ed., *Promoting the Total Newspaper* (Reston, Va.: International Newspaper Marketing Association, 1984), 1–4.

6. Goltz, "Financial Executives," *Presstime,* January 1987, 32.

7. Meyer, *Survival Book,* 5.

8. Marion Lewenstein, "Editors in Business Schools," *Presstime,* November 1986, 12–14.

9. Goltz, "Financial Executives," 32.

10. Fancher, "Metamorphosis," 73–74.

11. Gene Roberts, interview with the author, Seattle, Wa., September 1987. See Goltz, "A Twist to the Usual Organization Chart," *Presstime,* May 1987, 50, 52.

12. Roberts, speech to Investigative Reporters and Editors convention, San Francisco, Ca., October 19, 1991.

13. David Lawrence, telephone interview with the author, November 1987.

14. Sedgwick, "Putting the Customer First," 28–35.

15. The *Wall Street Journal* announced on October 3, 1988 that it had been redesigned and was adding a third section to the newspaper. The press release said the new design followed months of development work with readers. According to Angela Santoro, corporate relations associate for Dow Jones, readers were also asked after the redesign what they thought of it.

16. Morgenstern, "Fat Paper," 33–34. Chris Anderson, the executive editor of the *Orange County Register,* noted during a telephone interview with the author in November 1987 that the *Times*'s Orange County edition contained layout and makeup designs that were imitative of the *Register.* Some of those changes were later incorporated in the *Times*'s redesign of the entire newspaper.

17. Cose, *The Press.* References to the *New York Times*'s management changes, 231–279. In fact, even the grand old *Times* has seen its newspaper management "MBA-ized," so to speak. In the late 1970s, then *Times* publisher Arthur O. Sulzberger commissioned McKinsey and Company, a management consulting firm that has also worked with the *Los Angeles Times* and the *Washington Post* and NBC-TV, to help him restructure top management. The management moves came on the heels of readership studies in the mid-1970s that led to a much celebrated repackaging of the *Times,* featuring graphics and featurelike, what-to-do sections, designed to appeal to upscale readers. According to Cose, these changes, combined with Frankel's ascension, have meant a greater attention to financial details in the *Times*'s newsroom and greater newspaperwide coordination of marketing efforts. When Frankel came in, he began handing out copies of their budgets to department heads. Under Frankel, a CPA even worked with the news staff fulltime on the budget, Cose reports.

18. Porter, " 'Max' Factor," 30–31.

19. Jim Gannon, telephone interview with the author, November 1987.

20. Jonathan Kwitny, "The High Cost of High Profits," *Washington Journalism Review,* June 1990, 28.

21. Ibid., 29.

22. Stepp, "Readers Design," 23. Richard Shumate's analysis of the two Atlanta newspapers provides an excellent account of the conflict between the marketer's vision of Martin and Kovach's more traditional vision of journalism as public service. Under Kovach, the two newspapers emphasized informative and often hard-hitting coverage of local and regional news, often with a national or international perspective. The use of color was limited, color photos didn't appear on page one, leads were often elaborate, stories ran up to 70 inches long, and the newspaper took on the look and tone of the *New York Times*. Under Martin, there is more use of color and graphics, longer pieces are broken into shorter stories and sidebars, there is more emphasis on lifestyle and personal health and finance matters, a traffic and "around the town" column are featured, and reporters work as part of a team with editors and artists to design "packages" for the news pages. According to Shumate, Martin believes newspapers need to compete with television and other media sources; Kovach says dailies should provide the strong, in-depth perspective that television doesn't. However, Shumate says that, under Martin, enterprise and hard-hitting journalism are still featured parts of the newspapers. Shumate also notes that circulation has increased since Martin took over. Still, Shumate illustrates the distaste some journalists have for Martin's approach with this newsroom joke: "How many people does it take to write a story at the AJC? Fifty-three. One to write it, 50 to edit it and two to write the correction." (Shumate, "Life after Kovach," *Washington Journalism Review*, September 1992, 28–32.)

23. Stepp, "Of the People, by the People, Bore the People," *Washington Journalism Review*, March 1992, 23–24.

24. Ibid., 26.

25. Kwitny, "High Profits," 19–29.

26. Ben A. Franklin, "The News and Daily Advance," in Loren Ghiglione, ed., *The Buying and Selling of America's Newspapers* (Indianapolis: R. J. Berg, 1984), 144.

27. Ghiglione, "The Transcript," in *Buying and Selling,* 184–187.

28. Eugene C. Patterson, "Newspapers' Bottom-Line Mentality Threatens Vigorous Journalism," *Presstime,* July 1987, 49. See also C. K. McClatchy quoted in *The Next Newspapers* (Washington, D.C.: American Society of Newspaper Editors, 1988), 44. McClatchy, whose own small chain of West Coast newspapers is known for its hard-nosed management style but commitment to quality journalism, said, "One can say that good newspapers are almost always run by good newspaper people; they are almost never run by good bankers or good accountants. . . . American conglomerates have demonstrated special contempt for the press and its responsibility to inform the public. I fear it is just a matter of time before newspapers will be considered the same as any business, a fit prize for investment by interests that do not care about the principles of good journalism."

29. Underwood, "MBAs," 30.

30. George Wilson, telephone interview with the author, November 1987.

31. Gerald Stone, *Examining Newspapers: What Research Reveals about America's Newspapers* (Newbury Park, Ca.: Sage, 1987), 99–104.

32. Benjamin M. Compaine, "The Expanding Base of Media Competition," *Journal of Communication* 35 (Summer 1985): 88.

33. Ben Bagdikian, "The Myth of Newspaper Poverty," *Columbia Journalism Review,* March/April 1973, 24; Bagdikian, "The U.S. Media: Supermarket or Assembly Line?" *Journal of Communication* 35 (Summer 1985): 109.

34. Bagdikian, "Supermarket," 100.

35. Mary A. Anderson, "Ranks of Independent Newspapers Continue to Fade," *Presstime,* August 1987, 17.

36. Bagdikian, "The Lords of the Global Village," *The Nation,* June 12, 1989, 820.

37. Underwood, "MBAs," 27–28.

38. William L. Winter, "A Caution on the Road to Efficiency," *Presstime,* March 1988, 38.

39. Underwood, "MBAs," 28.

3. Inside the Managed Newsroom

1. Mark Richardson, "The McPapering of London, Ontario," *Ryerson Review of Journalism,* Spring 1989, 17.

2. Ibid., 14.

3. Don Gibb, "Profit Motive Driving Paper into Journalistic Bankruptcy," *Content,* November/December 1988, 33–35.

4. Richardson, "McPapering," 19.

5. Kreig, *Spiked,* 16.

6. Mark Hertsgaard, *On Bended Knee: The Press and the Reagan Presidency* (New York: Farrar Straus Giroux, 1988), 80.

7. Jennings, "The Changing Workplace," 2.

8. Louis Peck, "Anger in the Newsroom," *Washington Journalism Review,* December 1991, 24; Ted Pease, "Newsroom 2000: Not My Kid! Journalists Leery of Industry's Future," *Newspaper Research Journal* 13 (Winter/Spring 1992): 34–53.

9. Bill Gloede, "Stress Has a Significant Presence in Newsrooms," *Editor and Publisher,* November 12, 1983, 12–13.

10. Ibid., 12.

11. Giles, *Newsroom Management.*

12. It should be noted that Giles has presided over a startling circulation plunge at the *News* since the Gannett-owned newspaper joined in a much disputed joint operating agreement with the Knight-Ridder-owned *Detroit Free Press.* Within less than a year and a half after the agreement was approved, the *News*'s circulation fell from 700,000 to slightly more than 500,000, and both papers are losing money. While the *News* is still praised for occasional pieces of aggressive journalism, critics say the two papers are becoming homogenized, increasingly having the same graphics and same kind of writing. "*News* readers are getting a *USA Today* dosage," complained one disgruntled *News* reporter. "Good stories become 12–inch stories." (Howard Kurtz, "Detroit's Unhappy Media Marriage," *Washington Post,* March 17, 1991, pp. L1, L4.)

13. Underwood, "MBAs," 24–25. It should be pointed out that Burns was

the managing editor of the Gannett-owned *State Journal* in Lansing, Mich., when I was hired there as a reporter in 1974.

14. John W. C. Johnstone, Edward J. Slawski, William W. Bowman, *The News People: A Sociological Portrait of American Journalists and Their Work* (Urbana: University of Illinois Press, 1976); David H. Weaver and G. Cleveland Wilhoit, *The American Journalist: A Portrait of U.S. News People and Their Work* (Bloomington: Indiana University Press, 1986); Ted Joseph, "Reporters' and Editors' Preference Toward Reporter Decision Making," *Journalism Quarterly* 59 (Summer 1982): 219–222, 248; Cecile Gaziano and David C. Coulson, "Effect of Newsroom Management Styles on Journalists: A Case Study," *Journalism Quarterly* 65 (Winter 1988): 869–880.

15. Johnstone et al., *News People*, 149–154, 184–185.

16. Johnstone, "Organizational Constraints on Newswork," *Journalism Quarterly* 53 (Spring 1976): 12.

17. Weaver and Wilhoit, *American Journalist*, 88–103; Weaver and Wilhoit, *The American Journalist in the 1990s*, preliminary report (Arlington, Va.: The Freedom Forum, 1992), 1, 10.

18. Weaver and Wilhoit, *American Journalist*, 75, 99; Weaver and Wilhoit, *American Journalist in the 1990s*, 1, 11, 14. In their most recent study, Weaver and Wilhoit said 21 percent of their sample—almost double that of 1981–82— say they plan to exit the profession within the next five years. Weaver and Wilhoit say they see this tied to a significant decline in job satisfaction, with complaints about pay and the need for a new challenge most often cited.

19. Lee J. Guittar, "Winning Back Management Rights," *Newspaper Controller*, March 1980, 2.

20. John H. McMillan, "It's Time to Reinvent the City Editor," *Gannetteer*, special issue, January 1982, 2–3.

21. Johnstone et al., *News People*, 142; Weaver and Wilhoit, *American Journalist*, 88.

22. Frank Quine, "What People Think of Their Jobs: Newspapers and Bosses," in Lee Stinnett, ed., *The Changing Face of the Newsroom* (Washington, D.C.: American Society of Newspaper Editors, 1989), 10, 39–54.

23. Ibid., 41.

24. Fred Fedler, Tom Buhr and Diane Taylor, "Journalists Who Leave the News Media Seem Happier, Find Better Jobs," *Newspaper Research Journal* 9 (Winter 1988): 15–23.

25. George Blake, "Examining the Vital News-Circulation Relationship," *Gannetteer*, special issue, July 1981, 2–5.

26. Guittar, "Management Rights," 2.

27. Karen Schneider, telephone interview with the author, November · 1987.

28. Francis Pollock, "Knight-Ridder Wants to Know the *Real* You," *Columbia Journalism Review*, January/February 1978, 25–28.

29. Patricia P. Renfroe, "Productivity: Technology Helps, but People Are the Key," *Presstime*, September 1987, 32–33.

30. Mark Ingham, "Performance Reviews," *Presstime*, August 1986, 18–19. See also Goltz, "Newspapers Try Formal Methods of Evaluating Performance," *Presstime*, October 1989, 30–32.

31. Renfroe, "Productivity," 32.

32. Chris Argyris, *Behind the Front Page: Organizational Self-Renewal in a Metropolitan Newspaper* (San Francisco: Jossey-Bass, 1974), 1–33, 267–268.

33. Ibid., 244.

34. Kenneth Edwards, "Improving the Profit Plan by Evaluating Newsroom Efficiency," *Newspaper Controller*, September 1980, 4–5.

35. It is interesting to note how these ideas have been absorbed by the newspaper industry. Consider these sample questions taken from *Constructing the Future: A Self-Test for Editors* (Washington, D.C.: American Society of Newspaper Editors, 1989): "Do you know enough about the 'business' side to be an effective editor? Have you spent time learning about the advertising and circulation departments? Are you effectively explaining to your staff the corporate decisions that impact on the newspaper and the newsroom? Are you thinking about new ways to package and deliver information, in the context of the technological revolution? Does your paper, through survey research, carefully track the shifting needs and interests of your audience? Do you have a top editor or team of editors assigned to longer-ranged planning? Are you redefining news, redesigning sections and re-examining beats to meet your readers' changing needs and interests?"

36. Paul McMaster, "Management Techniques," in *Newsroom Management Handbook*, Chapter 15, pp. 1–5.

37. See David Halberstam, *The Reckoning* (New York: Avon, 1987). Although in this book Halberstam isn't writing about the newspaper business, many of his conclusions about the profit-mongering, bureaucratic rigidity, and short-term thinking of the American auto industry apply to the U.S. daily newspaper industry.

38. Joseph Nocera, "Making It at the *Washington Post*," *Washington Monthly*, January 1979, 10–22.

39. Miller, "Managing the Newsroom: Trading Tough Talk for TLC," *Washington Journalism Review*, March 1986, 30–33.

40. Ibid., 31.

41. Patrick R. Parsons, John Finnegan, Jr., and William Benham, "Editors and Their Roles," in Robert G. Picard, James P. Winter, Maxwell E. McCombs, and Stephen Lacy, eds., *Press Concentration and Monopoly: New Perspectives on Newspaper Ownership and Operation* (Norwood, N.J.: Ablex, 1988), 100.

42. Tom Goldstein, *The News at Any Cost* (New York: Simon and Schuster, 1985), 93.

43. Underwood, "MBAs," 28–29.

44. Ibid., 29.

45. Ibid.

46. Ibid.

47. Ibid.

48. Ibid.

49. Ibid., 30. See also Tom McNichol, "Proliferating Prizes," *Washington Journalism Review*, July 1986, 35–37.

50. Underwood, "MBAs," 30.

51. Ibid.

52. Ibid.

4. The Historical Roots of the Marketing and Management Revolution

1. F. M. Ball, "Circulation Problems," in Merle Thorpe, ed., *The Coming Newspaper* (New York: Henry Holt, 1915), 308.

2. Alfred McClung Lee, *The Daily Newspaper in America: The Evolution of a Social Instrument* (New York: Octagon, 1973), 642.

3. Ibid., 642–643.

4. Ibid., 643.

5. Carl E. Lindstrom, *The Fading American Newspaper* (Gloucester, Ma.: Peter Smith, 1964), 9.

6. Chakravarty and Torcellini, "Citizen Kane," 82. See also John Morton, "It Can't Get Any Worse, Can It?" *Washington Journalism Review*, March 1992, 66. Morton notes that despite the recession and the disappearance of more than 130 daily newspapers in the 1980s and 1990s many newspapers still maintained profit margins of 20 and 30 percent or even higher.

7. For example, see Anne Burris and Bob Puhala, "The Thomson Machine: Small Papers, Big Profits," *Columbia Journalism Review*, May/June 1987, 12, 16.

8. Halberstam, *The Powers That Be* (New York: Laurel, 1979), 1007–1008.

9. Bagdikian, "Newspaper Poverty," 19–20.

10. Underwood, "Retail Stores," 33–35.

11. Nelson, "Riding Out the Storm," 15–17. Nelson notes that the American Newspaper Publishers Association reports U.S. daily newspaper average operating margins declined from 20.2 percent in 1985 to 16.5 percent in 1990. But Nelson also quotes Morton as noting that many other industries don't do that well during a boom. "The real financial problem that the newspaper industry is having is its difficulty in meeting the profit expectations established in past years," Morton says. "Institutional investors, family shareholders, banks and others with a direct stake in newspaper operations do not like it when profits slip, even if from lofty levels to nearly lofty levels. The only real danger in this problem is that some newspapers might therefore try to do too much to shore up profitability, by trimming staff, news hole and journalistic effort. Some moves in these directions may be advisable, but going even a few steps too far damages product quality, a consequence liable to far outlast the difficulties of the current recession."

12. Gerald J. Baldasty, *The Commercialization of News in the Nineteenth Century* (Madison: University of Wisconsin Press, 1992). Excerpts come from chapter 3 ("Advertising and the Press") and chapter 5 ("Shaping and Packaging the News: Luring Readers and Advertisers") as well as from an earlier draft of the manuscript.

13. Jack R. Hart, "Horatio Alger in the Newsroom: Social Origins of American Editors," *Journalism Quarterly* 53 (Spring 1976): 14–20.

14. Lee, *The Daily Newspaper*, 206.

15. Ted Curtis Smythe, "The Reporter, 1880–1900: Working Conditions and Their Influence on the News," *Journalism History* 7 (Spring 1980): 1–10.

16. J. Herbert Altschull, *Agents of Power: The Role of the News Media in Human Affairs* (New York: Longman, 1984), 66–67.

17. Ibid., 65.

18. Ibid.

19. Stuart Ewen, *Captains of Consciousness: Advertising and the Social Roots of the Consumer Culture* (New York: McGraw-Hill, 1977), 213–214.

20. Michael Schudson, *Advertising, The Uneasy Persuasion: Its Dubious Impact on American Society* (New York: Basic, 1986), 175–176.

21. Schudson, *Discovering the News: A Social History of American Newspapers* (New York: Basic, 1978), 88–106.

22. Smythe, "The Reporter," 3, 8.

23. Schudson, *Discovering the News*, 106–120.

24. Upton Sinclair, *The Brass Check: A Study of American Journalism* (Pasadena, Ca.: Published by the author, 1920), 22.

25. Ibid., 125.

26. Altschull, *Agents of Power*, 64.

27. John M. Harrison and Harry H. Stein, *Muckraking: Past, Present, and Future* (University Park: Pennsylvania State University Press, 1978), 21.

28. Carey McWilliams, "Is Muckraking Coming Back?" *Columbia Journalism Review*, Fall 1970, 8–15.

29. Leonard Downie, Jr., *The New Muckrakers* (New York: Mentor, 1978).

30. Ibid., 257.

31. Harrison and Stein, *Muckraking*, 142.

32. Walter Lippmann, *Public Opinion* (New York: Free Press, 1965).

33. Ibid., 229, 233–249.

34. Edwin Diamond, *Good News, Bad News* (Cambridge: MIT Press, 1980), 232–240.

35. Douglass Cater, *The Fourth Branch of Government* (New York: Vintage, 1959), 2.

36. James Boylan, "Newspeople," *The Wilson Quarterly*, special issue, 1982, 74.

37. Ibid., 80.

38. Schudson, *Discovering the News*, 181.

39. Clayton Kirkpatrick, "A Practical Matter of Philosophy," *Bulletin* of ASNE, October 1983, 38. Kirkpatrick says of the survey, "The disquieting results disclosed an image problem. . . . Many described the paper as partisan and biased and, therefore, lacking credibility. Young people described it as unattractive and old-fashioned. Its most loyal readers were found in the upper age brackets."

40. Bagdikian, *The Effete Conspiracy and Other Crimes by the Press* (New York: Harper and Row, 1972), 3–17.

41. Anthony Smith, *Goodbye Gutenberg: The Newspaper Revolution of the 1980s* (New York: Oxford University Press, 1981), 183–186.

42. Diamond, " 'Reporter Power' Takes Root," *Columbia Journalism Review*, Summer 1970, 13.

43. Ron Dorfman, "Democracy in the Newsroom: Notes on the Movement Towards Non-Seigneurial Journalism," in Charles C. Flippen, ed., *Liberating*

the Media: The New Journalism (Washington, D.C.: Acropolis, 1974), 118–124.

44. Edmund B. Lambeth, *Committed Journalism: An Ethic for the Profession* (Bloomington: Indiana University Press, 1986), 116.

45. Boylan, "Newspeople," 79–85.

46. Michael J. O'Neill, "A Newspaper Editor Looks at the Press," *Wall Street Journal,* May 6, 1982, p. 28.

47. O'Neill, "The Ebbing of the 'Great Investigative Wave,'" *Bulletin* of ASNE, September 1983, 26–27.

48. First and foremost, U.S. newspapers are money-making ventures, and their coverage of government often reflects it. The underlying economic motives of the press can shape newspaper content as they did, for example, when the *Detroit Free Press* and the *Miami Herald* (both Knight-Ridder newspapers) withheld or softened editorial criticism of former attorney general Edwin Meese while Meese was considering Knight-Ridder's petition to link the *Free Press* with Gannett's *Detroit News* in a joint operating agreement. (See "Darts and Laurels," *Columbia Journalism Review,* September/October 1988, 25.) And yet the press has traditionally been most aggressive in pursuing the wrongdoings of government. Cynics would say that this is because the activities of government seldom directly threaten the economic interests of newspapers, at least compared to the activities of important businesses in the community, large advertisers, or influential business people. But even here, the inertia of the press often seems to pull it back into a passive relationship with government, despite cyclical upsurges of aggressive coverage.

49. Peter Dreier, "The Corporate Complaint Against the Media," *The Quill,* November 1983, 17–29.

50. Bagdikian, *The Media Monopoly* (Boston: Beacon, 1983), 58.

51. Dreier, "Corporate Complaint," 26–29.

52. Dreier, "The Position of the Press in the U.S. Power Structure," *Social Problems* 29 (February 1982): 298–307.

53. David Paletz and Robert M. Entman, *Media*Power*Politics* (New York: Free Press, 1982), 12.

54. Robert Cirino, *Don't Blame the People* (New York: Vintage, 1972), 197.

55. Michael Parenti, *Inventing Reality: The Politics of the Mass Media* (New York: St. Martin's, 1986), 55–56.

56. Edith Efron, *The News Twisters* (Manor, 1972), 207. Efron's study has been criticized by researchers who claim that the networks showed no systematic bias in covering the 1968 presidential candidates. (See Robert L. Stevenson, Richard A. Eisenger, Barry M. Feinberg, and Alan B. Kotok, "Untwisting The *News Twisters*: A Replication of Efron's Study," *Journalism Quarterly* 50 (Summer 1973): 211–19.)

57. Austin Ranney, *Channels of Power: The Impact of Television on American Politics* (New York: Basic, 1983), 42–50.

58. James K. Batten, "Press-Enterprise Lecture," Riverside, Ca., April 3, 1989.

5. *Imitations of the Tube*

1. Ranney, *Channels of Power*, 22.

2. Sydney H. Schanberg, "More and More, Newspapers Follow TV," *The Seattle Times* (reprint from *Newsday*, distributed by Los Angeles Times-Washington Post News Service), May 23, 1991, p. A17.

3. Walker, "Quit," 41.

4. Harry F. Waters, "The Future of Television," *Newsweek*, October 17, 1988, 85.

5. William J. Small, "Network News Is: Dead, Dying, King of the Mountain!" *Washington Journalism Review*, May 1989, 27.

6. Jon Katz, "Beyond Broadcast Journalism," *Columbia Journalism Review*, March/April 1992, 19–23. Katz isn't entirely pessimistic in his assessment of the future of television broadcast news. Even though the news operations at the networks and local stations are under heavy economic pressure, he notes that television news is "hardly becoming extinct" and is "spreading all over the place" at C-SPAN, CNN, and new cable channels with everything from twenty-four-hour local news operations to live coverage of a wide range of events. "Commercial broadcast journalism is freer to experiment and innovate than at any time since its inception," he says. "News divisions may have lost much of the virtual monopoly on the daily presentation of news they came to hold through their evening newscasts, and they may no longer be able to compete effectively on breaking stories. But that leaves a lot of room—for real commentary, more reports, and reporting away from the media clusters in Washington and New York, a revival of investigative units looking at crime, waste, and corruption, and closer looks at largely untapped subjects like science, technology, popular culture, and religion."

7. Patrick Maines, "Save the Networks to Save the Stations," *Washington Journalism Review*, January/February 1991, 57.

8. Waters, "Television," 85.

9. Ibid., 94.

10. John Hart, "TV's Identity Crisis," *The Quill*, December 1988, 30–31. See also John McManus, "Local TV News: Not a Pretty Picture," *Columbia Journalism Review*, May/June 1990, 42–43. McManus spent three days a week for a month in the newsrooms of four Western television stations where he analyzed news programing. He concluded that 56 percent of the stories he viewed were inaccurate or misleading—with many containing major errors.

11. John Engstrom, "News Flash: Anything Goes as the Big Three Slug It Out to Be Seattle's No. 1," *Seattle Post-Intelligencer*, May 30, 1991, pp. C1, C7.

12. Kit Boss, "Julie Blacklow Quits KING-TV," *Seattle Times*, January 28, 1992, p. F7.

13. Julie Blacklow, "10–Second Sound Bites May Be the Undoing of Real TV Journalism," *Seattle Times/Seattle Post-Intelligencer*, February 9, 1992, p. A19.

14. Patricia Clem, "TV Outlook for the '90s," *The Quill*, September 1990, 32–35. Perhaps the most dramatic illustration of the impact of network budget cuts and staff reductions occurred during the Gulf war. The reputations of the

network news operations, which have cut back their foreign news bureaus, suffered badly from their spotty coverage of the war while the reputation of Cable News Network soared. (See Katz, "Collateral Damage to Network News," *Columbia Journalism Review,* March/April 1991, 29.)

15. Edward Jay Epstein, *Between Fact and Fiction: The Problem of Journalism* (New York: Vintage, 1975), 186–198.

16. Ibid., 193.

17. Waters, "Television," 84.

18. Ted Dracos, "News Directors Are Lousy Managers," *Washington Journalism Review,* September 1989, 40.

19. Ibid., 41.

20. Diamond, *The Tin Kazoo: Television, Politics, and the News* (Cambridge: MIT Press, 1980), 75.

21. Harry J. Skornia, *Television and the News: A Critical Appraisal* (Palo Alto: Pacific Books, 1974), 50.

22. Epstein, *News from Nowhere: Television and the News* (New York: Vintage, 1974).

23. Les Brown, *Televi$ion: The Business behind the Box* (New York: Harvest, 1971), 16.

24. Tony Schwartz, "Why TV News Is Increasingly Being Packaged as Entertainment," *New York Times,* October 17, 1982, Arts and Leisure section, pp. 1, 33.

25. John Weisman, "Network News Today: Which Counts More—Journalism or Profits?" *TV Guide,* October 26, 1985, 7.

26. Peter J. Boyer, *Who Killed CBS?: The Undoing of America's Number One News Network* (New York: Random House, 1988), 114, 146, 157.

27. Ibid., 328.

28. Diamond, "News by the Numbers," *New York,* May 25, 1987, 20–21.

29. Brown, *Televi$ion.* Erik Barnouw, *Tube of Plenty: The Evolution of American Television* (New York: Oxford University Press, 1982).

30. Barnouw, *The Sponsor: Notes on a Modern Potentate* (New York: Oxford University Press, 1979), 127.

31. Ibid., 82.

32. Conrad Smith, "News Critics, Newsworkers and Local Television News," *Journalism Quarterly* 65 (Summer 1988): 341–346.

33. Marshall McLuhan, *Understanding Media: The Extensions of Man* (New York: Mentor, 1964).

34. Gladys Engel Lang and Kurt Lang, *Politics and Television Re-viewed* (Beverly Hills, Ca.: Sage, 1984), 29–57.

35. Epstein, *News from Nowhere,* 3–43.

36. Joshua Meyrowitz, *No Sense of Place: The Impact of Electronic Media on Social Behavior* (New York: Oxford University Press, 1986).

37. Ibid., 173–183.

38. Neil Postman, *Amusing Ourselves to Death: Public Discourse in the Age of Show Business* (New York: Penguin, 1986), 111.

39. Lawrence Lichty, "Video Versus Print," *The Wilson Quarterly,* special issue, 1982, 49–57.

40. Urban, "10 Myths," 20.

41. Walter Ong, *The Presence of the Word: Some Prolegomena for Cultural and Religious History* (Minneapolis: University of Minnesota Press, 1986).

6. Managers and the Mind of the Computer

1. Pegie Stark's presentation at the Journalism Workshop on Teaching, Writing, Reporting, and Editing (Funded by the Gannett Foundation), School of Journalism, Indiana University, July 29, 1988.

2. "Mac" technology has almost become a generic word for computer graphics and design. "Mac" refers to Apple's MacIntosh computer system, which has been the leading system among newspapers converting to computer graphics and pagination technology although other systems now have strong presences in the market.

3. Underwood, "The Desktop Challenge," *Columbia Journalism Review,* May/June 1989, 43–45. See also Goltz, "The Workforce Reorganization," *Presstime,* September 1989, 18–23. Goltz reports that computers dominate the news and advertising departments and are well on the way to controlling the complete production process. This, he says, has led to a "sea change" in the newsroom work force, where reporters and editors at terminals are taking over the old typesetting functions and are taking on many of the responsibilities of the old composing room.

4. Rosalind C. Truitt, "Systems Editors," *Presstime,* March 1988, 8.

5. Barbara Garson, *The Electronic Sweatshop: How Computers Are Transforming the Office of the Future into the Factory of the Past* (New York: Simon and Schuster, 1988).

6. Her points can certainly be applied to the newspaper industry where computerization has led newspapers to give their readers the news in a less timely fashion—rather than the other way around. There is hardly a daily newspaper whose printing schedule has not been shoved forward because of the computerization of the production process. Newspapers use computers to save money and organize the news process more efficiently. If that means earlier deadlines—and more stale news—so be it.

7. Garson, *Sweatshop,* 155–156.

8. This is not true of the backshop. Newspaper unions have been steadily losing the battle to retain traditional printing and paste-up jobs in the face of the new computer technologies.

9. For two examples of newspaper coverage of VDTs, see Peter H. Lewis, "Trying to Assess the Potential Hazards of Video Terminals," *New York Times,* April 21, 1991, p. F9; David Streitfeld, "Debating the Perils of VDTs," *Washington Post,* March 18, 1991, p. D5.

10. Weaver and Wilhoit, *The American Journalist,* 152.

11. Ibid.

12. Ibid., 153.

13. Stone, *Examining Newspapers,* 59–61.

14. Weaver and Wilhoit, *The American Journalist,* 155–156.

15. John M. Shipman, Jr. "Computerization and Job Satisfaction in the Newsroom: Four Factors to Consider," *Newspaper Research Journal* 8 (Fall 1986): 69–78.

16. Ibid., 75.

17. Richard P. Cunningham, "Privacy and the Electronic Newsroom," *Columbia Journalism Review*, November/December, 1984, 32–34.

18. I know this from my own career in newspaper work. All were general violations of the companies' computer policies. But the point was that the computer system was capable of the task—and somebody was able to figure out how to put it to use. Cunningham concluded that, while newspapers have tried to protect the privacy of their computer system, no one should assume privacy is foolproof. For example, he notes that there must always be one person who retains a password to everyone's computer files—the systems manager.

19. Tim Miller, "The Data-Base Revolution," *Columbia Journalism Review*, September/October 1988, 35–38.

20. Peter Prichard, *The Making of McPaper: The Inside Story of USA Today* (Kansas City, Mo.: Andrews, McMeel and Parker, 1987), 113–114. To its credit, *USA Today* has begun to expand its use of computers into some sophisticated investigative areas. In recent years the newspaper has produced some interesting computer-investigative articles.

21. *The Future of Newspapers* (Proceedings of an American Society of Newspaper Editors conference, April 8, 1987), 28.

22. A. J. Liebling, *The Press* (New York: Pantheon, 1981), 32.

23. Underwood, "Desktop," 44.

24. Ibid., 45.

25. Ibid., 44.

26. Ibid., 43.

27. William Rinehart, telephone interview with the author, October 1989.

28. Gary Gumpert, *Talking Tombstones and Other Tales of the Media Age* (New York: Oxford University Press, 1988), 163.

29. Theodore Roszak, *The Cult of Information: The Folklore of Computers and the True Art of Thinking* (New York: Pantheon, 1986), 22.

30. Ong, *The Word*, 260.

31. Meyrowitz, *No Sense of Place*, 322.

32. Smith, *Goodbye Gutenberg*, 300.

33. Ibid., 305.

7. *The Think Tanks Spread the Word*

1. "Reinventing Newspapers," 28–38, 40–47.

2. Ibid., 30.

3. Ibid., 42.

4. "American Press Institute: 1988 Seminars," *Bulletin of the American Press Institute* (Reston, Va., 1988).

5. 1988 Catalogue, *The Poynter Institute for Media Studies* (St. Petersburg, Fla., 1988).

6. Brown, "First-Level Editors," 21.

7. Mario Garcia, telephone interview with the author, December 1987.

8. Stone, *Examining Newspapers*, 93–94.

9. Ibid., 89–90.

10. Quine, "Training," *Presstime*, January 1985, 33.

11. Smith, *Goodbye Gutenberg*, 77–78.

12. *Directory of Media Studies Centers, Midcareer Fellowship and Training Programs for Journalists*, Gannett Center for Media Studies, 1989. The debt owed by communications academics to the altruism of the newspaper industry was wonderfully illustrated at a reception given by the Freedom Forum at the 1992 Association for Education in Journalism and Mass Communication convention in Montreal. The reception was held to honor programs in teaching, ethics, and advertising that the foundation sponsors at Indiana University, University of North Carolina, and University of South Carolina and was attended by most of the "heavy-weights" in academic communications. Unfortunately, the amount of money available from the foundation for university-related programs is relatively small compared to the demand—particularly when it comes to support of academic research of the communications industry. For example, a Freedom Forum–sponsored program of $5,000 grants at the University of Illinois is virtually the only industry program that directly supports university communications research. As one academic left the reception, he was overheard to grumble, "It's too bad they can get us so cheaply."

13. See the series in *Presstime* written by Jean Gaddy Wilson, who heads the New Directions for News. For example: Wilson and Iris Igawa, "Strategy No. 6: 'Target New and Different Readers,'" *Presstime*, June 1991, 72–73.

14. Ted Natt, telephone interview with the author, August 1989.

15. Logan, "Newspaper Odyssey," 40.

16. Ibid.

17. "API Seminars," 1988.

18. Gary Blonston, "SND at 10: A Healthy Search for Identity," *The Louisville Chronicles: The News from the Society of Newspaper Design Workshop in Louisville, Kentucky*, October 15, 1988, 21.

19. Ibid.

20. *APME '87* (Associated Press Managing Editors convention agenda, September, 15–18 1987), 14–17. Again this convention is a good example of a typical industry gathering during the reader-oriented 1980s.

21. These are my conclusions based on attending the program. Many of the seminars were very valuable to people like myself making the transition from journalism into teaching. But there was also a strong emphasis on marketing values during the program.

22. Dorfman, "Learning Cashbox Journalism," *The Quill*, July/August 1986, 12–13.

23. Kathy Kozdemba, telephone interview with author, December 1987.

24. Bill Pukmel, "Budget Building," in the *Newsroom Management Handbook*, Chapter 22, p. 1.

25. *American Press Institute: Catalog 1991* (Reston, Va., 1991); *American Press Institute: Catalog 1992* (Reston, Va., 1992).

26. I was in attendance for this seminar.

27. Matthew Cooper, "Hot Chain Nixes Wingo, Buscapades—Nabs Pulitzers, Big Bucks," *Washington Monthly*, September 1987, 17–22.

28. Ibid., 21.

29. "Reinventing Newspapers," 41.

30. Ibid., 41, 44.

31. Ibid., 28, 43.

32. Joel Benenson, "Identity Crisis," *NewsInc.*, April 1991, 22–24.

33. Ibid., 23.

8. The Cult of Colorful Tidbits

1. *Creative Marketing Strategies*, 28.

2. Robert A. Logan, "*USA Today*'s Innovations and Their Impact on Journalism Ethics," *Journal of Mass Media Ethics* 1 (Spring/Summer 1986): 74–87.

3. Prichard, *McPaper*, 22.

4. *Creative Marketing Strategies*, 11. Also see George Albert Gladney, "The McPaper Revolution?: *USA Today*-style Innovation at Large U.S. Dailies," *Newspaper Research Journal* 13 (Winter/Spring 1992): 54–71. Gladney analyzed 230 dailies with circulations over 50,000 and concluded that smaller dailies and those in chains tended to imitate *USA Today* more strongly in the use of color, graphics, capsules, brief text, fluff, and trivia. Larger dailies—including such prestige newspapers as the *Philadelphia Inquirer,* the *Providence Journal,* the *New York Times,* the *Washington Post,* and the *Boston Globe*—tended more strongly to "resist" *USA Today*-style innovations. However, Gladney said there is evidence that even the elite, traditional newspapers have "made some accommodation" to "reader-friendly" journalism and the "tighter-and-brighter approach."

5. Prichard, *McPaper*, 146.

6. Ibid., 91.

7. Ibid., 117; *Creative Marketing Strategies*, 28.

8. Miller, "Lost Readers," 62.

9. Daniel C. Hallin, "Cartography, Community, and the Cold War," in Robert Karl Manoff and Michael Schudson, eds., *Reading The News* (New York: Pantheon, 1986), 124.

10. Weiss, "Gannettoids," 18.

11. Despite its losses, the newspaper has made some positive gains in advertising and circulation. *USA Today* executives have noted with optimism that the newspaper hasn't seen its advertising linage drop as far as most other newspapers during the recession. (See Paul Farhi, "Gannett Says a Profit in '89 Is Unlikely at *USA Today,*" *Washington Post,* October 12, 1989, pp. E1, E5; Farhi, "Gannett's Profit Up a Fraction: *USA Today* Is Lone Star for Media Giant," *Washington Post,* April 18, 1990, pp. F1, F10; Joanne Lipman, "Newspapers' Results Bode Ill for Economy," *Wall Street Journal,* April 24, 1991, p. B8.)

12. Underwood, "Identity Crisis," 25.

13. Underwood, "MBAs," 25–26. Some journalists at Gannett's newspapers say the *USA Today* management approach has been spread to their newspapers in the form of News 2000. They say that the marketing-oriented values of the company are adhered to by newsroom managers like an ideology and those who are not true believers have a rough go of it. "It's like living in a communist

country," says a reporter about newsroom life at one local Gannett newspaper. "That's how I describe it."

14. McMasters, "Management Techniques," in *Newsroom Management Handbook,* Chapter 15, p. 1.

15. McMillan, "Reinvent," 2–3.

16. Barbara Henry, "Communication: A Breakdown That's Fixable," *Gannetteer,* special issue, January 1982, 4.

17. Sheryl Bills, "Good Reporters Deeply Concerned about Commitment," *Gannetteer,* special issue, January 1982, 5.

18. Larry Fuller, "How to Improve City Desk Operations," *Gannetteer,* special issue, January 1982, 6–7.

19. Peter Katel, "The New Mexican," in Ghiglione's *The Buying and Selling,* 114–135. It should be noted that Gannett resold the newspaper to former owner Robert McKinney in 1989 after McKinney prevailed in a court contest. McKinney alleged Gannett had violated its contractual agreement to allow him to retain editorial control over the newspaper after the sale to Gannett.

20. Since the JOA, the *News*'s circulation during the week has plummeted. This isn't a surprise. The *News,* by returning to its slot as an afternoon newspaper (it produced a morning edition prior to the JOA), has followed the trend of fading afternoon newspapers. In addition, Gannett has not done well in other competitive situations. After struggling with the Oakland *Tribune* (which it renamed *East Bay Today* for a time after acquiring it in a merger with Combined Communications), Gannett finally turned the newspaper over to publisher Robert Maynard as a way of escaping the highly competitive Bay area market. Gannett has also struggled in Little Rock where its *Arkansas Gazette* was sold and closed after the company lost a two-fisted competition with the independently owned *Arkansas Democrat.*

21. Bagdikian, *Media Monopoly,* 69–91.

22. Al Neuharth, "Air Travel Priority: Return of 'Sky Girls,' " *USA Today,* July 28, 1989, p. 9A.

23. Bagdikian, *Media Monopoly,* 78.

24. Kurtz, "Paper Known for 'News Bites' Offers Heartier Fare," *Washington Post* (distributed by the Los Angeles Times-Washington Post News Service), December 28, 1991.

25. Sheila Owens, "Gannett New Business Expands Its Niche," *Gannetteer,* May 1991, 1–3.

26. James W. Carey, *Communication as Culture: Essays on Media and Society* (Boston: Unwin Hyman, 1989), 13–35.

27. Ibid., 21.

9. What Newspapers—and Newspaper Researchers—Don't Tell Us About Newspapers

1. Liebling, *The Press,* 36.

2. I recall that this call came in the summer of 1989. My notes on the telephone call aren't clear on the date. The reporter indicated that he was aware

of the *Wall Street Journal*'s use of readership research in its remake of its format in 1988.

3. A Dow Jones' press release says the new design was based on, among other things, "discussions with readers in various regions of the United States." The *DJ Bulletin* (the Dow Jones employee newsletter) of October 3, 1988, says the changes came after "months of planning" and "some 20 test editions" of the redesigned newspaper. "The changes and improvements we are making are responses to the evolving needs and interests of our readers," associate publisher Peter Kann was quoted as saying.

4. The reporter who originally interviewed me wouldn't discuss what had happened to the story when I called later. He said the decision about the story had been made in New York, and he referred me to Rout.

5. Christine Reid Veronis, "Research Moves to Center Stage," *Presstime,* November 1989, 20–26.

6. The *Seattle Times* is one newspaper that has released some details of a newsroom staff morale survey. Then *Times* ombudsman Frank Wetzel disclosed in a column that the newspaper's marketing-minded editors were most often described as "arrogant" and "aloof" by employees in the survey, followed closely by adjectives like "insecure," "isolated," and "superfluous." (Underwood, "Marriage of Convenience," 45.) See also Kreig, *Spiked,* 125–127. In a *Courant* staff morale survey, Kreig says, executives were "shocked" at employee complaints of too much bureaucracy, too much direction from "absent landlords," too close links between editors and the business community, too many stories written to mollify advertisers, and a "total disregard for humane values" by top management in their treatment of employees.

7. Carol Smith, "Running Newspapers or Building Empires: Analysis of Gannett's Ideology," *Newspaper Research Journal* 9 (Winter 1988): 37–47.

8. For a nonacademic analysis of Gannett's shaping of its public image, see Bagdikian, *Media Monopoly,* 69–91.

9. How would a researcher cut to the heart of the tactic Gannett uses so brilliantly—both within the company and outside it—to avoid an open discussion of the way the bottom line shapes the editorial operations of its properties? It would be very hard. It would take time and creativity and follow-up. And it hasn't been done.

I think back to a time in the late 1970s when I was sitting in on a Gannett regional management meeting in southern California. In the room were executives from the company's home office querying Gannett's California editors and business managers about their newspapers' performance. Time and again, the Californians would cheerfully present contradictory pictures of their operations: the business folk touting their efforts to trim newshole, hold down hiring, and freeze salaries; the editors just as cheerfully talking about the accomplishments of the news side, the reportorial successes, the big projects, the prizes. The Gannett executives didn't seem the least bit fazed by the upbeat and evasive talk, nor did they seem interested in asking anybody to reconcile these apparently antithetical versions of life at Gannett's California newspapers.

10. Stone, *Examining Newspapers,* 77–99. Among the newspaper management studies that do exist, Ogan (1983) found that 90 percent of male and 83 percent of female managers had participated in some form of management

training, primarily seminars. Chusmir (1983) found that many newsroom jobs are associated with high power needs. Kaufman (1981) said extensive interdepartmental cooperation could promote better relationships at the top executive level but would result in more dissension among lower-level personnel. Joseph (1981) found that as newspapers increase in size, management becomes more centralized, and centralized management systems are less permissive with employees. The Burgoons and Atkin (1982) found journalists love their work, but there was greater job satisfaction among journalists with greater autonomy, particularly younger journalists. In his study of California editors, Bennett (1985) found that 78 percent had been in their current position less than five years and called the turnover rate excessive.

Some of the studies do point to the trends of MBA management, but sometimes they are contradicted by other studies. For example, Jim Willis concludes in a survey of 52 editors that, despite the upsurge of interest in market research, most editors are still judging news value on the basis of professional standards and not based on what they feel their readers want to read. (Willis, "Editors, Readers and News Judgment," *Editor and Publisher*, February 7, 1987, 14–15.) On the other hand, Weaver and Wilhoit found that significantly more journalists—and editors, in particular—accepted the importance of entertaining the audience. (Weaver and Wilhoit, *American Journalist*, 122–123.) In their study, Weaver and Wilhoit also found that the median age of managing editors had dropped by ten years between 1971 and 1982. (Weaver and Wilhoit, *American Journalist*, 71.)

11. Stone, *Examining Newspapers*, 99. Like Stone, the communications research community has concluded, based on its surveys, content analysis, and methodological examinations, that the relationship between monopoly and the decline in newspaper content is "rather inconclusive and scanty." (A. Carlos Ruotolo, "Monopoly and Socialization," in Picard et al., eds., *Press Concentration*, 117.)

In fact, researcher F. Dennis Hale goes even further in his study in the same volume. (Hale, "Editorial Diversity and Concentration," in Picard et al., eds., *Press Concentration*, 161–176.) He found that editorial pages do not deteriorate under chain ownership (although neither do they improve, he concedes). Hale notes that some people feel chain ownership is a "dead issue" in an era of growing consolidation in virtually every industry. And he concludes, just as Gannett would like him to conclude, that "the all-time giant, Gannett, makes a difficult target for those who wish to limit the size of chains. For Gannett, with 91 newspapers and numerous other holdings in 1986, is a progressive corporate leader in the promotion of women and minorities and in the protection of the First Amendment. To attack Gannett is to attack a civil liberties crusader." (Hale in Picard, et al., *Press Concentration*, 176.)

My intuition—and my five-year experience as a Gannett News Service employee—tells me that Gannett *does* very consciously craft its journalistic crusades and the public relations efforts that back them up to create a corporate image that makes it harder to attack the company's monopolistic practices. Like *Playboy* and *Penthouse*, which are careful to put socially redeeming reading material around the pictorial layouts, Gannett has kept congressional critics, tax reformers, and antitrust enforcers off balance by promoting itself as a champion of open government and First Amendment principles and the cause of women and minorities. This isn't to say the company doesn't have sincere reasons for pushing the causes. But its motives are mixed at best, I believe.

12. Stone, *Examining Newspapers,* 99–104.

13. I wish to thank my colleague Richard Kielbowicz at the University of Washington for his insights into this issue.

14. Sharon H. Polansky and Douglas W. W. Hughes, "Managerial Innovation in Newspaper Organizations," *Newspaper Research Journal* 8 (Fall, 1986): 1–11.

15. Mark Fishman, *Manufacturing the News* (Austin: University of Texas Press, 1988), 51, 138.

16. Gaziano and Coulson, "Effect of Newsroom Management Styles," 869–880.

17. Steve Pasternack and Sandra H. Utt, "Subject Perception of Newspaper Characteristics Based on Front Page Design," *Newspaper Research Journal* 8 (Fall 1986): 29–35.

18. Ruth C. Flegel and Steven H. Chaffee, "Influences of Editors, Readers, and Personal Opinions on Reporters," *Journalism Quarterly* 48 (Winter 1971): 645–651.

19. Hale, "An In-Depth Look at Chain Ownership," *Editor and Publisher,* April 28, 1984, 30, 88, 90.

20. Most of these studies—funded by the newspaper industry, as they were—are heavy in analyzing such "market-oriented" issues as reader response to color front pages, readership habits of the public, demographics on young readers, the habits of nonreaders, the relationship of content and appearance to circulation.

21. Ernest F. Larkin and Gerald L. Grotta, "A Market Segmentation Approach to Daily Newspaper Audience Studies," *Journalism Quarterly* 56 (Spring 1979): 37.

22. The proprietary studies done by newspapers also should caution academic researchers about drawing grand conclusions about the newspaper business based on the examination of just one or two newspapers. For example, Tom Curley, then Gannett's director of information, said the company's PILOT research project found that in seven Gannett markets readers in different markets behaved and responded very differently. (Curley, "Audience Selectivity Can Be the Key to Newspaper Marketing," *Newspaper Controller,* March 1980, 4–5.)

23. David Pearce Demers and Daniel B. Wackman, "Effect of Chain Ownership on Newspaper Management Goals," *Newspaper Research Journal* 9 (Winter 1988): 59–68.

24. C. N. Olien, P. J. Tichenor and G. A. Donohue, "Relation between Corporate Ownership and Editor Attitudes about Business," *Journalism Quarterly* 65 (Summer 1988): 259–266.

25. For additional discussion of the studies of newspapers that may shed some light on the marketing and readership revolution, see Stone, *Examining Newspapers,* and Picard et al., eds., *Press Concentration.* Some of their conclusions include:

Newsroom Management: Researchers hint at the changes that have come to newsrooms—and the tensions they have created—but the studies create a very incomplete picture. Most studies do conclude that employees prefer participatory systems and want a voice in their work. See Stone, *Examining Newspapers*, 93–99.

Chain Newspapers: Newspaper analysts generally say that chains seldom damage, but also seldom improve, the editorial content of newspapers. However, they do note that chains tend to lead to higher advertising and circulation prices. And there are studies showing some negative influences of chain ownership. See Stone, *Examining Newspapers*, 99–104; Picard, "Pricing Behavior of Newspapers" and Hale, "Editorial Diversity," in Picard et al., eds., *Press Concentration*, 66–67, 161–176.

Competitiveness and Monopoly: In general, researchers have also found that there is no clear relationship between newspaper competition and newspaper performance. While the studies do note a move toward a more homogeneous news product, they blame it on factors other than lack of competition. See McCombs, "Concentration, Monopoly, and Content," in Picard et al., eds., *Press Concentration*, 129–137; Stone, *Examining Newspapers*, 100.

Management Training: The escalation in the use of management training techniques and programs is well-documented by researchers. See Stone, *Examining Newspapers*, 89–90, 98–99.

Professional Satisfaction: Researchers have concluded that journalists, as a group, are satisfied with their work, but they are also jealous of their professional values and autonomy. See Stone, *Examining Newspapers*, 97–98; Johnstone et al., *News People*, 110; Weaver and Wilhoit, *American Journalist*, 100–101.

Writing, Graphic Design, and Packaging: Research in this area has encouraged newspapers in their push toward briefer writing and more colorful presentations of the news. The studies indicate that longer, more complex writing is difficult for readers to comprehend. But the addition of more creative and dramatic prose, packaged with more color, graphics, and modern design, is well-received by readers. See Stone, *Examining Newspapers*, 47–54, 68–72.

26. Steve Weinberg, "Bridging the Chasm," *The Quill*, October 1990, 26–28. Weinberg says that journalists and communications researchers have traditionally viewed each other with suspicion. "Each side is cautious; and each, unsure. . . . Working journalists are fond of declaring that media researchers are out of touch with reality, while researchers accuse the working media of striking the classic ostrich pose—head in the sand—and refusing to advance with the times." It should be noted that Stamm and I delivered a portion of our study as a paper at the 1991 AEJMC convention.

10. The "New" Daily Newspaper Newsroom—and What Our Research Tells Us About It

1. "The State of the Industry," special supplement. Among other things, the editors surveyed indicated that they were focusing more on local news, listening to readers more, using shorter stories, running more graphics and less

investigative reporting, cutting newshole and newsroom budgets, and paying more attention to administrative tasks than to editing.

2. Underwood and Stamm, "Balancing Business with Journalism," 301–317.

3. Underwood, "MBAs," 23–30.

4. Either Keith Stamm or I or both of us conducted the site visits in Washington and Idaho. Edward Bassett, the director of the University of Washington School of Communications, carried out the field work for us in California.

5. Initially a list of management policies was constructed from a series of interviews conducted with both newsroom managers and reporters. Our initial list of statements was circulated for comment to a number of active journalists and communication scholars. This list was revised to make it more inclusive and to correct wording that was perceived as biased. The revised list was circulated several more times and further revised until our advisers appeared to be satisfied. We then tested the statements on a small sample of practicing journalists who confirmed that the statements were reasonably clear and unbiased and accurately reflected actual newsroom policy.

6. Completion rates varied from a high of 93 percent to a low of 51 percent. Generally, the higher rates were obtained at the smaller newspapers. This last point does not appear to be due to any difference in the number of staff willing to participate. At the larger newspapers, a greater percentage of staffers was absent on the day of the site visit because of shift and beat requirements.

7. We were told, among other things, that:

- "We already know our staffers think we focus too much on marketing and readership at the expense of journalism. We don't need your survey to tell us that."
- "We don't want to stir up people by raising philosophical questions."
- "I look at these questions, and I can tell you now how all those dissidents in the newsroom would answer them."
- "We're putting in a new system this summer, and we don't have time for anything that doesn't relate directly to business."
- "We don't want to provide the Guild with anything that could be used against us in contract negotiations."

Although we did eventually succeed in gaining access to some large newspapers, we believe that this self-selection process does bias our findings. Our sample consists primarily of newspapers that were not threatened by the prospect of having their management policies investigated.

8. For the most part, the recession of the early 1990s hadn't yet hit the newspapers we surveyed. According to Stepp and Bagby, the effects of the recession have only intensified the pressures for newspapers to adopt reader-oriented marketing techniques. This also would tend to understate the impact of market-oriented journalism in our findings.

9. Bagby, "Transforming Newspapers," 18–25; Stepp, "Readers Design," 20–24; Goltz, "Reviving a Romance," 16–22.

10. See Fink, *Strategic Newspaper Management*; Lavine and Wackman, *Managing Media Organizations*; Giles, *Newsroom Management*.

11. In our open-ended questions, changes were coded as business-oriented if they reflected the business or marketing goals of the newspaper—i.e., profits, treating readers as customers, integration of business and editorial departments, or tighter management control. The following are sample quotes coded as business-oriented changes: "shorter, more people-oriented stories," "more focus on marketing paper over journalism," "editors preconceive ideas instead of reporters," "more giving readers what we perceive they want, rather than what editors or reporters think may be important," "reduction in traditional coverage techniques causing us to miss stories or find out about them long after the fact," "relentless 'dumbing down' of news content, making it short, pretty, and entertaining," "incredible emphasis on quarter-to-quarter profit gains [makes financial budget for newsroom very unstable—subject to wild swings]," "too many senior editors with very little reporting experience."

Changes were coded as journalistic if they reflected such goals as serving the community, treating readers as citizens, preserving editorial autonomy, or improving newsgathering efforts. The following are sample quotes coded as journalistic changes: "push to open up section fronts without ads," "emphasize regional coverage," "split news and feature/sports operations into completely separate departments," "more detailed election coverage," "weekend coverage of events by bureaus," "expanded zoned editions of the paper," "strong emphasis on what is local," "a decision to hone a sharper edge to metro copy." For further discussion of the methodology of our study, see Underwood and Stamm, "Balancing Business with Journalism," methods section, 305–308.

12. Stamm and Underwood, "Job Satisfaction."

13. In the questionnaire, we asked newsroom staffers to read a list of fifty-two policy statements, indicating degree of emphasis in each case. (A five-point scale was provided on which 1 = no emphasis and 5 = a great deal.)

In the analysis, items were grouped into seven policy indexes. Grouping of the items was based upon each item's relationship to the conceptual typology of policy areas and upon intercorrelations.

1. Emphasis on profits: five items, alpha = .75. Sample item—"How much emphasis does your newspaper give to: put the bottom line first?"

2. Emphasis on serving the reader as a customer: seven items, alpha = .66. Sample item—"How much emphasis does your newspaper give to: make it your first priority to entertain our readers?"

3. Emphasis on integration of business and editorial functions: five items, alpha = .63. Sample item—"How much emphasis does your newspaper give to: encourage the news and business sides of the newspaper to work closely together?"

4. Emphasis on management control over newsroom: seven items, alpha = .67. Sample item—"How much emphasis does your newspaper give to: hire administrators to be newsroom managers?"

5. Emphasis on serving needs of community: six items, alpha = .68. Sample item—"How much emphasis does your newspaper give to: cover the news as we see it, even when people might be offended?"

6. Emphasis on serving reader as citizen: five items, alpha = .67. Sample item—"How much emphasis does your newspaper give to: strive to produce a serious and informative paper?"

7. Emphasis on editorial autonomy: six items, alpha = .72. Sample item—"How much emphasis does your newspaper give to: give reporters some say in decisions about news coverage?"

Indexes for each of the seven dimensions of management policy were constructed by summing responses across items and dividing by the number of items. Cronbach reliability coefficients were then calculated for each of the indexes. In most cases the indexes met or were near to acceptable levels of reliability.

14. The scales were developed by our former University of Washington colleague, Merrill Samuelson. Approximate wording of the items is shown in table 11. See Samuelson, "A Standardized Test to Measure Job Satisfaction in the Newsroom," *Journalism Quarterly* 39 (Summer 1962): 285–291.

15. Lori A. Bergen and David Weaver, "Job Satisfaction of Daily Journalists and Organization Size," *Newspaper Research Journal* 9 (Winter 1988): 1–13; Weaver and Wilhoit, *American Journalist*, 65–103; Johnstone et al., *News People*, 133–156; Gaziano and Coulson, "Newsroom Management Styles," 869–880; Judee K. Burgoon, Michael Burgoon, and Charles K. Atkin, "The World of the Working Journalist," New York: Newspaper Advertising Bureau, 1982; Joseph, "Reporters Decision Making," 219–222, 248; Joseph, "Existing Decision-Making Practices on American Dailies," *Newspaper Research Journal* 2 (Summer 1981): 13–19; Cary B. Ziter, "Commentary: More Effective People Management through QWL," *Newspaper Research Journal* 2 (Spring 1981): 64–69; Gilbert L. Fowler and John Marlin Shipman, "Pennsylvania Editors' Perceptions of Communication in the Newsroom," *Journalism Quarterly* 61 (Winter 1984): 822–826; Polansky and Hughes, "Managerial Innovation," 1–11; Boylan, "Newspeople," 71–85; Fedler, Buhr, and Taylor, "Journalists Who Leave," 15–23.

16. Grace H. Barrett, "Job Satisfaction among Newspaperwomen," *Journalism Quarterly* 61 (Autumn 1984): 593–599; Edwin A. Locke, "The Nature and Causes of Job Satisfaction," in Marvin D. Dunnette, ed., *Handbook of Industrial and Organizational Psychology* (Chicago: Rand McNally, 1976), 1297–1349.

17. In our questionnaire, staffers were asked to rank the management style in their newsroom on a scale ranging from authoritarian to democratic. Strongly authoritarian styles correlated negatively with job satisfaction; democratic styles correlated positively.

18. Miller, "Managing the Newsroom," 30–33. In recent years, there has been a trend toward so-called corporate therapy programs to improve morale and ease tensions in the newsroom. However, some journalists feel these programs smack too much of the same corporate values that helped create the morale problems in the first place.

19. Since we conducted our study before the impact of the recession had hit many West Coast newspapers, any mention by our respondents about decline in newspaper quality should not, for the most part, be related to the recession. Although some of the California newspapers were beginning to feel the effects of the downturn in the economy, the big retrenchments and other cutbacks in newsrooms hadn't occurred at the time we did our field research in the summer and fall of 1990.

20. Bagby, "Transforming Newspapers," 18–25.

11. How Much News Is News?

1. Polly Lane, "Another Airline Cites Defects in Boeing Jets," *Seattle Times*, April 9, 1988, pp. A1, A6.

2. Les Gapay, "Japan Air Lines Rips Boeing Defects," *Seattle Post-Intelligencer*, April 5, 1988, pp. A1, A4; Wire service account of same story carried in the business section of the *Seattle Times*, April 4, 1988, p. D1.

3. *P-I* account of press conference, April 13, 1988, pp. A1, A4.

4. As with many things they cover, the *Times*'s and *P-I*'s coverage of Boeing is spotty and inconsistent. (See Underwood, "The Boeing Story and the Hometown Press," *Columbia Journalism Review*, November/December 1988, 50–52, 54, 56.) Some of the coverage during this period was quite good. Both Seattle newspapers eventually carried stories that included complaints from union officials and employees who cited a series of assembly line "horror stories" and blamed them on stepped-up production schedules, poor training of new workers, and excessive overtime. Two enterprise pieces stand out: Gapay, "A Question of Quality," *Seattle Post-Intelligencer*, April 18, 1988, pp. B4, B8; Lane and James E. Lalonde, "Overtime, Training Are Issues," *Seattle Times*, April 13, 1988, pp. A1, A12. Nevertheless, at least in the *Seattle Times*, the newspapers' reaction was typified by Lane who wrote just a few weeks after the press conference that Boeing's "blue-chip image as a well-run company" had weathered the wave of airline protests about poor workmanship "with barely a ripple." (Lane, "Boeing's Image Weathers Accident, Criticism," *Seattle Times*, May 6, 1988, p. B1.) Critics of the coverage of Boeing include, ironically, at least one Boeing worker who complains that the Seattle media are reluctant to probe very deeply inside the company. "They are a kind of Pollyanna," said Mike McMullin, a test program writer at Boeing's Everett, Washington, plant. "They'll tell about orders and they'll tell management's side of things. But, as far as talking to people [in the plant], they're no more inclined to do that than our own management. And that's zilch." (Underwood, "Boeing," 54.)

5. Dreier, "Corporate Complaint," 18.

6. David Johnston, telephone interview with the author, December 1987.

7. Ken Gepfert and Richard Oppel, "The Competitive Environment," in *The Next Newspapers*, 51–54.

8. Fancher, "Finding What the Readers Want, Then Changing the Section," *Bulletin* of ASNE, May/June 1983, 13.

9. Steve Dunphy, interview with the author, April 1988. See Underwood, "Marriage of Convenience," 44.

10. The emphasis on marketing was illustrated at the *Seattle Times* when on the day the Gulf war ended the *Times* enclosed the entire newspaper (including the front page) in a marketing wrap touting its newly expanded suburban coverage. (See the article by the *Times* reader advocate, Colleen Patrick, "*Times* 'Adwrap': Was It Promotion—or Demotion?" *Seattle Times*, March 3, 1991, p. A19.) Although Patrick questioned whether the *Times* had become "more interested in promotion than journalism," the *Times* was in tune with other newspapers in its stress on the suburbs. Everyone at 168 dailies in a 1986 survey said they had made some content changes, such as supplements

or zoned editions, to woo suburban readers. (Anderson, "Doing Battle in the Suburbs," *Presstime,* June 1987, 9.)

11. The company apparently learned a lesson from the spate of quality control stories in 1988. First, Boeing hired a research firm to do a study of the company's relationship with the press. In 1991, when the federal government discovered more quality control problems at Boeing, the company decided to take the offensive. Before the press "discovered" the story, Boeing revealed its difficulties in a press conference. This tactic limited the coverage to a day of bad press rather than the additional days that were generated in 1988.

12. As Bagdikian notes, there are very few business reporters who consider themselves to be investigative reporters. Usually, what little investigative reporting about companies occurs is done by reporters on the news side who make forays into the business realm. But even when that happens, those reporters often run into obstacles from both the business community and their bosses. For good examples of the clash between market-oriented editors and reporters who tried to probe corporate misdeeds, see Kreig, *Spiked,* and Manning, *Last Stand.*

13. Underwood, "Retail Stores," 33–35. See also Barbara Gyles, "Ringing Up Retail," *Presstime,* August 1992, 14–18.

14. "Darts and Laurels," *Columbia Journalism Review,* November/December 1989, 21.

15. Eric Dexheimer, "Cover-Up: The Story the *Oregonian* Didn't Want to Publish," *Willamette Week,* May 9–15, 1991, 1, 10–14; Sarah Bartlett, "Gambling with the Big Boys," *New York Times Magazine,* May 5, 1991, 38, 56–57, 69–70.

16. G. Pascal Zachary, "Many Journalists See a Growing Reluctance to Criticize Advertisers," *Wall Street Journal,* February 6, 1992, pp. A1, A6.

17. "Darts and Laurels," *Columbia Journalism Review,* September/October 1984, 25.

18. "Darts and Laurels," *Columbia Journalism Review,* November/December 1984, 20. See also Ronald K. L. Collins, "Press Freedom Vs. Advertising Pressure," special to the *Seattle Times,* April 4, 1992, p. A19. Collins quotes John Robert Starr, the recently retired managing editor of the *Arkansas Democrat,* as saying, "Our policy is no different from every other paper I know about: People hired as columnists by the paper don't trash advertisers."

19. "Darts and Laurels," *Columbia Journalism Review,* November/December 1989, 22.

20. Underwood, "Retail Stores," 34. The two newspapers operate in a joint operating agreement with the *Times* handling the business and circulation matters for both newspapers.

21. Underwood, "Retail Stores," 35.

22. Mary Ellen Schoonmaker, "The Real Estate Story: Hard News or Soft Sell?" *Columbia Journalism Review,* January/February 1987, 25–30.

23. Elizabeth Lesly, "Realtors and Builders Demand Happy News . . . and Often Get It," *Washington Journalism Review,* November 1991, 20–23.

24. Wendy Swallow Williams, "Two New Surveys Show the Industry's Research," *Washington Journalism Review,* November 1991, 24–25.

25. For examples of newspapers' treatment of car dealers, see *CJR*'s "darts"

aimed at the *Chicago Sun-Times* ("Darts and Laurels," *Columbia Journalism Review,* September/October 1985, 22) and the *Southern Illinoisan* of Carbondale, Illinois, ("Darts and Laurels," *Columbia Journalism Review,* July/August 1990, 14). See also Steve Singer, "Auto Dealers Muscle the Newsroom," *Washington Journalism Review,* September 1991, 24–28. Singer details a series of incidents of daily newspapers placing coverage of the automotive field under the control of the advertising department and/or bowing to car dealers unhappy with consumer-oriented auto coverage. "It doesn't make much sense to . . . piss off advertisers," Singer quotes Frank Daniels III, the executive editor of the Raleigh, North Carolina, *News and Observer.* "There are other places to get information, like *Consumer Reports.* I would never look to newspapers to decide what model to buy. . . . Newspapers never did a good job at this in the first place." Singer says the trend could undermine newspapers' credibility with readers and means readers "must now understand that caveat emptor applies" not only to car dealers but also to the newspapers that publish their advertising. "There is mounting evidence that advertisers nationwide are increasingly taking advantage of weak newspaper ad revenues to pressure papers into more positive coverage of their activities," Singer concludes. "The trend also raises questions about the slow erosion of the walls around the newsroom and, ultimately, about what readers should expect from newspapers."

26. Michael Moore, "How to Keep 'Em Happy in Flint," *Columbia Journalism Review,* September/October 1985, 40–43.

27. "Darts and Laurels," *Columbia Journalism Review,* September/October 1990, 15.

28. "Darts and Laurels," *Columbia Journalism Review,* March/April 1989, 20.

29. "Darts and Laurels," *Columbia Journalism Review,* November/December 1989, 21.

30. "Darts and Laurels," *Columbia Journalism Review,* May/June 1990, 24. See also Wetzel, "Why is the *Times* Stonewalling on Prodigy?" *Seattle Times/Seattle Post-Intelligencer,* November 26, 1989, p. A23.

31. "Darts and Laurels," *Columbia Journalism Review,* January/February 1991, 24.

32. Mark Silk, "Who Will Rewire America?" *Columbia Journalism Review,* May/June 1991, 45–48.

33. Ibid., 48.

34. "Darts and Laurels," *Columbia Journalism Review,* March/April 1988, 22.

35. "Darts and Laurels," *Columbia Journalism Review,* March/April 1990, 21.

36. "Darts and Laurels," *Columbia Journalism Review,* January/February 1988, 20–21.

37. "Darts and Laurels," *Columbia Journalism Review,* January/February 1986, 25.

38. Daniel Lazare, "Vanity Fare," *Columbia Journalism Review,* May/June 1989, 6, 8.

39. Michael Hoyt, "When the Walls Come Tumbling Down," *Columbia Journalism Review,* March/April 1990, 35–41.

40. Bob Sonenclar, "The VNR Top Ten," *Columbia Journalism Review,* March/April 1991, 14.

41. Joanne Angela Ambrosio, "It's in the *Journal.* But This Is Reporting?" *Columbia Journalism Review,* March/April 1980, 34–36.

42. Collins, "Press Freedom," p. A19.

43. Harry Hammitt, "Advertising Pressures on Media," *Freedom of Information Center Report No. 367,* February 1977, 1–7.

44. However, there are notable exceptions to this. Note the repeated darts various Gannett newspapers have received for their fulsome and overblown coverage of the corporate doings of Al Neuharth and other top Gannett officials. (See "Darts and Laurels" in *Columbia Journalism Review:* July/August 1989, 18; March/April 1986, 25; March/April 1985, 26; May/June 1983, 24–25; July/August 1980, 26.)

45. At most newspapers—such as the *Seattle Times,* for example—any mention of the newspaper in the news columns requires advance clearance with top editors. Newspaper editors will argue that this isn't a double-standard (although what other business gets this treatment?) but simply an assurance that they are aware in advance of what the newspaper says about itself. However, many staffers don't see it this way.

46. James Aronson, *Packaging the News: A Critical Survey of Press, Radio, TV* (New York: International Publishers, 1971), 44–47.

47. Warren Breed, "Social Control in the Newsroom: A Functional Analysis," *Social Forces,* 33 (May 1955): 326–335.

48. For example, see Lee Sigelman, "Reporting the News: An Organizational Analysis," *American Journal of Sociology* 79 (July 1973): 132–151; Gaye Tuchman, *Making News: A Study in the Construction of Reality* (New York: Free Press, 1980).

49. Todd Gitlin, *The Whole World Is Watching: Mass Media in the Making and Unmaking of the New Left* (Berkeley: University of California Press, 1980), 262.

50. Carlin Romano, "The Grisly Truth about Bare Facts," in *Reading the News,* 75.

51. Herbert J. Gans, *Deciding What's News: A Study of CBS Evening News, NBC Nightly News, Newsweek, and Time* (New York: Vintage, 1980), 206.

52. Ibid., 46–48. *Village Voice* writer Jack Newfield expressed much the same thing in "Journalism: Old, New, and Corporate," *Bread and Roses Too* (New York: Dutton, 1971), 269. Newfield says, "The men and women who control the technological giants of the mass media are not neutral, unbiased computers. They have a mind-set. They have definite life styles and political values, which are concealed under a rhetoric of objectivity. . . . Among those unspoken, but organic, values are belief in welfare capitalism, God, the West, Puritanism, the Law, the family, property, the two-party system, and perhaps most crucially, in the notion that violence is only defensible when employed by the state. I can't think of any White House correspondent, or network television analyst, who doesn't share these values. And at the same time, who doesn't insist he is totally objective."

53. Gans, *Deciding What's News,* 246–247.

54. Leon V. Sigal, *Reporters and Officials: The Organization and Politics of Newsmaking* (Lexington, Ma.: Heath, 1973), 3–5.

55. Ibid., 54.

56. Ibid., 34.

57. Stone, *Examining Newspapers,* 40–42.

58. Sigal, *Reporters,* 121.

59. Schudson, "Deadlines, Datelines, and History," in *Reading the News,* 81. See also Edward S. Herman and Noam Chomsky, *Manufacturing Consent: The Political Economy of the Mass Media* (New York: Pantheon, 1988), 22. Herman and Chomsky, two leftist media critics, say journalists are, in effect, bought off by their sources. "In effect, the large bureaucracies of the powerful *subsidize* the mass media, and gain special access by their contribution to reducing the media's costs of acquiring the raw materials of, and producing, 'news,' " they say. "The large entities that provide this subsidy become 'routine' news sources and have privileged access to the gates."

60. Daniel J. Boorstin, *The Image: A Guide to Pseudo-Events in America* (New York: Athenaeum, 1987), 255–259.

61. Ibid., 197.

62. Walker, "Quit," 40.

63. Johnston, telephone interview with the author, December 1987.

64. Joseph S. Fowler and Stuart W. Showalter, "Evening Network News Selection: A Confirmation of News Judgment," *Journalism Quarterly* 51 (Winter 1974): 712–715.

65. Donald Kaul, telephone interview with the author, November 1991.

66. Hertsgaard, *On Bended Knee,* 52. Hertsgaard details the way the networks softened their coverage of Reagan in deference to the "market" of viewers who television executives believed wanted more of the "feel-good" coverage that Reagan inspired. "The media did more than merely get caught up in the 'It's morning again in America' mood; it actively embraced and helped to spread it," Hertsgaard wrote. "Who in the press wanted to interrupt the national orgy of self-congratulation and remind Americans of the downside of the Reagan Revolution? That was no way to sell newspapers." (Hertsgaard, *On Bended Knee,* 258.)

67. The media coverage of the Gulf war illustrates how completely the public relations wizards can dominate today's press and how marketing concerns have come to shape even the media's coverage of war. John MacArthur documents the way the public relations officials at the Pentagon were able to control the public's perception of the war by limiting the press's access to the fighting. He tells how Kuwait manipulated press and public attitudes in favor of U.S. involvement by hiring the influential public relations firm Hill and Knowlton. But MacArthur's most telling accounts involve the timid efforts by today's marketing-minded news executives in protesting the Pentagon's press restrictions. In explaining this, Robert Ingle, executive editor of Knight-Ridder's *San Jose Mercury News,* said, "I can only pose a possible theory and that is [that] newspapers all over the country, including the *New York Times,* the *Los Angeles Times,* and all the others, are terribly concerned about losing touch with their readers and losing the support of their readers. . . . You have to keep in mind that this was a terribly popular war by all of the polls I've seen. . . . I

think the conflict between needing to stay relevant and in touch with readers, and independent of those readers, is a terribly difficult one." (Ingle quoted in MacArthur, *Second Front: Censorship and Propaganda in the Gulf War* (New York: Hill and Wang, 1992), 21.)

68. Halberstam, *The Reckoning.*

69. Halberstam appearance before Northwest business journalists, May 1988. See Underwood, "Boeing," 56.

12. Fear and the Future of Newspapers

1. Underwood, "Identity Crisis," 24.

2. Janis, "News 2000," 4–5; "Gannett's News 2000 Project," 50; Green, "Featuring NEWS 2000," 2.

3. Benenson, "Shook Up," 20–23; Deneen, "Doing the Boca," 15; "Boca Watch," 19–23. Benenson says the *Register*'s New Age management techniques included the hiring of Synetics, an innovative management consultant team; "collaborative" news budget meetings where design and topics editors work closely together; and the selection of "feel-good" topics for reporters to cover. She says *Register* executives insist that the amused reaction by the industry to the *Register*'s revamped, "reader-friendly" newsroom has been exaggerated and distorted. However, she notes that many *Register* reporters and lower level editors haven't been amused—and have been leaving the newspaper in increasing numbers.

4. Underwood, "Identity Crisis," 25. See also Walt Potter, "A Modest Role Emerges for Videotex Systems," *Presstime,* August 1991, 12–15.

5. Owens, "Gannett New Business," 1–2; Kari Granville, "CNN, Gannett among American Firms Exploring Interactive Media," *The Quill,* September 1991, 26.

6. Bill Baker, telephone interview with the author, November 1991.

7. Roger Fidler, "Mediamorphosis, or the Transformation of Newspapers into a New Medium," *Media Studies Journal* 5 (Fall 1991): 115–125.

8. Underwood, "Identity Crisis," 25.

9. Bagby, "Transforming Newspapers," 18–25.

10. Ibid. See also Urban, "Myths," 19–21; Bogart, *Press and Public.*

11. Baker, telephone interview with the author, November 1991.

12. Daniel Pearl, "Florida Newspaper Fires Two in Flap over Circulation," *Wall Street Journal,* August 12, 1991, p. B5.

13. The *Olympian*'s "News 2000" strategy obtained from a newspaper employee.

14. Phil Currie, telephone interview with the author, November 1991. Currie also appeared at the 1992 AEJMC convention in Montreal, where his comments about "News 2000" amply illustrated the tightening of Gannett's corporate control over its local newspapers. Currie and News 2000 director Mark Silverman explained that Gannett editors are evaluated every six months for how well their newspapers have adapted to the "News 2000" news pyramid—a graphically presented formula that emphasizes interaction with readers, community interest, compelling presentation, and useful information. A company

that once prided itself on granting "local autonomy" to its editors now uses a 100-point grading system to judge its editors on how well they are "managing change," as Currie put it. Currie acknowledged that the company knew it would lose some newsroom employees as a result of "News 2000." "We don't see everybody buying into this," he said. At the same time, Gannett executives say it is too soon to tell if the program will translate into increased circulation. At the AEJMC meeting, Currie and Silverman pointed to some individual success stories but acknowledged that no hard data has been developed on the success of the program.

15. Miller, telephone interview with the author, November 1991. As part of its 25/43 program, Knight-Ridder has embarked on an experimental newsroom restructuring project at the Gary, Indiana, *Post-Tribune*. Like the Boca Raton *News*, the Gary newspaper's new design emphasizes brief stories, bulleted items, few story jumps, and targeting reader groups. Editors at the *Post-Tribune* have also shuffled and renamed beats, downplayed meeting coverage, and encouraged reporters to work in teams and write for various sections of the newspaper. But the most notable changes involved a decision to do away with traditional newsroom titles. The former managing editor is now called "newsroom manager," the chief photographer "photographic image manager," the copy desk "news production group." The reason for this, says *Post-Tribune* executive editor Betty Wells Cox (who has retained her traditional title) is that "we wanted to flatten out the management. We needed to give more power and autonomy to the people on the front lines and reduce the distance between editors and reporters." The moves have been applauded in some quarters, although not everyone is convinced. "I don't see a lot of impact good or bad. . . . You can call yourself the Grand Poobah of News for all I care," says *Post-Tribune* reporter Chris Isidore. (Mark Fitzgerald, "Tranformation Under Way in Gary, Indiana," *Editor and Publisher,* May 2, 1992, 46, 48, 50.)

16. Underwood, "Identity Crisis," 26.

17. Tina Brown, "Magazine Editor Urges Tough, Lively Papers," (Adaptation of her speech to ANPA's 1991 annual convention in Vancouver, B.C.), *Presstime,* June 1991, 58–59, 61.

18. Potter, "How to Build Your Own Audiotex System," *Presstime,* July 1991, 10–12.

19. Underwood, "Identity Crisis," 26.

20. David Carlsen, telephone interview with the author, November 1991.

21. Scott Whiteside, telephone interview with the author, November 1991.

22. Terry Maguire, telephone interview with the author, November 1991.

23. Underwood, "Identity Crisis," 26.

24. One explanation for this is that while the average circulation for daily newspapers has been relatively flat, free and subscription weeklies have seen their circulation grow substantially in the last decade. A fast-growing portion of that consists of Reagan-Bush-era versions of the old underground publications that, as city magazines or slick tabloids, have carved out a healthy circulation niche through a combination of in-depth reporting with "building-the-better-bagel" coverage of the yuppie scene. At least one newspaper company, Gold Coast Publications, a wholly owned subsidiary of the News and Sun-Sentinel Company of Fort Lauderdale, Florida (itself owned by the Tribune Company

of Chicago), has gone into the alternative media business by launching a new alternative weekly, named *XS*, of its own. In attempting to tap the lucrative market developed by alternative publications, *XS* uses language and produces antiestablishment journalism not found in its more sedate, parent daily publication. Some see an irony in this. (Jeff Truesdell, "Alternative Strategy," *Columbia Journalism Review*, July/August 1991, 15–16.) Also see Schoonmaker, "Has the Alternative Press Gone Yuppie?" *Columbia Journalism Review*, November/December 1987, 60, 62–64.

25. Rinehart, "Technology Is Spawning the Tailored Newspaper," *Presstime*, June 1989, 56.

26. Logan, "Newspaper Odyssey," 38, 40. The potential competition by the telephone companies is considerable. For example, AT & T is in competition with Time Warner and IBM to bring to market a "video-on-demand" system that would provide electronically compressed data contained in a TV signal so cable subscribers could order movies and other programs any time of day.

27. O. Casey Corr, "U.S. West to Offer Electronic News," *Seattle Times/ Seattle Post-Intelligencer*, October 6, 1991, p. A1, A8. See also "Blethen Hits RBOCs at Telecommunications Forum," *Bulletin* of the Pacific Northwest Newspaper Association, June 10, 1991, 4–5. Blethen charged the Bell companies with running a "disinformation campaign" and acting in a "vindictive" and "mean spirited" manner in their battle with the newspaper industry to get into the electronic information business.

28. Experimental systems at Stanford University and the University of Missouri, for example, are already bringing digitalized, multimedia versions of the campus newspapers—complete with text, sound, video, and animation in Stanford's case—to students and other computer users. (Maryellen Driscoll, "Big Medium on Campus," *Presstime*, September 1992, 18–20.) Tandy, Sony, and other companies are bringing TV-based multimedia systems to the market that include a variety of word processing programs, dictionaries, newspaper data bases, and other data base software.

29. Fidler, "Mediamorphosis," 122–124. At a research and development level, these multimedia developments are moving at a breathtaking speed. For example, one computer company has developed an electronic device the size of a credit card that could store prodigious amounts of computer data and replace tapes and discs as a way to play sound and video and movies as well as display text.

30. Underwood, "Identity Crisis," 27. It should be noted that a major threat to the future of newspapers is the one presented by the new technologies to traditional concepts of retailing and advertising. Some futurists see the new home video shopping networks as precursors to developments that will accelerate with fiber optics and digital television. In this wired world, people will have easy access to direct purchasing of items through their home video screens. Many observers believe this will be a boon to direct sellers of merchandise, manufacturers, and package delivery services but could have negative impacts on traditional retailers and advertisers. Needless to say, these developments could also profoundly affect daily newspapers. While the new electronic information delivery systems offer the possibility for new forms of targeted newspa-

234 · 12. Fear and the Future of Newspapers

per advertising, they also portend the possibility of greatly diminished advertising revenues for newspapers.

31. Jane Ciabattari, "Of Time and Integrity," *Columbia Journalism Review*, September/October, 1989, 27–34. Ciabattari noted the difficulties that Jason McManus, the editor-in-chief of Time Inc.'s magazines, had in wearing two hats during the merger. Insiders were stung, she said, by *Time*'s decision not to cover the merger when it was announced on March 4, 1989—allowing *Newsweek* to scoop *Time* in that week's issues of the magazines. McManus justified the decision on the grounds that he didn't want it to look like *Time* was part of the public relations rollout. But he also outlined a somewhat tortured ethical policy where he said he'd prefer to keep information out of print rather than to reveal information he knew as a corporate insider to a *Time* or *Fortune* reporter.

32. Television critic Katz has argued that news, in fact, has become so merged with entertainment that the "New News"—"dazzling, adolescent, irresponsible, fearless, frightening and powerful"—has replaced the traditional "Old News"—balanced, ossified, paralyzed by new technologies—among the young. (See Katz, "Rock, Rap and Movies Bring You the News," *Rolling Stone*, March 5, 1992, 33, 36–37, 40, 78.) Katz argues that the "New News" is a "heady concoction" of Hollywood films and television culture, pop music and pop art, celebrity magazines, tabloid telecasts, and home video that stresses passion and hyperbole and makes more sense to the young than the old, dying media. However, there are signs that the "New News" may be as much—or even more—market-driven than the "Old News" has become. For example, the rock music channel, MTV, now has a news staff and includes news clips in its broadcasts. But Dave Sirulnick, director of MTV news, says the channel doesn't try to cover national or international stories that won't interest young people. "We also have to stay in touch with what they (MTV viewers) want and the issues they care about," adds Tom Freston, chairman of MTV Networks. (Judith Miller, "The News on MTV," reprinted from the *New York Times Magazine* in the *Seattle Post-Intelligencer* focus section, *Seattle Times/Seattle P-I*, October 11, 1992, p. D1.)

33. Baker, telephone interview with the author, November 1991.

34. Urban, telephone interview with the author, November 1991.

35. Underwood, "Identity Crisis," 27.

13. Fighting the Good Fight Within

1. Underwood, "The Pulitzer Prize-Winner Who Became a Private Eye," *Columbia Journalism Review*, September/October 1989, 41–45.

2. Sigal, *Reporters and Officials*, 19.

3. William Davis, telephone interview with the author, December 1987.

4. Michael Wagner, telephone interview with the author, November 1987.

5. Underwood, "MBAs," 29.

6. Stanford Sesser, "Journalists: Objectivity and Activism," *Wall Street Journal*, October 21, 1969, p. 22; Diamond, "Reporter Power 'Takes Root,' " 12–18; Richard P. Nielsen, "Pluralism in the Mass Media: Can Management

Participation Help?" *Journal of Business Ethics* 3 (November 1984): 335–341.

7. Irving Kristol, "Is the Press Misusing Its Growing Power?" *More*, January 1975, 28, 26.

8. Stein, " 'Gloss' Is Taken Off Investigative Reporting," *Editor and Publisher*, October 22, 1983, 10–11.

9. Bill Bellows, "Why Investigative Reporting Is Dying," *Editor and Publisher*, March 14, 1981, 60.

10. Manning, *Last Stand*, 81.

11. Ibid., 157, 159–160.

12. McWilliams, "Muckraking," 13.

13. Underwood, "MBAs," 30.

14. Curtis D. MacDougall, *Newsroom Problems and Policies*, (New York: Dover, 1963), 152.

15. Gans, *Deciding What's News*, 68–69.

16. S. Robert Lichter, Stanley Rothman, Linda S. Lichter, *The Media Elite* (Bethesda, Md.: Adler and Adler, 1986).

17. Mitchell Stephens, *A History of News* (New York: Viking, 1988), 268.

18. Fancher, "Metamorphosis," 73.

19. Breed, "Social Control"; Bernard Roshco, *Newsmaking* (Chicago: University of Chicago Press, 1975); Sigal, *Reporters and Officials*. Breeds' study shows what most working reporters would confirm: newsroom pressures, like the fear of reprisal, the desire to be accepted among peers, and the hope for career advancement, insure coverage that is acceptable to the organization. Roshco focuses on the broader social pressures that shape the news: the newspaper's organizational needs, the newsworker's occupational dilemmas, and the audience's predominant social assumptions. Sigal portrays the newspaper as a bureaucracy where the product of a journalist's work is heavily influenced by office politics, the organizational structure, and the formal hierarchy of the organization.

20. Hillier Krieghbaum, *Pressures on the Press* (New York: Crowell, 1972), 95.

21. Tuchman quoted in Schudson, *Discovering the News*, 1986 (see also Altschull, *Agents of Power*, 128–129); Schudson, *Discovering the News*, 184; Carey, "The Communications Revolution and the Professional Communicator," in Paul Halmos, ed., "The Sociology of Mass Media Communicators," *The Sociological Review*, 13 (January 1969): 36; Gans, *Deciding What's News*, 191–192, 39–69. Tuchman calls journalists' claim to objective powers a "strategic ritual" designed to camouflage the political and financial agenda of news organizations. Schudson refers to the belief in objective reporting as the form of a news story concealing content. Carey says the acceptance of an obsolete concept like objectivity is "a silent conspiracy . . . to keep the house locked up tight even though all the windows have been blown out." Gans talks of journalists' nonideological pose as "self-serving . . . for it blinds them to the fact that they also have ideologies, even if these are largely unconscious."

22. Lippmann, *Public Opinion*, 229.

23. Paletz and Entman, *Media*Power*Politics,* 19, 251.

24. Douglas Birkhead, "News Media Ethics and the Management of Professionals," *Journal of Mass Media Ethics* 1 (Spring/Summer 1986): 37–46.

25. Altschull, *Agents of Power*, 273.

26. Epstein, *Between Fact and Fiction*, 17.

27. David S. Broder, *Behind the Front Page: A Candid Look at How the News Is Made* (New York: Simon and Schuster, 1987), 324–326.

28. Gay Talese, *The Kingdom and the Power* (New York: Laurel, 1986), 459–461.

29. Merrill's views are summarized in Altschull, *Agents of Power*, 193.

30. Fancher, "Metamorphosis," 69.

31. A. Kent MacDougall, "Memoirs of a Radical in the Mainstream Press," *Columbia Journalism Review*, (March/April, 1989), 36–41.

32. Schudson, *Discovering the News*, 192.

33. McWilliams, "Muckraking," 15.

34. Smith, *Goodbye Gutenberg*, 183; Broder, *Behind the Front Page*, 325; Halberstam, *The Powers That Be*.

35. Lambeth, *Committed Journalism*, 79.

14. *The Future of the Word*

1. Ted Solotaroff, "The Literary-Industrial Complex," *The New Republic*, June 8, 1987, 38.

2. Michael Arlen, *Living-Room War* (New York: Viking, 1969), 57–58.

3. Henry David Thoreau, *Walden and Civil Disobedience* (New York: Penguin, 1984), 95.

4. Roszak, *The Cult of Information*, 88.

5. McLuhan, *Understanding Media*, 73.

6. Boorstin, *The Image*, 257.

7. Boorstin, *Democracy and Its Discontents: Reflections on Everyday America* (New York: Random House, 1974), 12–21.

8. Ibid., 3–11.

9. Ibid., 8–9.

10. Harold A. Innis, *Empire and Communications* (Toronto: University of Toronto Press, 1972), 43.

11. Postman, *Amusing Ourselves*, 9.

12. Ong, *Word*, 313.

13. Herbert G. May and Bruce M. Metzger, *The Oxford Annotated Bible with the Apocrypha* (New York: Oxford University Press, 1965), 1284.

SELECTED BIBLIOGRAPHY

This bibliography contains the books of scholars, researchers, journalists, and other writers who have touched upon related aspects of the marketing phenomenon in the media. Citations for articles and newspaper industry publications can be found in the notes.

Altschull, J. Herbert. *Agents of Power: The Role of the News Media in Human Affairs*. New York: Longman, 1984.

Argyris, Chris. *Behind the Front Page: Organizational Self-Renewal in a Metropolitan Newspaper*. San Francisco: Jossey-Bass, 1974.

Arlen, Michael J. *Living-Room War*. New York: Viking, 1969.

———. *The Camera Age: Essays on Television*. New York: Penguin, 1982.

Aronson, James. *Packaging the News: A Critical Survey of Press, Radio, TV*. New York: International Publishers, 1971.

Bagdikian, Ben H. *The Information Machines: Their Impact on Men and the Media*. New York: Harper Colophon, 1971.

———. *The Effete Conspiracy and Other Crimes by the Press*. New York: Harper and Row, 1972.

———. *The Media Monopoly*. Boston: Beacon, 1983.

Baldasty, Gerald J. *The Commercialization of News in the Nineteenth Century.* Madison: University of Wisconsin Press, 1992.

Barnouw, Erik. *The Sponsor: Notes on a Modern Potentate.* New York: Oxford University Press, 1979.

———. *Tube of Plenty: The Evolution of American Television.* New York: Oxford University Press, 1982.

Bogart, Leo. *Press and Public: Who Reads What, When, Where, and Why in American Newspapers.* Hillsdale, N.J.: Erlbaum, 1981.

———. *Preserving the Press: How Daily Newspapers Mobilized to Keep Their Readers.* New York: Columbia University Press, 1991.

Boorstin, Daniel J. *Democracy and Its Discontents: Reflections on Everyday America.* New York: Random House, 1974.

———. *The Image: A Guide to Pseudo-Events in America.* New York: Athenaeum, 1987.

Boyer, Peter J. *Who Killed CBS?: The Undoing of America's Number One News Network.* New York: Random House, 1988.

Broder, David S. *Behind the Front Page: A Candid Look at How the News Is Made.* New York: Simon and Schuster, 1987.

Brown, Les. *Televi$ion: The Business behind the Box.* New York: Harvest, 1971.

Burnham, David. *The Rise of the Computer State.* New York: Vintage, 1984.

Carey, James W. *Communication as Culture: Essays on Media and Society.* Boston: Unwin Hyman, 1989.

Cater, Douglass. *The Fourth Branch of Government.* New York: Vintage, 1959.

Cirino, Robert. *Don't Blame the People.* New York: Vintage, 1972.

Cose, Ellis. *The Press.* New York: Morrow, 1989.

Crouse, Timothy. *The Boys on the Bus.* New York: Ballantine, 1974.

Dennis, Everette E., Arnold H. Ismach, and Donald M. Gillmor, eds. *Enduring Issues in Mass Communication.* St. Paul: West, 1978.

Diamond, Edwin. *Good News, Bad News.* Cambridge: MIT Press, 1980.

———. *The Tin Kazoo: Television, Politics, and the News.* Cambridge: MIT Press, 1980.

Downie, Jr., Leonard. *The New Muckrakers.* New York: Mentor, 1978.

Dunnette, Marvin D., ed. *Handbook of Industrial and Organizational Psychology.* Chicago: Rand McNally, 1976.

Efron, Edith. *The News Twisters.* Manor, 1972.

Epstein, Edward Jay. *News from Nowhere: Television and the News.* New York: Vintage, 1974.

———. *Between Fact and Fiction: The Problem of Journalism.* New York: Vintage, 1975.

Ewen, Stuart. *Captains of Consciousness: Advertising and the Social Roots of the Consumer Culture.* New York: McGraw-Hill, 1977.

Fenton, Charles A. *The Apprenticeship of Ernest Hemingway: The Early Years.* New York: Viking, 1954.

Fink, Conrad C. *Strategic Newspaper Management.* New York: Random House, 1988.

Fishman, Mark. *Manufacturing the News*. Austin: University of Texas Press, 1988.

Flippen, Charles C., ed. *Liberating the Media: The New Journalism*. Washington, D.C.: Acropolis, 1974.

Gans, Herbert J. *Deciding What's News: A Study of CBS Evening News, NBC Nightly News, Newsweek, and Time*. New York: Vintage, 1980.

Garson, Barbara. *The Electronic Sweatshop: How Computers Are Transforming the Office of the Future into the Factory of the Past*. New York: Simon and Schuster, 1988.

Ghiglione, Loren, ed. *The Buying and Selling of America's Newspapers*. Indianapolis: R. J. Berg, 1984.

Giles, Robert H. *Newsroom Management: A Guide to Theory and Practice*. Indianapolis: R. J. Berg, 1987.

Gitlin, Todd. *The Whole World Is Watching: Mass Media in the Making and Unmaking of the New Left*. Berkeley: University of California Press, 1980.
———. *Inside Prime Time*. New York: Pantheon, 1985.

Goldstein, Tom. *The News at Any Cost: How Journalists Compromise Their Ethics to Shape the News*. New York: Touchstone, 1986.

Gumpert, Gary. *Talking Tombstones and Other Tales of the Media Age*. New York: Oxford University Press, 1988.

Halberstam, David. *The Powers That Be*. New York: Laurel, 1986.
———. *The Reckoning*. New York: Avon, 1987.

Harrison, John M. and Harry H. Stein. *Muckraking: Past, Present, and Future*. University Park: Pennsylvania State University Press, 1978.

Herman, Edward S. and Noam Chomsky. *Manufacturing Consent: The Political Economy of the Mass Media*. New York: Pantheon, 1988.

Hertsgaard, Mark. *On Bended Knee: The Press and the Reagan Presidency*. New York: Farrar Straus Giroux, 1988.

Innis, Harold A. *Empire and Communications*. Toronto: University of Toronto Press, 1972.

Johnstone, John W. C., Edward J. Slawski, and William W. Bowman. *The News People: A Sociological Portrait of American Journalists and Their Work*. Urbana: University of Illinois Press, 1976.

Kreig, Andrew. *Spiked: How Chain Management Corrupted America's Oldest Newspaper*. Old Saybrook, Conn.: Peregrine, 1987.

Krieghbaum, Hillier. *Pressures on the Press*. New York: Thomas Y. Crowell, 1972.

Lambeth, Edmund B. *Committed Journalism: An Ethic for the Profession*. Bloomington: Indiana University Press, 1986.

Lang, Gladys Engel and Kurt Lang. *Politics and Television Re-viewed*. Beverly Hills, Ca.: Sage, 1984.

Lavine, John M. and Daniel B. Wackman. *Managing Media Organizations: Effective Leadership of the Media*. New York: Longman, 1988.

Lee, Alfred McClung. *The Daily Newspaper in America: The Evolution of a Social Instrument*. New York: Octagon, 1973.

Lichter, S. Robert, Stanley Rothman, and Linda S. Lichter. *The Media Elite*. Bethesda, Md.: Adler and Adler, 1986.

Liebling, A. J. *The Press*. New York: Pantheon, 1981.

Lindstrom, Carl. *The Fading American Newspaper*. Gloucester: Peter Smith, 1964.

Lippmann, Walter. *Public Opinion*. New York: Free Press, 1965.

MacArthur, John R. *Second Front: Censorship and Propaganda in the Gulf War*. New York: Hill and Wang, 1992.

MacDougall, Curtis D. *Newsroom Problems and Policies*. New York: Dover, 1963.

McLuhan, Marshall. *Understanding Media: The Extensions of Man*. New York: Mentor, 1964.

Manning, Richard. *Last Stand: Logging, Journalism, and the Case for Humility*. Salt Lake City: Peregrine Smith, 1991.

Manoff, Robert Karl and Michael Schudson, eds. *Reading the News*. New York: Pantheon, 1986.

May, Herbert G. and Bruce M. Metzger, eds. *The Oxford Annotated Bible with the Apocrypha*. New York: Oxford University Press, 1965.

Meyer, Philip. *The Newspaper Survival Book: An Editor's Guide to Marketing Research*. Bloomington: Indiana University Press, 1985.

Meyrowitz, Joshua. *No Sense of Place: The Impact of Electronic Media on Social Behavior*. New York: Oxford University Press, 1986.

Newfield, Jack. *Bread and Roses Too*. New York: Dutton, 1971.

Ong, Walter J. *The Presence of the Word: Some Prolegomena for Cultural and Religious History*. Minneapolis: University of Minnesota Press, 1986.

Paletz, David L. and Robert M. Entman. *Media*Power*Politics*. New York: Free Press, 1982.

Parenti, Michael. *Inventing Reality: The Politics of the Mass Media*. New York: St. Martin's, 1986.

Picard, Robert G., James P. Winter, Maxwell E. McCombs, Stephen Lacy, eds. *Press Concentration and Monopoly: New Perspectives on Newspaper Ownership and Operation*. Norwood, N.J.: Ablex, 1988.

Postman, Neil. *Amusing Ourselves to Death: Public Discourse in the Age of Show Business*. New York: Penguin, 1986.

Prichard, Peter. *The Making of McPaper: The Inside Story of USA Today*. Kansas City, Mo.: Andrews, McMeel and Parker, 1987.

Ranney, Austin. *Channels of Power: The Impact of Television on American Politics*. New York: Basic, 1983.

Roshco, Bernard. *Newsmaking*. Chicago: University of Chicago Press, 1975.

Roszak, Theodore. *The Cult of Information: The Folklore of Computers and the True Art of Thinking*. New York: Pantheon, 1986.

Schudson, Michael. *Discovering the News: A Social History of American Newspapers*. New York: Basic, 1978.

——. *Advertising, The Uneasy Persuasion: Its Dubious Impact on American Society*. New York: Basic, 1986.

Seldes, George. *Lords of the Press*. New York: Julian Messner, 1938.

Sigal, Leon V. *Reporters and Officials: The Organization and Politics of Newsmaking*. Lexington, Ma.: Heath, 1973.

Sinclair, Upton. *The Brass Check: A Study of American Journalism*. Pasadena: Published by the author, 1920.

Skornia, Harry J. *Television and the News: A Critical Appraisal*. Palo Alto: Pacific Books, 1974.

Smith, Anthony. *Goodbye Gutenberg: The Newspaper Revolution of the 1980s*. New York: Oxford University Press, 1981.

Stephens, Mitchell. *A History of News: From the Drum to the Satellite*. New York: Viking, 1988.

Stone, Gerald. *Examining Newspapers: What Research Reveals about America's Newspapers*. Newbury Park, Ca.: Sage, 1987.

Talese, Gay. *The Kingdom and the Power*. New York: Laurel, 1986.

Thoreau, Henry David. *Walden and Civil Disobedience*. New York: Penguin, 1984.

Thorpe, Merle, ed. *The Coming Newspaper*. New York: Holt, 1915.

Tuchman, Gaye. *Making News: A Study in the Construction of Reality*. New York: Free Press, 1980.

Weaver, David H. and G. Cleveland Wilhoit. *The American Journalist: A Portrait of U.S. News People and Their Work*. Bloomington: Indiana University Press, 1986.

White, E. B. *Writings from the New Yorker 1927–1976*. New York: Harper Perennial, 1990.

INDEX